UNDERSTANDING HUMAN EVOLUTION AND THE NINE HUMAN ENDEAVORS

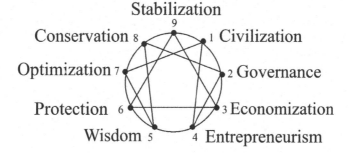

REVEALS THE PURPOSE AND MEANING OF LIFE

RICHARD COLTER

A PUBLICATION OF

UNIVERSAL PARADIGMS

Library of Congress Cataloging-in-Publication Data
Colter, Richard Glen
Understanding Human Evolution : And The Nine Human Endeavors : Reveals The Purpose And Meaning Of Life / Universal Paradigms (2019)

Library of Congress Control Number:2019907636

ISBN: 9781733197700

Printed in the United States of America

Cover design by Bespokebookcovers.com

This book is dedicated to the Conservationists, Stabilizers, Civilians, Governors, Economists, Entrepreneurs, Advisors, Protectors, and Optimizers who endeavored to find the purpose and meaning of life.

CONTENTS

PREFACE

The story of human evolution begins with the adoption of a multidisciplinary perspective that encompasses anthropology, economics, sociology, and psychology. Each perspective provides a piece to the puzzle that, when properly assembled, analyzed, and interpreted within the Enneagram framework, reveals the three distinct phenomena of human evolution. This knowledge provides a proper context for the nine human subtypes, and the nuances of their behavior, to reveal the blueprint and evolutionary mechanisms of humanity.

The philosophical ideas and teachings of George Gurdjieff provided knowledge that was indispensable to unraveling the mystery that surrounds the human phenomenon. Gurdjieff espoused the nine distinct human subtypes, and that he could discern them, which led to the premise that skill was involved. After developing this skill, a quest began for teaching others how to differentiate the nine human phenotypes. The knowledge contained in this book is the result of that quest.

The contributions of many scientists appear throughout this book, including Sigmund Freud's framework of the human psyche, and Carl Jung's archetypes of the unconscious mind. The Enneagram theories of Don Riso and Russ Hudson provided a starting point for the eventual development of a scientific framework for evolution. Many others were influential, including A.H. Almaas and Ken Wilber, for their explicit, detailed, and thorough account of the inner aspects of human psychology.

Most important was the adoption of a multidisciplinary perspective which led to the conceptualization and depiction of the Nine Factors of Extinction and the Nine Human Endeavors. These depictions synthesize the applicable principles of psychology, economics, anthropology, criminology, theology, sociology, and cosmology with the scientific framework of the Enneagram. Thus, it was the adoption of an evolutionary view of the Enneagram, coupled with the applicable scientific predicates, that reveals how, why, and for what purpose humans evolved.

The adoption of a multidisciplinary approach also provides a deeper understanding of the human condition, because it reveals the specialization for each of the nine subtypes and the functional roles that allow each type to achieve their evolutionary purpose. Taking this information with the physiological characteristics for each type, it then becomes possible to identify the phenotype of every human being, revealing their evolutionary Endeavor, specializations, primary roles, and functional adaptations. The integration of this knowledge, when catalyzed by experiences in the world, sets in motion a metamorphosis of the individual that reveals the beauty, purpose, and meaning of life.

Richard Colter

Pleasanton, California

August 2019

CHAPTER 1

INTRODUCTION

The enigma surrounding human evolution has been the topic of much research, conjecture, and debate for millennia. An aura of mystery persists, especially on the questions of how and why humans came into existence. And without an explanation for how and why humans came into existence, a workable theory that explains the phenomenon of human evolution has been elusive.

Of the many attempts to advance the subject of human evolution, most are in the form of conjecture, pointing to such social behaviors as cooking, conquering, hunting, sharing, toolmaking, and trading. Some of these conjectures contain essential points; however, they are not theories, but merely observations and analysis related to the sociology, psychology, and economy of humans. The main point is that conjecture alone cannot be the basis for the study of a complex subject such as human evolution: A scientific framework is not only essential; it is critical for the formulation of a comprehensive theory on this unassailable topic.

This book moves beyond conjecture by presenting a theoretical framework that explains how, why, and for what purpose humans evolved. The Enneagram is the scientific framework that explains the three distinct phenomena of human evolution: The Nine Factors of Extinction (NFE), the Nine Human Endeavors (NHE), and the Nine Human Virtues. When taken together, these phenomena provide a comprehensive understanding of the human condition.

The NFE were the causative factors, and the intractable problems, responsible for the extinction of multiple species of Early Humans. Evolution responded to the NFE with the introduction of the Enneatypes. Each of the Enneatypes possesses a specialization that is a necessary remedy for the factor of extinction from which it evolved, meaning that each of the Enneatypes is adapted to solve one of the NFE. When viewing the Enneatypes from this perspective, the Nine Human Endeavors reveal themselves. In turn, the Nine Human Endeavors reveal the evolutionary purpose of every human being.

Understanding the origin, structure, and purpose of the Enneatypes requires a multidisciplinary perspective that includes evolution. That is because the modus operandi of the Enneatypes, such as the Nine Human Endeavors, are the functional endpoint of a discrete, rational, and complex psychological and physiological evolutionary mechanism. Later, the relevant functions for each of the Enneatypes are delineated, with their respective physiological and psychological adaptations, to provide a detailed account of the evolutionary purpose for each Enneatype.

Chapter Two introduces the NFE, Chapter Three introduces the Enneagram framework, and then a full chapter is devoted to each of the Enneatypes. The final chapters discuss advanced concepts, with details of how the Enneatypes function within the Enneagram framework, and how this knowledge informs the evolutionary purpose and meaning of human life. The remainder of this chapter introduces the basic concepts of human evolution, including a developmental overview of the human psyche, along with definitions of some key concepts that appear throughout this book.

Evolution of the Survival Mechanisms

DNA evidence supports the theory that humans evolved from the Higher Primates, as does the fact that gorillas, chimpanzees, orangutans, bonobos, and other Higher Primates are psychologically more sophisticated than all other non-human members of the animal kingdom. Examples of their sophistication include their use of tools, symbols, and gestures. And there are many other similarities between humans and the Higher Primates, including a sophisticated social hierarchy, anatomy, and emotional behaviors. But the similarities do not end there.

Humans share a triadic psychological structure with the Higher Primates consisting of three faculties: Instincts, Cognition, and Emotion; after this referred to as the Instinctive Center, Thinking Center, and Emotional Center, respectively. It's important to understand these three basic faculties, and how they shape and control behavior, as they form the foundations of human behavior.

The Instinctive Center within every mammal is responsible for the day to day functions of the organism, including hunger, thirst, reproduction, migration, imitation, fight/flight, and so on. Because these functions are codependent with various types of stimuli, the Instinctive Center must be hardwired through the central nervous system, to give survival the highest priority. The Instinctive Center ensures survival by controlling behavior with preprogrammed responses to various types of scenarios. In this way, the Instinctive Center serves to guide, protect, and perpetuate the organism. In the Higher Primates, there is greater depth and diversity in how the instincts function. And those capabilities continued to evolve until the arrival of humans.

The Thinking Center is responsible for cognitive functioning, including memory, self-awareness, language-symbol processing, creativity, reasoning, and problem-solving; and varying degrees of object relationships. The level of consciousness inherent to the organism places limits on the skills, functions, and object relations that are developed by the Thinking Center. Here, the implication is that the Thinking Center, and the level of consciousness observed in the Higher Primates, is more developed than in other animals; which partly explains why the Higher Primates have exceptional cognitive skills and functions relative to the rest of the animal kingdom.

The Higher Primates also possess a faculty for feeling, which allows for more complex interactions, which in turn leads to more sophisticated social structures. One way to understand this is to differentiate some of the primary functions within the Feeling Center, such as empathy and nurturing.

Researchers have determined that the Higher Primates possess empathy, allowing them to sense and intuit when others are distressed, enabling more sophisticated responses such as emotional support, affection, nurturing, and sharing. Some animals are preprogrammed to provide nurturing and support. However, there is a difference between nurturing that is instinctively programmed and nurturing that flows from a locus of feeling that operates within the moment.

A key to understanding the Emotional (Feeling) Center is that it provides intelligence for acting appropriately to events as they are unfolding moment to moment. It is a particular type of intelligence that operates on a completely different frequency from the Thinking Center and Instinctive Center. Although the Higher Primates and humans both possess a Feeling Center, caution should be used in making direct comparisons, because the Emotional Center is exponentially more advanced in humans.

Although apes and Humans each possess an ego, composed of an Instinctive, Thinking, and Feeling center, that is where the similarities end. Apes have evolved and developed very little in the past several million years, mostly because they don't need to adapt, given the stability they enjoy in their native habitat. However, this means that apes are vulnerable to extinction from significant changes in their climate, local ecology, and habitat; and it was these vulnerabilities and weaknesses in the Higher Primates that led to the evolution of creatures that would be more adaptive to change and adversity. After approximately 5 MY, creatures that could walk upright emerged.

The arrival of Homo Erectus, approximately 2 million years ago, marked the end of the Australopithecine era. The brain of Homo Erectus was substantially larger than the brain of the Australopithecines, and this allowed the addition of two fundamental survival mechanisms, the Id and Superego. The combination of the Id, Ego, and Superego formed a potent triadic survival mechanism. Armed with the most versatile survival mechanism on Earth, Homo Erectus managed to emigrate out of Africa, and conquer much of the European and Asian continents.

(As a side note, the Id explains the emigrating tendencies of Homo Erectus. An introduction to the Id, and the corresponding theoretical framework that explains the emigrating behaviors of Homo Erectus are both given in Appendix A.)

Although Sigmund Freud was the first to identify the Id, Ego, and Superego, this book furthers the development of these mechanisms, which requires a slightly different approach. For example, two separate and autonomous instinctive faculties exist: There is the Id, which Freud described as the instinctual center of the Ego. And there are the instincts that function within the inherent structure of the Ego. Although Freud failed to differentiate them, a distinction must be made to arrive at the correct understanding.

Although Freud described the Id as the instinctual apparatus of personality, his work focused on the Instinctive Center of the Ego. And because Freud neglected to differentiate the instincts that arise within the Id, from the instincts that occur within the Ego, he missed an opportunity to illuminate the precise structure and functioning of these human survival mechanisms.

Most of the work devoted to the study of personality has focused on the Ego survival mechanism, while the Id has mostly been ignored, or merely undifferentiated from the other survival mechanisms. The neglect of the Id is understandable, because the Ego mechanism has more depth and complexity, especially when compared to the Id and Superego. And the Ego provides a sense of identity, which in turn provides a fundamental foundation for human function. For these reasons, the Ego survival mechanism is considered synonymous with personality, and this emphasis has led to the emergence of two modern-day psychological models which are compared and analyzed in Appendix B.

THE ARRIVAL OF HUMANS

Neanderthals were probably the most successful species of Early Humans. However, their success was quite limited, based on a consensus estimate of their population over time, indicating that the Neanderthal population peaked at around 70,000 members. There is also a consensus that Neanderthals numbered less than 10,000 in the latter phases of their existence, despite the availability of vast ranges of fertile land that provided an abundance of natural resources.

Neanderthals are described as *Early Humans* because they belong to a select group of late-period hominids that includes Denisovans and Floresiensis. There are many distinctions between these Early Human species and Modern Humans, but the most notable difference is that Modern Humans can be further delineated by nine distinct phenotype categories, with each phenotype marked by a unique set of characteristics. These characteristics include the Endeavor, specializations, primary role, and functional adaptations that are unique to Modern Humans.

There is some evidence to suggest the extinction of Neanderthals occurred soon after the arrival of humans; and that they coexisted, intermingled, and in some cases interbred with humans. Notable is that Early Humans and Modern Humans shared a common ancestor, perhaps with Homo Erectus, or as recent as Homo Heidelbergensis. Although some of these points are debatable, there is a consensus that Modern Humans were the last species to arrive.

Although the exact date that Modern Humans arrived remains a mystery, two critical observations regarding the arrival of humans can be made, with the first being that humans are the progeny of a species that existed sometime between 20,000 YA to 400,000 YA. Second is that humans are the product of a distinct evolutionary mechanism known as Enneciation. Understanding Enneciation requires an understanding of Environmental Archetypes.

Environmental Archetypes are the symbols and structures that formed within the collective psyche of Early Humans based on experiential impressions that took place over vast periods. Experiences having the most gravity, and that occur with enough repetition, are the most likely to become an Environmental Archetype. The data created by Environmental Archetypes resides in the DNA, where the unconscious mind accesses it when needed. This information plays a vital role in human functioning because it provides the psyche with a rich source of the contextual knowledge that is necessary for survival. The Nine Factors of Extinction presented in the next chapter are examples of Environmental Archetypes.

Enneciation is an evolutionary mechanism for semi-sapient life forms, that provides for the reconciliation of intractable Environmental Archetypes, by the differentiation of nine distinct phenotypes. Each phenotype (Enneatype) is uniquely adapted to address one of the nine intractable Environmental Archetypes. For this to occur, a critical mass of Environmental Archetypes must develop within a species, especially archetypes that pose direct and indirect threats.

> **Enneciation:** The differentiation of a species into nine distinct phenotypes, each having unique physiological and psychological characteristics, within a system that evolved to address nine intractable Environmental Archetypes.

There are a few things to note about Enneciation. First is that each of the nine types evolved from, and has the specializations necessary to eliminate, one of the Nine Factors of Extinction. Second is that Enneciation is possible because of the Environmental Archetypes that formed in the psyche of Early Humans. This phenomenon was described by Carl Jung, who theorized that the archetypes represented functional roles, each derived from the collective interpersonal experiences of humanity. Jung saw that archetypes provide the human psyche with a rich source of contextual information concerning interpersonal roles. However, Jung failed to link the phenomenon of archetypes to a specific evolutionary mechanism or framework such as the Enneagram.

If Jung were here today, he would no doubt have a great appreciation that his work on archetypes was useful from the perspective of human evolution. However, the Jungian archetypes would not include each of the Nine Factors of Extinction, as some are not entirely related to interpersonal experiences. Thus, the Jungian archetypes are a subset of the Environmental Archetypes. A good starting point for understanding the phenomenon of Environmental Archetypes is to study the Nine Factors of Extinction presented later.

Although Enneciation is a potent mechanism of evolution, it does have some limitations, especially concerning its reach, scope, and application. The critical point is that Enneciation is a local phenomenon, as opposed to a universal phenomenon, which has important implications. Consider that if Enneciation were a universal phenomenon, then all life forms in every corner of the universe would evolve to have the same form, function, and appearance. But since Enneciation is a local phenomenon, operating as a distinct paradigm of adaptation, it produces life forms that reflect a specific locale. It necessarily follows that humans are a uniquely evolved and individuated product of Earth.

Enneciation also depends on time, as the Environmental Archetypes themselves are period-specific, which carries significant implications. Consider the hypothetical situation of Higher Primates evolving during the mid-Jurassic era of dinosaurs. The Environmental Archetypes would have been substantially different for that period, in turn affecting the Nine Factors of Extinction, resulting in the Enneciation of Enneatypes that were radically different in form, function, and appearance from humans. For these reasons, Enneciation is a function of time, location, and circumstances.

Enneciation is the phenomenon responsible for creating a new species, composed of nine distinct phenotypes, with each type purposefully matched to one of the Nine Factors of Extinction. This discussion continues with an analysis of the Nine Factors of Extinction, followed by a chapter for each of the Enneatypes.

CHAPTER 2
THE NINE FACTORS OF EXTINCTION

The Nine Factors of Extinction (NFE) are a phenomenon having two fundamental dimensions. The first dimension describes the point of origin, which can be either exogenous, endogenous, or intrinsic. Exogenous refers to factors that are generally outside the direct control of Early Humans, endogenous refers to factors within the direct control of Early Humans, and intrinsic factors are those that are under the control of the individual. The second dimension describes the locus of impact on the Thinking, Emotional, and Instinctive Centers: Three factors of extinction affect the Thinking Center, three affect the Emotional Center, and three affect the Instinctive Center. In consideration of both dimensions, the following matrix emerges:

Type One: Endogenous/Instinctive

Type Two: Exogenous/Emotional

Type Three: Intrinsic/Emotional

Type Four: Endogenous/Emotional

Type Five: Exogenous/Thinking

Type Six: Intrinsic/Thinking

Type Seven: Endogenous/Thinking

Type Eight: Exogenous/Instinctive

Type Nine: Intrinsic/Instinctive

The most expedient way to organize the discussion of the NFE and the nine phenotypes is to group them into triads composed of three Enneatypes. The logical way to group them is according to the second dimension, resulting in three triadic themes: Barbarism is the common theme for the 8-9-1 triad, Stagnation for the triad of 2-3-4, and Conundrums for triad 5-6-7. For these reasons, the best way to proceed is according to the groupings created by the Instinctive, Emotional, and Thinking Centers.

Triad 8-9-1: Barbarism

The universe exists, functions, and evolves according to three fundamental laws known as The Law of Three, the Law of Seven, and the Law of Nine. Each law plays a vital role in the phenomenology of the universe, especially for the evolution of life forms. Thus, understanding the three fundamental laws of the universe in more detail is a prerequisite to understanding the phenomenon of evolution.

The law of three, also known as the law of three forces, is the most fundamental law of nature because it determines the basic structure of all matter in the universe. There are many examples of the law of three, but perhaps the best example is the atomic model because it demonstrates the three primal forces of nature. Electrons are particles with a positive force, neutrons are a neutralizing force, and protons have a negative force. The atomic model illustrates how three distinct forces, working together in harmony, can provide the structure for a multitude of diverse elements.

Apart from the atomic model, there are many other examples of the law of three, with the most notable examples appearing in the natural sciences. For example, Geologists have identified three types of rock: Igneous, metamorphic, and sedimentary. Physicists have identified three natural states of matter: Solid, liquid, and gas. Zoologists classify animals as herbivores, carnivores, and omnivores. Indeed, clouds, flowers, plants, and celestial bodies all conform to the Law of Three. There are many more, but those are left to the reader to discover on their own. Next is the relationship between matter and the law of seven.

Everything in the universe is vibrating. Fortunately, vibration is an observable phenomenon, which has allowed scientists to confirm that the vibration level of all objects in the universe is continually changing. The law of seven, also known as the law of harmonics, is the mechanism that determines the changes in vibrational frequency that scientists have observed. The Law of Seven determines the timing, magnitude, and direction that vibrational frequencies change. The best example of the Law of Seven is the musical scale, which contains eight notes within each octave: Do, Re, Mi, Fa, So, La, Ti, Do.

The musical scale demonstrates the seven steps of an octave, with the understanding that each step in an octave corresponds to a distinct change in vibration. This phenomenon manifests as an increase, decrease, or monotone change in frequency. The tonality of the music scale follows a pattern predicated on the Law of Seven. Moreover, because the Law of Seven determines all manner of change in the universe, it necessarily follows that the law of seven governs evolution.

The Law of Nine is known as the Law of Higher Orders. Higher Orders become possible when a life form, such as those endowed with consciousness, reaches a certain level of vibrational frequency. When the vibrational level becomes critical, the Law of Nine will produce a new life form consisting of nine distinct phenotypes. Perhaps the best example of the Law of Nine can be found in the Enneciation of life forms.

The three fundamental laws govern the order, structure, and evolution of matter. As matter evolves into life forms, there is a oneness and unity with nature that allows all life forms to live in peace and harmony with one another, as each adapts, bonds, and conforms to their environment. Each life form is respectful of the laws of nature, but most importantly, each has an inherent respect for life itself. That was the situation on Earth for hundreds of millions of years, at least until the arrival of Early Humans.

At a critical point in the chain of human evolution, sometime before the arrival of Homo Erectus, Early Humans developed a new level of consciousness that was not bound by the laws of nature. Concurrent with this development was the evolution of new psychic structures, including a more advanced ego that brought a higher degree of independent thought, action, and behavior. Independent thinking was a seminal event in human evolution, as a primitive consciousness oriented toward the survival of the individual displaced the instinctive drives of the organism that had been dominant for millions of years.

Although the arrival of consciousness was a substantial step forward in evolution, it amplified the narcissism that had already developed. The amplification of narcissism meant that each specimen would seek to selfishly maximize rewards whenever possible, doing so without respect for the laws of nature or the sanctity of life. The failure to recognize the laws of nature, especially with due regard for the sanctity of life, introduced a state of lawless barbarism that had not existed before.

The introduction of barbarism created a default state of rampant inter-personal violence, savagery, and chaos that is a defining characteristic of primitive beings and their progeny. Barbarism is not an intuitive outcome, as an expansion of consciousness would generally be expected to align with more evolved character traits and behaviors. The following discussion of barbarism provides some answers.

Factor Eight: Exogenous Barbarism

Exogenous Barbarism is the intentional infliction of violence, exacted for survival, on an individual or social group by an opposing group of individuals. Although the victims of Exogenous Barbarism have no direct relationship with their attackers, they generally have an implicit understanding that the violence serves the purpose of reallocating the resources necessary for survival. The resources reallocated in this manner include food, weapons, tools, precious metals, technology, shelter, and personnel.

Acquiring resources by force was necessary for several reasons, with the foremost being that Early Humans lacked a mechanism that sponsored barter or trade between groups. Trade benefits all participants for a multitude of reasons, including the efficiency gains that occur from specialization, productivity gains that are achieved by economies of scale, and the collateral boosts in innovation that are secondary to long-term trading activities. Had there been a mechanism that sponsored trading activities between social groups, much of the violence between groups would have been unnecessary, thus curtailing or limiting the degree of Exogenous Barbarism. This point will be revisited in more detail later.

Exogenous Barbarism would still be problematic even if intertribal trade were a regular practice because Exogenous Barbarism aims to reallocate resources to those who are the fittest, strongest, and most intelligent, due to the evolutionary phenomenon of natural selection: The Darwinian process that ensures survival by the selective endorsement of superior traits. Natural selection helps to ensure that traits conferring a survival advantage, as determined by reproductive success, are passed forward to future generations.

By carefully examining the evolution of humans, it is clear that natural selection had endorsed the aggressive traits associated with Exogenous Barbarism. And if resources were reallocated to the fittest, strongest, and most intelligent, then Exogenous Barbarism could be considered an essential component in the natural selection process because it recognizes, rewards, and endorses the traits associated with competitive behaviors. However, the reallocation and redistribution of resources among Early Humans, despite the prevalence of Exogenous Barbarism, was not according to the fittest, strongest, and most intelligent. It was a chaotic phenomenon based mostly on random chance. Some examples will illustrate this point.

Early Humans existing 1.5 MYA would have been very successful hunter-gatherers, thus allowing them to support nuclear families composed of several members. Exogenous Barbarism was a primary threat to these subsistence hunters, mostly due to the scarcity of resources, as other individuals and groups that were less successful were motivated to expropriate their resources. Unfortunately, there would be no way to predict, prepare, or defend against these expropriations, as they were typically the result of random, spontaneous, uncoordinated interceptions. The reality was that a small team of successful hunters, when ambushed by superior numbers, would be forced to hand over the fruits of their labor. These types of scenarios meant the reallocation of resources to those who had less talent, skill, and intelligence often occurred. This result runs contrary to the edicts of natural selection.

Another problem was the many coordinated, premeditated, and barbaric attacks that aimed to decimate a nuclear family. Attacks on nuclear families that possessed a superior location, tools, weapons, food stocks, clothing, or other resources occurred frequently. An excellent example of a superior location would be a cave located near a river because it would afford protection from environmental threats while providing an efficient source of water. Such a location would be subject to competition, and thus would have changed hands frequently, sometimes by the aggressive elimination of the inhabitants. Violence often leads to collateral casualties, which in this context meant that substantial numbers of Early Human lives were wasted rather than conserved, yielding a result that runs contrary to the successful evolution of a species.

In the example of the cave by the river, the individuals who were successful in acquiring the cave were not necessarily the fittest, strongest, and most intelligent. What they often did have was a coordinated attack based on the advantage of surprise, which allowed them to overcome the previous inhabitants of the cave in ways that were independent of talent, skill, and intelligence. Examples like this demonstrate the reallocation of resources from those with superior traits to those with inferior traits, skills, and abilities. Again, this result runs contrary to the edicts of natural selection.

Although Exogenous Barbarism was a form of competitive resource allocation, it failed to select, reward, and endorse those who possessed exceptional talent, skill, and intelligence. Because of this failure, natural selection failed to enhance, strengthen, and improve the genes of Early Humans. Because the natural selection mechanism failed, Exogenous Barbarism became both an impediment and a limiting factor in the success of Early Humans. That is because the failure to allocate resources according to the principles of competitive behaviors results in the endorsement of traits that are random, regressive, and deleterious. The endorsement of regressive traits, coupled with the waste of resources that occurred over protracted periods, caused or contributed to the extinction of multiple Early Human species.

Exogenous Barbarism was responsible for the persistent misallocation and wasting of resources, and the endorsement of regressive traits,

making it a primary factor in the extinction of multiple species of Early Humans.

Factor Nine: Intrinsic Barbarism

Intrinsic Barbarism is the extreme violence that stems from defects existing within the psyche. These defects include various disorders, regressive traits, nutritional deficiencies, arrested development of consciousness, antiquated survival mechanisms, and many others. In the interest of brevity, this discussion will be restricted to the intra-psychic regressive traits, because they are a substantial cause of Intrinsic Barbarism.

Early Humans possessed a great diversity of traits and behaviors that were necessary for surviving harsh, extreme, and very primitive conditions. Some of these traits, such as envy, jealousy, and hostility, can be traced to the Higher Primates. However, many of these traits, including deception, greed, lust, anger, and hate developed sometime after humans diverged from the Higher Primates. These traits and behaviors eventually reached an evolutionary threshold, where they became a constant source of intraspecies conflict that had devastating consequences for human evolution. The consequences of conflict include the misallocation of resources, the loss of innocent lives, and the fracturing of nuclear families and groups.

Hate is probably the most ubiquitous cause of conflict, and it plays a central role in the phenomenology of Intrinsic Barbarism. Object relations theory defines hate as an emotional effect. According to object relations theory, the Ego functions by dividing reality into distinct objects, and then assigns an emotional effect between all external objects and the self. By dividing reality into small pieces, and attaching an emotion to each piece, the ego creates the framework that is necessary to function in the world. However, this necessarily restricts and objectifies everything in the physical universe, including the self and others, while at the same time it further restricts the relationship potential to that of predefined emotional effects: Love, hate, joy, peace, disappointment, trust, distrust, attraction, disgust, excitement and so on.

The Universal Qualities, such as love, joy, and peace, operate mostly on a conscious level; whereas, hate and other regressive traits operate mostly on a subconscious level. To understand why the regressive traits are a subconscious phenomenon, an understanding of these traits within the context of the Superego is necessary.

The Superego is a defensive mechanism within the psyche, functioning as an inner coercive agency, whose primary role is to protect a species from harm. Although the Superego controls the thoughts, behaviors, and actions of an individual, the individual is generally unaware of when, how, and why their Superego is operating. That is because the Superego is designed to work on a subconscious level, which gives the Superego default control over the thoughts, behaviors, and actions of the individual. Thus, the individual is under the jurisdiction of and is subordinate to, the dictates of their superego.

As a coercive agency, the Superego is the primary protective mechanism of the individual. The Superego protects the individual by avoiding harmful situations, such as physical violence, by coercing and controlling the instinctive and emotional behaviors. However, the Superego was generally only effective at sublimating the regressive traits, behaviors, and violent tendencies to the subconscious mind. Pushing the problem to the subconscious mind gave rise to individuals who were mostly unaware that they possess any of the regressive traits, behaviors, or violent tendencies. Unfortunately, several intra-psychic defense mechanisms such as projection only made matters worse.

Projection is a defensive mechanism that helps maintain the integration of the ego. Projection occurs when an individual displaces (projects) one of their character traits onto another object as a way of eliminating this trait from their own ego identity. Projection becomes necessary due to conflicts between two or more ego identity structures, such as when there is an identification with love that coincides with hate. The concurrent identification with love and hate creates a conflict, which threatens the integration of the Ego because of the polarity that exists between these two traits. Projecting the trait of hate onto another individual allows the suppression of this trait to the subconscious, thereby allowing the ego to maintain its identification with the trait of love, which strengthens the overall integrity of the ego.

From an evolutionary perspective, the suppression of the regressive traits to the subconscious mind was necessary, because otherwise they might be ignored or rendered irrelevant by the conscious mind. And that would be an untenable outcome, as the regressive traits provide distinct advantages and protections for the individual, and this is especially true for the trait of hate.

From an object relations perspective, hate is the most potent form of rejection that is possible within the psyche; thus, it is the most potent emotional effect that can be assigned by the Superego. Although hate is an emotion that is generally controlled by the Superego, it is fueled and exacerbated by other regressive traits such as envy, jealousy, and aggression that originate from the Ego. Thus, hate is difficult to predict, and difficult to isolate, due to its infinite variations. For these reasons, no other emotion has as much variation, from a mild rejection on one end of the continuum to unspeakably barbarous acts at the other end.

The continuum of hate serves several purposes. However, the primary purpose of hate is to change the behavior of a target, because when targeted individuals feel rejected, they are more likely to adapt to the edicts of their social circle. In this respect, hate serves the purpose of ensuring behavioral conformity within a social group. For individuals who do not conform, hate serves to isolate, alienate, and reject those perceived as a threat. The process of escalation may continue, sometimes ending in the annihilation of nonconforming individuals.

Other purposes for hate include the reallocation of resources and the protection of the organism. However, the purpose here is not to illuminate the evolutionary functions of regressive traits such as hate. The purpose is to understand that all regressive traits, including hate, are a direct cause of Intrinsic Barbarism. The phenomenon of hate was used as an example because most people have direct knowledge of the collateral damage that it causes. These damages include the loss and alienation of valuable human resources and the fracturing of nuclear families and social groups. Thus, the damages of Intrinsic Barbarism range from minor disruptions to the catastrophic decimation of families and communities.

There is a certain irony here because the causes of Intrinsic Barbarism trace back to the human psyche. Part of the problem traces back to the regressive traits of primates, but from this discussion, it becomes clear that some of the regressive traits evolved much later. So, the irony is that evolution had created advanced mechanisms for survival that, at a certain point in evolution, had become an impediment to further evolution.

Another irony is that the phenomenon of Intrinsic Barbarism is self-evident by merely pointing to the regressive traits and behaviors of primates, and the regressive traits and behaviors of Modern Humans while realizing that Early Humans had the worst elements of both groups. Indeed, the regressive traits were responsible for a high degree of intra-species corruption, having the potential to affect all individuals, by sponsoring rampant deception, theft, assault, rape, and murder. The conditions imposed by Intrinsic Barbarism were so extreme, and so devastating to Early Humans that it earned a place among the Nine Factors of Extinction.

Intrinsic Barbarism is the result of an incomplete, redundant, or conflicted integration of psychic mechanisms, resulting in significant collateral damage and loss of life, thereby contributing to the extinction of multiple Early Human species.

Factor One: Endogenous Barbarism

Endogenous Barbarism is the savage, inexplicable, chaotic, and lawless violence that occurred in the domestic affairs of semi-conscious beings. Endogenous Barbarism includes the assault, rape, torture, murder, and genocides that were responsible for the loss of many lives and communities. Because chaos is both a defining feature and a direct cause of Endogenous Barbarism, it is important to understand the fundamentals of chaos, especially its origin, history, and phenomenology.

In the context of Endogenous Barbarism, chaos is the unpredictable, disorderly, unruly, and primeval behaviors that persist in a consequence-free environment. Chaos is generally not observed in the animal kingdom, because most creatures exist in harmony with nature, although episodes of chaotic behavior have been known to occur in some primates. However, even primates have near absolute respect for the laws of nature, as they are rarely observed committing random acts of aggression that serve no survival purpose. Unfortunately, this inherent respect for the laws of nature did not apply to semi-conscious beings such as Homo Erectus.

The arrival of semi-conscious beings brought a fundamental disregard for the laws of nature, mostly because the laws of nature have no influence, control, or jurisdiction over consciousness. That is because consciousness is an independent phenomenon, existing on its own accord, without regard to the physical dimension. Consciousness has no boundaries, morals, edicts, ethics, principles, or standards that pertain to the physical world, so it is not subject to the laws of nature.

The expansion of consciousness that occurred with Homo Erectus was made possible by a more sophisticated psychic structure consisting of an ID, Ego, and Superego. The Ego was of special importance because the identity of the individual was enhanced, refined, and expanded. Together, the expansion in consciousness, coupled with the advancements in the Ego, brought new-found freedom to think, act, and behave independently of the laws of nature.

The laws of nature derive from the authority of a higher power. Having independence from the laws of nature meant that Early Humans had greater freedom to think, act, and behave because they could conceptualize them-selves in a way that was independent of a higher power. This separation and independence from the jurisdiction of a higher power meant that Early Humans had effectively substituted themselves to replace God. The substitu-tion of the self in place of God had significant consequences!

The substitution of God with the Ego is perpetuated by a fundamental inability to perceive the existence of God. The inability to perceive God is the result of an intra-psychic bias known as Atheism. Atheism was problematic to Early Humans for several reasons, but primarily because it eliminated all regard for a higher power, which in turn sponsored all manner of chaos. The problems associated with Atheism are confirmed by history, which has proven that the absence of respect for a higher power breeds chaos. Conversely, respect for a higher power eliminates chaos. Thus, atheism is the predicate for chaos.

A critical inference has surfaced from the relationship between Endogenous Barbarism, chaos, and atheism, which is that atheism is one of the fundamental causes of Endogenous Barbarism. If a higher power does exist, it seems to have anticipated the phenomenon of atheism and instituted measures to counteract it. That will become clear upon reading Chapter Six. The main point here is that evolution has not favored atheism, as social groups that are respecting of a higher power have been more successful, especially when compared to atheistic groups. A key reason is that respect for a higher power replaces chaos with order, structure, and lawful behavior; while the opposite is true for atheism.

Endogenous Barbarism is the extreme violence, mayhem, and chaos that prevails, in the absence of social order, structure, and civilization, due to a primitive disdain for the laws of nature.

Triad 2-3-4: Economic Stagnation

The period marked by the arrival of Homo Erectus approximately 2 MYA, and ending with Neanderthals approximately 24,000 YA, can be viewed as a period of very little cultural, economic, and technological growth. The lack of economic growth partly explains why Early Humans were functioning at a subsistence level of existence during this period. However, it does not mean that Early Humans were not evolving during this period, as many changes did occur, such as the anatomical changes that have been documented by many anthropologists. However, despite significant increases in brain size, and a more sophisticated psyche, Early Humans continued to function at a subsistence level for a very extended period.

There is no question that Early Humans functioned at less than a subsistence level, based on the number of extinct species that have been littered along the path of human evolution during the past 2 MY, which includes Homo Neanderthalensis, Homo Floresiensis, Homo Heidelbergensis, Paranthropus Robustus, and Paranthropus Boisei. With evidence of so many failures among Early Human species, it is important to investigate all factors that might be responsible for their failure to thrive. The first step in this investigation requires an understanding of what is meant by a *failure to thrive*.

The observation that Early Humans *failed to thrive* means that they failed to improve, progress, or make advancements in living standards. All of these were true for Early Humans because their economic status was dire. Thus, a pivot to an economic perspective is necessary for further analysis.

A failure to advance living standards means, in economic terms, the failure to increase the per capita production of goods and services. The Gross Species Product (GSP) refers to the total value of all goods and services produced by a species per period. The GSP includes the value of all food, clothing, tools, shelters, weapons, jewelry, accouterments, miscellaneous goods, and services that are produced by a species. The GSP can then be divided by population to arrive at the per capita GSP, which is tracked over time to indicate whether the standard of living is increasing, stagnating, or declining.

Although it would be interesting to compute the per capita GSP for every species of Early Humans, it is not required in this case, because the focus is on the factors that shaped the overall trend in per capita GSP during the 2 MY period of Early Human evolution. Based on the episodic nature of Early Human evolution, there is no question that the overall trend for GSP was flat, hovering just above the level necessary for subsistence. Indeed, there is no evidence of significant cyclical trends; nor evidence of a positive trend that might have produced appreciable changes in GSP. Economists define a flat trend in average economic output as stagnation.

Economic theory informs that many factors might lead to stagnation in modern economies. On a macroeconomic level, changes in the money supply, inflation, input prices, interest rates, international trade, and confidence levels are among the most important. As a general factor, the average productivity of labor is the most important. However, each of these factors becomes irrelevant, with one exception, in the context of the primitive Early Human economies. The average productivity of labor is the one exception, because economic productivity is the most fundamental of factors affecting economic output in the long term, and this is especially true for the output trends observed in primitive Early Human economies. Because there were no other significant factors that affected Early Human GSP, the average productivity of labor likely had a substantial causal relationship with per capita GSP.

There were undoubtedly other factors that affected per capita GSP. A short list of important factors would include the economies of scale, which in turn would affect the degree of specialization that was possible. Both factors are dependent on population densities, and the availability of resources, especially human resources. Language efficiency also played a role. However, these factors are subsumed by the average productivity of labor, at least for this discussion.

In the context of economic theory, the average productivity of labor is the primary explanatory variable for changes in GSP. Because there is a strong causal relationship between these variables, the flat trend in GSP can be attributed primarily to a flat trend in average productivity. Thus, the average labor productivity is the key to understanding the flat trend observed in the GSP of Early Humans.

The average productivity of labor is a function of three distinct economic factors: Cultural innovation, Intrinsic innovation, and Entrepreneurial innovation. Cultural innovation refers to the development of new behaviors that support Commerce. Intrinsic innovation refers to the economic psychology of a species, and how that psychology supports the economization of resources, resulting in greater economic efficiency, productivity, and growth. Entrepreneurial innovation refers to the risk-taking initiatives that are necessary for the creation and advancement of new technologies.

An absence of innovation in all three economic spheres will result in Cultural, Intrinsic, and Entrepreneurial stagnation. Each of these corresponds to a distinct factor of extinction. This discussion continues by taking a closer look at the three distinct economic factors of extinction corresponding with Enneatypes 2-3-4.

Factor Two: Cultural Stagnation

Human culture is composed of the specific social norms and behaviors that persist within a homogenous population. The reference to social norms and behaviors refers to many types of intangible phenomena, including the ethics, etiquette, and integration standards endemic to a social group. Ethics refs to the moral values that are agreed and enforced within a social group; and etiquette pertains to the customs, practices, and traditions. The integration standards determine the order, structure, language, and composition of social groups.

Because culture is mostly an intangible phenomenon, it is difficult to analyze without direct observation, documentation, or related artifacts. Complicating matters is the fact that artifacts unearthed to date indicate very little or no significant cultural advancement over the final 2MY of human evolution. Thus, an understanding of cultural stagnation requires an analysis of the factors that prevented innovation in the ethical, etiquette, and integration standards of Early Humans.

Cultural stagnation persisted as a significant factor of extinction in Early Human populations due to the operation of many interrelated cofactors. In the interest of brevity, the focus will be on the cofactor of fracturing, because it was a predominant cause of cultural stagnation.

> **Fracturing**: Divisions between individuals, nuclear families, and social groups that stem from real, perceived, or imagined conflicts.

Fracturing occurs when a bond between two individuals, or the cohesion within a social group, is broken by real, perceived, or imagined conflicts. Although fracturing traces to conflicts with other survival traits such as envy, greed, hate, jealousy, and lust, it also occurs because of perceived violations in the standards of etiquette, ethics, and integration. Each of these factors played an important role because of their ubiquity among Early Human populations. The persistence of regressive traits, coupled with a lack of social standards, was a persistent cause of fracturing among Early Human social groups.

Fracturing limited the size of Early Human social groups to that of small tribes composed of inter-related nuclear families, with the nuclear families consisting of two generations existing in small groups of four to twenty individuals. Although contact between nuclear families would have been a frequent occurrence, especially within the confines of a tribal organization, nuclear families tended to limit contact with those outside their nuclear group. However, closer integration of nuclear families certainly did occur from time to time, especially in locations of abundant resources, but this would have been a temporal phenomenon. The main point is that the lack of integration between nuclear families was a limiting factor in the scale that could be achieved by social tribes.

The lack of integration between nuclear families, meaning horizontal integration, meant that the social (horizontal) channel of learning between nuclear families was limited or closed. The lack of a horizontal learning channel had a crippling effect on cultural innovation because it prevented the sharing of ideas, experiences, customs, traditions, methods, language, and practices necessary for increases in productivity. The lack of sharing meant that the primary channel for passing cultural traditions was by way of the vertical channel. Parents would teach their children how to create tools, weapons, and survival gear; and then provide instruction for the ways of subsistence living. Thus, the vertical channel of social learning was the primary means, and perhaps the only means, of cultural innovation for Early Humans: A fact that had significant economic implications.

Economic theory tells us that innovation is a horizontal phenomenon, as it depends on the competitive advantages inherent to competing groups. Without some degree of integration, cooperation, communication, and competition between groups, cultural innovation opportunities would have been minimal in Early Human communities. Indeed, their primitive psychology did not provide a mechanism that sponsored integration, cooperation, communication, and competition between groups. Thus, Early Humans had a very primitive standard of integration that did not lend itself to advancements in culture.

It is important to remember that cultural innovations do not occur in a vacuum. They occur within the social environment endemic to the social group, which in this case happened to be vacillating conditions of extreme barbarism. Due to the prevalence of barbarism, there would have been an absence of ethical standards to guide Early Human behavior. Although there may be some debate on the magnitude, there is no question that barbarism also impeded the operation of horizontal channels of learning that would have sponsored cultural innovations in Early Human populations.

Emerging from this discussion is an understanding that Early Humans possessed a very primitive culture that did not lend itself to innovation. The problems associated with a primitive culture were compounded by fracturing, which created additional problems, such as language dialects, learning impediments, and an overall stagnation in economic productivity. So without a mechanism that inspired more sophisticated behaviors, every species of Early Humans was doomed to fail.

The lack of ethical, etiquette and integration standards was responsible for the division, fracturing, and eventual economic stagnation of Early Human economies, making them a significant factor in the extinction of multiple Early Human species.

Factor Three: Intrinsic Stagnation

The arrival of consciousness meant that Early Humans had greater freedom in where, when, and how they performed the intrinsic activities of daily living. These activities included foraging and hunting, building comfortable shelters, and the activities necessary for procreation. These are the intrinsic activities of survival since a persistent failure in just one of these activities is a one-way road to extinction. Some further discussion may help to illuminate the gravity of these critical functions.

The television series titled Naked and Afraid documents the struggle to survive that ensues, as couples brave the challenges of a remote wilderness location for a period of up to twenty days in the nude. The couple that appears in each episode is typically allowed one tool, one accouterment, and perhaps a map of their location. Many do not make it three weeks, sometimes because of medical issues, but mostly because they surrender from a broken will. For those individuals who have the will to endure, they lose significant amounts of body mass each day due to extreme caloric deprivation. Thus, all indications are that nearly 100% of the participants would eventually perish in a real-world survival scenario, an astonishing failure rate, even considering how far removed humans are from the wilderness experience. These results concur with other survival television programs.

Les Stroud is a self-described survivalist who produced perhaps the first survival television series. In each episode, he would arrive at a remote location with his clothes, harmonica, cameras, and a few accouterments. He would then document his struggle to survive in that location over several days. Les is certainly more capable of survival than the average person, and there are indications that he had researched and planned a survival strategy; but despite these advantages, he also failed to acquire enough calories for long term survival in most of his episodes.

The main point from these programs is that survival in the wilderness is a tough business. Survival requires strength, will, courage, and flexibility. These traits combine to form the work ethic that is necessary for the survival of a species. Because without a strong, well-defined, and persistent work ethic, advancements in the intrinsic activities of daily living are not forthcoming.

The work ethic in most organisms is hard-wired thru the instincts; but in the case of Early Humans, consciousness displaced the fundamental drive to survive. With consciousness came freedom, which meant that the work ethic for Early Humans was no longer a constant, as it depended on the cultural norms, behaviors, and ethics of the social group. The problem with this arrangement is that the cultural norm for Early Humans was to achieve a subsistence level of existence.

From an economic perspective, the culture of Early Humans was not conducive to economic growth because there were no mechanisms, incentives, or traits that sponsored greater productivity in the intrinsic activities of daily living. But perhaps the most important factor was that the work ethic was subsumed by, and a direct reflection of, the Early Human cultural norms of mediocrity, sloth, and laziness.

The regressive traits of mediocrity, sloth, and laziness are behavioral phenomena explained by two economic principles. The first principle is the substitution effect, which demonstrates the substitutions that individuals make when they have a choice between two goods. In this example, Early Humans had a choice between leisure time and additional food supplies. Because Early Humans had no way to preserve food, and there were no markets to barter excess food supplies, any food accumulated beyond the daily rations would have very little value because of spoilage. Thus, food had a marginal value approaching zero, resulting in the substitution of leisure for food at the margin. As a consequence, the substitution effect of leisure prevented Early Humans from further economic advancement.

The second economic principle is known as the income effect, which describes how a change in income affects the economic choices that are made by individuals. In this example, an increase in income will increase the amounts of both leisure and food; however, the increase in leisure will be proportionally greater than the increase in food, because the marginal value for food approaches zero for the reasons cited above.

There are other factors at play, such as the opportunity costs of taking leisure. The opportunity cost of taking leisure offsets the income effect, but the offset would be negligible in extremely primitive economies because the opportunity cost of additional food is negligible. From this discussion, an understanding emerges that small changes in standard of living would have a relatively greater marginal effect on the increased consumption of leisure.

The income and substitution effects inform that Early Humans were naturally predisposed to favor leisure over the acquisition of additional food supplies, better shelter, and additional procreation. These phenomena can be observed in primates, as their behavior also demonstrates a strong preference for leisure. From an economic perspective, the preference for leisure is a rational phenomenon. But from the perspective of evolution, the preference for leisure is irrational, due to the devastation it exacts upon a species in the long term.

The application of economic theory to the situation of Early Humans illuminates the role that economic factors played in human evolution. Economic theory suggests that Early Humans lived at a subsistence level primarily because they had a very high preference for leisure, meaning that after basic rations were acquired, they would dawdle much of their time away. Indeed, the preference for leisure was responsible for a work ethic that regressed toward subsistence, rather than a work ethic based on growth, prosperity, and achievement. Of course, other factors were operable such as the prevailing cultural norms and behaviors, the opportunities for improvement, and the incentives for innovation. But these factors generally favored mediocrity, sloth, and laziness.

Emerging from this discussion is an appreciation that Early Humans had a work ethic that regressed to a subsistence level due to economic, psychological, environmental, and cultural reasons. Moreover, the prevalence of a subsistence level work ethic impeded the advancements in efficiency, productivity, and economies of scale needed for improvement in the intrinsic activities of daily living. A primitive work ethic gave rise to the phenomenon of Intrinsic Stagnation, which occurs when a species fails to evolve the economic psychology needed to boost the per capita productivity of labor, thereby preventing economic progress beyond a subsistence level of existence. The cumulative effects of failure in the basic survival activities and the concurrent stagnation in the average productivity of labor include malnutrition, disease, bottlenecks, and extinction. Because of the grave consequences, Intrinsic Stagnation earned a place among the Nine Factors of Extinction.

Intrinsic Stagnation was the result of psychological and economic factors that combined to impede the growth, viability, and long-term success of Early Human economies.

Factor Four: Entrepreneurial Stagnation

The archaeological evidence suggests that Early Humans had, during the last 2 MY of their evolution, a very primitive ability to innovate new tools, weapons, clothing, cookware, and shelter. Even as environmental conditions deteriorated, there was very little innovation concerning the core technologies utilized by Early Humans. The failure to advance, innovate, and develop new technologies in the face of a harsh, primitive, rapidly changing environment had disastrous consequences for Early Humans. The consequences were so severe that in many cases, the failure to innovate new technologies was a significant factor of extinction.

Entrepreneurial innovations are new technologies that produce measurable changes in human behavior, such as using a cell phone camera or using the internet to obtain information. But many innovations are subtle, as with the introduction of new methods of painting such as pointillism, impressionism, or line and color. The important point is that in each case, entrepreneurial innovations produce a measurable change in human behavior. Thus, entrepreneurial innovation is a significant contributor to the evolution of human culture.

What is generally not understood is that entrepreneurial innovation is an economic behavior, specifically an economic risk-taking initiative, that is inherently prone to failure. Entrepreneurs invest their time and energy in the development of new technologies, in lieu of the immediate rewards of a stable career, in the hope that their innovations will change human behavior. Moreover, entrepreneurs seek rewards that compensate for the substantial risks of failure, the foregone income, and the inherent value of the innovation.

In modern times, entrepreneurs rarely receive compensation for the risks they undertake, and this would have been especially true for Early Humans. Consider that Early Human entrepreneurs had no market for their innovations. Even if there was demand for innovation, the lack of currency for exchange, and the limits of mobility prevented the development of geographically diverse markets. The lack of markets and mobility meant that the end consumer of an Early Human innovation was often the entrepreneur.

There are other reasons to explain the risk adversity of Early Humans. One is that Early Humans could not forgo their obligation to perform the intrinsic activities of daily living; therefore, risk-taking would have been a luxury that few could afford. And even if a new technology had magically presented itself, Early Humans had a limited means to share it, because the horizontal learning channels lacked sophistication. For these reasons, Early Human entrepreneurs had no way to capitalize on their innovations.

It is tempting to conclude that Early Humans failed to innovate because of risk adversity, a lack of learning channels, and a lack of economic markets. Indeed, there is every probability that Early Humans did make minor advances in critical areas such as tool making and weapons; a contention that is supported by archaeological evidence. But this does not mean that these advances were widely shared or disseminated. On the contrary, Early Humans were very primitive and short-sighted. They had no psychological mechanism that sponsored sharing, cooperation, and integration with other communities. Thus, most of the incremental advances made would have disappeared within the stretch of a few generations.

Although Early Humans had evolved in significant ways, a mechanism that sponsored innovation and other entrepreneurial behaviors had not developed, thereby limiting their ability to make advancements in tools, weapons, and other technologies. But perhaps their greatest weakness was their risk adversity, which ensured that entrepreneurial stagnation would earn a place among the Nine Factors of Extinction.

The failure to create positive changes in human behavior, by the innovation, advancement, and adaptation of new technologies, was responsible for the economic stagnation and eventual extinction of Early Humans.

Triad 2-3-4: Conundrums

With a significantly greater brain capacity, the arrival of Homo Erectus was a major step in human evolution for several reasons. First, the increase in brain size sponsored a much greater capacity for memory and solving problems. A larger brain meant that Homo Erectus was able to solve more problems related to survival than any of their predecessors. Moreover, the increase in brain size allowed the development of the Id, which sponsored new instinctive mechanisms for survival that are discussed further in Appendix A.

Having greater memory and problem-solving ability, coupled with the development of additional mechanisms in the psyche, propelled Homo Erectus out of Africa to the far reaches of Europe and Asia. The emigration of Homo Erectus was a remarkable moment in human evolution because it marked the arrival of new human behaviors, notably the behavior of exploration, that had not existed before. Indeed, human evolution had taken a major step forward.

The emigration from Africa subjected Homo Erectus to new challenges concerning the intrinsic activities of daily living. These were new challenges because the terrain and climate of the northern hemisphere differed in the types of resources that were available to Homo Erectus. A key challenge was in the acquisition of food and shelter, which would have been a daunting task at times, especially when the effects of climate and new terrain are factored in. Homo Erectus was able to meet these challenges because they possessed the necessary intellectual capacity for solving problems. But their success was not without limits.

There are several indications that Homo Erectus struggled to succeed and propagate as they emigrated from Africa. A key indicator was their maximum population, which is estimated to be less than 35,000 members at any one time. Another indicator was that Homo Erectus demonstrated a perpetual pattern of emigration, born of the effects of scarcity, driving them to discover areas having a greater density of resources. Had Homo Erectus been more successful, perhaps a much greater maximum population would have been achieved, coupled with a less robust emigration pattern. But the impediments to their success lie in the intractable problems corresponding to the triadic grouping of 5-6-7.

Homo Erectus faced three distinct categories of problems, with each category corresponding with a specific Factor of Extinction that appears within the triadic grouping 5-6-7. The following sections introduce each of these Factors of Extinction.

Factor Five: Fallacy

A fallacy is a false conclusion or belief that is rooted in a faulty premise or false logic. There are three types of fallacy: A concrete fallacy involves a faulty premise, an abstract fallacy involves faulty logic, and complex fallacies involve both a faulty premise and faulty logic. Many fallacies are harmless, such as various types of superstitions that have persisted for millennia. Whereas other fallacies may be deadly, such as the fallacy that bleeding is a natural remedy for a bacterial infection. Early Humans were vulnerable to fallacies, not just because they had a very primitive ability to use logic and reason, but because fallacies are expedient. Fallacies are expedient because they allow individuals to bypass the cumbersome, laborious, and time-consuming aspects of the scientific method.

The scientific method is a process for investigating facts, formulating a hypothesis, and conducting the tests necessary for endorsing or rejecting the hypothesis. As an example, assume there is a statistically positive correlation between calories consumed and measured blood pressure, which arouses curiosity for understanding the causes of high blood pressure (hypertension). A review of the data indicates that individuals who consume excessive calories have higher blood pressure, while those who consume substantially fewer calories have much lower blood pressure, allowing the formulation of a hypothesis that expresses this relationship: "There is a causal relationship between calories consumed and hypertension". Such a statement provides an example of an objective hypothesis that was formulated based on supporting data.

Regarding the subject of hypertension, an invalid hypothesis would be: There is a causal relationship between salt consumption and hypertension. This hypothesis would be invalid for multiple reasons, with the foremost reason being that there is no data to suggest a correlation between salt and hypertension. Indeed, there is no reason to believe that salt, a necessary dietary element, has any relationship with hypertension. To assert otherwise is to erroneously create a hypothesis when there are no facts or data to support it.

The scientific method also requires that objective methods are used to test a hypothesis. That is because researchers often carry a financial stake in the results of their testing. Overcoming this bias requires that researchers be blind to the testing process, to ensure objectivity in the conclusions reached. The double-blind clinical trials conducted by pharmaceutical researchers is one way to eliminate fallacies from the critical process of testing human drugs.

Fallacies persist because the scientific method is very time consuming, labor-intensive, and cumbersome. It is more expedient to look at some basic facts and conclude something that is immediately gratifying, rather than engage the scientific method. But what often occurs is that facts are set aside, in favor of wealth, fame, or adulation. The expedience, immediate gratification, and euphoria of fallacies explain why such fallacies as "salt causes hypertension" have persisted.

Fallacies have significant consequences because they create chaos, perpetuate ignorance, and slow the general accretion of knowledge. The best way to understand this is with examples, starting with the "Ad Hominin" fallacy, which is often used in politics to redirect attention away from a pertinent issue by making irrelevant criticisms of the victim's character for the sole purpose of deflecting attention away from the truth. This fallacy continues to persist, especially in today's modern politics, as many political candidates use the Ad Hominin fallacy to gain leverage over their opponents.

The "False Dichotomy" fallacy is an invalid argument, whereby only two possible conclusions are allowed, even though more than two conclusions are possible. A False Dichotomy often occurs in political polling of two possible choices, such as affirming or denying allegiance to a candidate, thus oversimplifying a complex political question. Later in this section, a fallacy similar to a false dichotomy will be given.

Another fallacy is the "Appeal to Authority" fallacy, which involves deflecting the conclusion of an argument to a higher authority, regardless of the qualifications of the authority. This fallacy is often used to prove a false conclusion because the reliance upon a higher authority introduces a subjective bias. The higher authority is biased because of a preexisting relationship with the person who invokes the Appeal to Authority, obligating the higher authority to take their side, thus allowing the fallacy to go unchallenged.

The Appeal to Authority Fallacy is in a similar vein with the Group Think fallacy. The main difference between these two is that, instead of appealing to a higher authority, the Group Think Fallacy appeals to a fallacy that is endorsed by the group. The Group Think Fallacy is very common in today's modern societies and likely has a very long history among Early Human populations, perhaps coinciding with the development of language.

Another example is the Sunk Costs Fallacy, which occurs when a false conclusion is endorsed based on historical events, rather than an assessment of current and future events. Hunting is a situation where the Sunk Costs

Fallacy might be used to justify continuing a hunt, based on the amount of time already expended (sunk costs), despite all indications that the hunt will not be successful. War is another example where decisions are often made based on the Sunk Costs Fallacy. The persistence of the Sunk Costs Fallacy, especially in situations of life and death, gives credence to the hypothesis that the Sunk Costs Fallacy has been one of the deadliest of all fallacies since recorded time.

The fallacies cited thus far are mostly complex fallacies, which can be debunked by examining the underlying premises and then critiquing the logic. Critiquing logic is the most challenging aspect for debunking fallacies because it requires the ability to apply deductive and inductive reasoning, which is not a universal skill. The following example will help to illustrate this point. In this example, three premises are stated, followed by possible conclusions:

P1: All people who eat a strict vegan diet have low total cholesterol (<150 mg/L).

P2: All people who maintain low total cholesterol (<150 mg/L) live longer than average.

P3: Consumption of animal products (meat, dairy, and eggs) raises cholesterol levels in all people.

Choose the best answer from the choices below:

    A. Eliminating animal products from the diet increases life expectancy in every case.

    B. The consumption of animal products decreases life expectancy in every case.

    C. The consumption of animal products is a risk factor for life expectancy.

    D. All the above.

    E. None of the above.

In this example, three premises are presented, followed by three hypothetical syllogisms. A hypothetical syllogism is a conclusion, in accord with logical reasoning, derived from one or more premises. Answer A is not correct because a carnivorous individual may live longer than average; and in some cases, they may gain no benefit from switching to a vegan diet. Thus, it is illogical to infer that switching to a strict vegan diet will increase a person's life expectancy; however, the inference that they will live longer than average is valid.

Answer B is also incorrect because a carnivorous diet may not increase cholesterol levels above 150 mg/L. With the limited information provided, which is that cholesterol levels only become a risk factor when they exceed 150 mg/L, a carnivorous diet does not necessarily reduce life expectancy. Indeed, a carnivorous diet may increase life expectancy in some individuals. And even if a carnivore has cholesterol levels exceeding 150 mg/L, there is insufficient information to form conclusions about their anticipated life expectancy. For example, carnivores having cholesterol levels exceeding 150 mg/L may enjoy a greater life expectancy than if they followed a strict vegan diet. (emphasis).

Answer C is the correct answer. Arriving at the correct answer recognizes the simultaneous conditions, which establishes a relationship between animal products and life expectancy. However, this relationship depends upon a 150 mg/L+ threshold, which has the effect of weakening the relationship between animal products and life expectancy. For these reasons, the only logical conclusion is that the consumption of animal products is a risk factor for life expectancy because it raises cholesterol levels in all people.

Although some fallacies are relatively harmless, many have deadly consequences, such as eating a poisonous mushroom, rendering an inappropriate treatment for an infection, or punishing a victim rather than the aggressor. And because fallacies are a function of imagination, nearly infinite variations are possible, with no mechanism to hold them in check. For these reasons, fallacies constituted both a direct and indirect threat to the viability of Early Human species, earning it a place among the Nine Factors of Extinction.

Although fallacious thinking continues to plague Modern Humans, it played a central role in the extinction of Early Human species because

it perpetuated the ignorance, malfeasance, and reckless disregard for the sanctity of life.

Factor Six: Risk

There were many hazards throughout human evolution that, severally and individually, constituted a terminal threat to the viability of Early Human populations. These hazards can be categorized as either endogenous, exogenous, or heterogenous, depending on the scale of the hazard. For example, microbial pathogens and parasites are an example of an endogenous hazard because they attack the internal systems of the body after an introduction via food, water, bodily contact, or a break in the skin. Contact with dangerous substances, such as poisonous plants, is another example of an endogenous hazard. The totality of all known endogenous hazards, including viruses, bacteria, parasites, and poisons, were responsible for a substantial percentage of the overall morbidity risk to Early Humans.

Exogenous hazards are the environmental threats that are generally outside the direct control of the individual and include all manner of activities, circumstances, and direct threats that have the potential for physical injuries. Hunting live game is a prime example of a hazardous activity that carried risks for being trampled, horned, bitten, stabbed, or otherwise traumatized. And there are many other hazardous activities, such as walking on thin ice, walking near sinkholes, climbing trees, and swimming. Hazardous circumstances would include inclement weather, floods, earthquakes, and tsunamis. Examples of hazardous direct threats include animal attacks, forest fires, housing fires, insect bites, falling tree limbs, rockfalls, and collapsing structures.

Early Humans were also subject to the felonious actions perpetrated by members of their social group. These felonious actions include theft, assault, and homicides. These intra-tribal crimes constitute the heterogenous hazards that undoubtedly became more and more frequent as Early Humans traveled the path of evolution. Indeed, intra-tribal violence was increasing over time, mostly because of the regressive traits and behaviors related to barbarism. It was these vices, coupled with acts of intra-tribal violence and crime, that undermined the cohesiveness, cooperation, and stability of Early Human social structures. Thus, it was the heterogenous hazards that were perhaps the most intractable, if not the deadliest, for Early Humans.

Each of the endogenous, exogenous, and heterogenous hazards that confronted Early Humans carried a quantifiable risk. In this context, risk means there was a probability of betrayal, harm, or death. And these risks were substantial, as they exacted a huge toll on the lives of Early Humans. Thus, the risk of an accident, or other unfortunate circumstance, became a significant limiting factor in the life expectancy of Early Humans. Unfortunately, Early Humans possessed a very limited ability for recognizing risk, and even if they could, they possessed no mechanism to prevent, mitigate, and manage it. Thus, risk became an important factor in the extinction of Early Humans.

Early Humans experienced a seemingly infinite array of deadly risks, accidents, and catastrophes that either precipitated contributed to or caused their extinction.

Factor Seven: Scarcity

Dinosaurs roamed the earth for most of the 180 million-year Mesozoic era as the period's dominant life form on earth. The diversity of life during the Mesozoic was differentiated from all other periods in history, as dinosaurs evolved to become the largest terrestrial animals ever to exist on earth. Having a large constitution confers many evolutionary advantages; but surviving extinction level events (ELE), such as the one that occurred in the Yucatan Peninsula, is not one of them.

The geologic evidence suggests that a meteor, approximately 15 km wide, hit the Yucatan Peninsula of Mexico approximately 65 million years ago. Volcanic activity was also occurring during this period; and it was the combined effects of the meteor and volcanoes that caused major disruptions in Earth's atmosphere and climate, resulting in the termination of food supplies for most animal life. The termination of food explains why the Yucatan ELE effectively ended approximately 76% of all life forms. And for those dinosaurs that did survive, such as birds and crocodiles, the Yucatan ELE had negative effects in almost every case.

There are five known ELE's, with 251 million years ago Permian-Triassic extinction as the most devastating example, based on an estimated extinction rate of 96%. When considering all known ELE's, an understanding emerges that each of them had an enormous influence on the evolution of life on Earth. Indeed, the evolution of all life forms on earth today were affected by past ELE's, including Early Humans, as they were especially vulnerable to even minor changes in climate. Neanderthals provide a case on point.

Perhaps more important to understand is that minor events, as opposed to ELE's, constituted a greater threat to survival for Early Humans. That is because minor changes occur more frequently, and over time they can have the same effect as a major event: In this context, the threat to survival was not from the events themselves, but from the collateral effects to habitats, such as foraging and hunting opportunities. Minor events such as earthquakes, volcanic activity, and severe weather patterns are known to cause mass animal migrations, resulting in a substantial disruption to local habitats. Even a moderate earthquake, or 5c change in average temperatures, could have disastrous collateral effects on local habitats.

The evidence of multiple bottlenecks in Early Human populations supports the contention that minor events, as opposed to ELE's, constituted a greater overall threat to Early Humans. A bottleneck is a reduction in species population, that if not corrected early enough, can cause irreparable harm, damage, or extinction of a species. Bottlenecks have coincided with relatively minor events such as earthquakes, volcanic activity, and rapid climate change. In each of these events, the habitat is disrupted, leading to malnutrition, disease, and a dwindling population. As a population dwindles, the probability of irreparable DNA damage increases, thus reducing the viability of the species.

Recent advances in DNA sequencing have opened the doors to the analysis of historical human DNA. Current research supports the contention that Early Humans suffered multiple population bottlenecks in the past. The implication here is that the disruption to habitats, whether by ELE's or minor events, was a very real and serious hazard to Early Humans. Moreover, the effects of these hazards were not limited to remote populations because there was always the possibility that an ELE could decimate the entire human population.

Apart from natural events, there are many other reasons to explain why Early Humans might experience an alteration, disruption, or destruction of their habitat. For example, overhunting might lead to the extinction of large-game, causing ecological imbalances that affected other wildlife. A natural shift in migratory patterns of large-game is another example. And disease processes that affected both plants and animals also occurred. These factors eliminate all doubt that local ecologies and habitats did change over time, and sometimes the changes were very rapid.

The factors that adversely affected habitats constituted a major threat to the viability of Early Humans. And because these threats were intermittent, they resided mostly in the subconscious mind, only resurfacing when triggered by an event. Over time, the threat of changing habitats, coupled with the negative impact that had on the Early Human way of life, gave rise to a persistent fear of environmental paucity. The persistence of this fear over eons of human evolution was the genesis of the fear of scarcity.

Scarcity implies an absence, specifically an absence of the necessities of survival that occurred at different scales. At the macrocosmic scale, there are vast areas of emptiness in the universe that stand apart from areas of infinite density such as black holes. Despite the inherent diversity of matter in the universe, it is possible to perceive the universe as empty, especially when the experience is limited to the areas devoid of matter. However, a broader perspective informs that scarcity is just a local phenomenon as opposed to a universal phenomenon.

At the scale of an individual planet, Earth has areas that are teeming with life such as in the tropics, accompanied by desert and arctic climates that are relatively less affluent. When the poles shift, as occurs every 800,000 years or so, rapid climate changes may occur. The pole shifts may cause massive changes in the density, diversity, and locations of life on earth. Thus, areas of scarcity may become the areas of abundance and vice versa. Regardless of these occurrences, scarcity remains a local phenomenon.

From the human perspective, scarcity first appears as a local phenomenon, and then it quickly becomes a catastrophic phenomenon. The ravaging effects of scarcity include malnutrition, disease, dwindling population, and death. Because scarcity carries such grave consequences, it constituted one of the major threats confronting Early Humans, thus becoming a major factor in their extinction.

There are several things to be learned from this discussion of scarcity. First, a scarcity of resources is a local phenomenon that often occurs because of changes in climate, ecology, and geologic events. But most important to understand is that when scarcity does occur, it often has disastrous consequences, leading to malnutrition, disease, and a dwindling population. Indeed, many of the population bottlenecks affecting Early Humans were primarily the result of scarcity. And because Early Humans did not have an effective mechanism for managing scarcity, they were ill-prepared for the temporal episodes of scarcity that played a role in their extinction.

Resource scarcity played an important role and in some cases was the primary cause of multiple bottlenecks and extinctions among Early Human species.

Operation of the Nine Factors of Extinction

The previous discussion highlighted the ways that the NFE directly undermined the evolution of Early Humans. However, just as important was how they indirectly undermined Early Human evolution. For example, each of the NFE had a synergistic effect upon the others, as in the synergies that are created by the combined effects of scarcity and a lack of resource conservation, which meant that there was no method for rationing resources to those who were best positioned to use those resources. As a consequence, a scant amount of resources would be allocated randomly, based on sheer luck, rather than rationed to those possessing superior survival traits such as intelligence.

Another example of synergy is between risks and fallacies. Consider the unfortunate situation of falling from a tree, resulting in a compound fracture to the right lower extremity. Dirt was sometimes applied to stop the bleeding, which in turn caused an infection that resulted in death. In this example, the risk of climbing a tree was a precipitating factor, while a fallacy was the actual cause of death.

The preceding examples demonstrate the synergies that exist between the NFE, and how minor problems can escalate into major problems, with devastating consequences. Here, it is important to emphasize that several factors of extinction acted simultaneously, creating an infinitely variable array of possible catastrophes, that were often too much for Early Humans to bear. The fact that significant numbers of Early Humans were able to survive at all is a testament to their spirit, physiology, and will to live.

Another important aspect of the NFE was the collateral effect that each had on the natural selection process. In the example of resource scarcity, resources were often allocated to the weakest and least intelligent, rather than to the fittest, strongest, and most intelligent. The absence of a Darwinian process meant that the natural selection process was regressive rather than progressive. Neanderthals provide a probative example of how the NFE had a regressive effect on a species, given that their numbers dropped precipitously, never to recover for many thousands of years before their extinction.

This discussion has highlighted the key aspects of the Nine Factors of Extinction that precipitated the Enneciation of the nine human phenotypes. The connections between these phenomena can be understood within, and are the product of, the scientific framework known as the Enneagram. Understanding the Enneagram, especially in the context of how the nine human phenotypes evolved, is the focus of the next chapter.

CHAPTER 3

THE ENNEAGRAM

Although the Law of Three establishes the basic internal and external structures necessary for life to evolve, it has many limitations, especially when a life form reaches a developmental plateau. In the case of Early Humans, that plateau was probably reached well before the arrival of Homo Heidelbergensis or Homo Neanderthalensis, both of whom made little progress against the Nine Factors of Extinction. When a developmental plateau occurs, and a species makes no further progress over a protracted period, evolution responds with the introduction of a higher-order process.

The Law of Nine is responsible for creating higher-order processes, which in the case of Early Humans was the creation of a system composed of nine forces (Endeavors), with each Endeavor matched to one of the Nine Factors of Extinction. The system that is created by the Law of Nine may take several forms, depending on the conditions predicate, and the solution that is required. From a cosmological perspective, the Law of Nine is an infinitely variable mechanism of intelligence that proactively solves the most intractable problems occurring in the universe.

The system created by the Law of Nine, specific to the NFE, is depicted by a hieroglyphic symbol (see front cover) known as the Enneagram. The Enneagram symbol has three parts. The outer circle represents the all-encompassing concept of unity. The inner equilateral triangle, intersecting at three points on the circle, is devoted to problems confronting humanity that are intrinsic to the psyche. The remaining inner symmetrical structure is devoted to solving the greater socio-economic problems confronting humanity.

The Enneagram symbol made its first appearance in the 1949 publication *In Search of the Miraculous*, authored by the Russian mathematician P.D. Ouspensky, who discovered the Enneagram by way of the teachings of George Ivanovich Gurdjieff. A noted Russian philosopher and mystic, Gurdjieff is credited as the earliest source of Enneagram knowledge. Gurdjieff described the Enneagram as a powerful tool, but he was careful not to discuss the subject of the nine human personality types in the same vein as the Enneagram, ostensibly to prevent his students from discovering the source and framework of the human phenomenon. Although Gurdjieff ostensibly withheld details of the human connection to the Enneagram, he certainly knew that the Enneagram was a perfect map of the human ego types, because multiple accounts describe his ability to diagnose the ego type of others.

Gurdjieff made a special point that is worth mentioning: That even with the help of the Enneagram, it is not possible to discern the ego type of others without first accurately typing oneself. This point underscores the fact that any bias against seeing the truth about oneself will necessarily introduce an impediment to seeing others objectively. Thus, seeing the truth about others always starts with seeing the truth about oneself, and so the Enneagram is first and foremost a tool for self-understanding.

The next milestone for the Enneagram came in 1982 when Oscar Ichazo published a paper titled *Interviews with Oscar Ichazo*, where he used the Enneagram to explain the nine ego-personality types. Ichazo claimed that he developed the Enneagram personality system in 1954, as part of an insight that led to the development of an entire human development program, ostensibly the basis to start the ARICA human development school in 1968. Ichazo is also notable for seeking to enjoin Helen Palmer in 1992, who purportedly learned the Enneagram by way of Ichazo's teachings, from publishing her version of the Enneagram.

The outcome of the lawsuit turned on Ichazo's 1982 publication, where he established the Enneagram to be of a scientific and factual origin, as opposed to his invention. Because the court recognized the scientific nature of the

Enneagram, they ruled that the Enneagram symbol cannot be copyrighted. The court also ruled that Palmer's publication, including parts which ostensibly were derivatives of Ichazo's work, did not rise to the level necessary to be considered an infringement of Ichazo's copyrighted intellectual property. These events were important milestones in the history of the Enneagram because they support the theory that the Enneagram is a phenomenon of science, rather than a fictitious system of thought.

The next milestone came from the work of Don Riso and Russ Hudson, who published multiple Enneagram books, each depicting the traits, behaviors, and psychology related to the Enneatypes. Their work provided an overall map of how the ego functions, such as the basic fears, desires, and motivations for each type. Their work was indispensable to the writing of this book, in that they provided the map of the human ego, which was the starting point for connecting the dots of human evolution.

This book represents the next milestone for the Enneagram, in that a multidisciplinary approach is taken to explain how and why humans evolved. This approach reveals the Nine Human Endeavors, specializations, primary roles, and functional adaptations for each of the Enneatypes. This knowledge gives great power because it informs the evolutionary purpose of every member of the human race. Thus, this knowledge is the foundation of all human wisdom.

THEORY OF THE ENNEAGRAM

Enneagram theory posits that every person is born as a unique point on the circle, and because every circle has an infinite number of points, the Enneagram allows for the individuality of every human being. The Enneagram also has nine points on the circle, the periodic points, which represent the nine human Enneatypes.

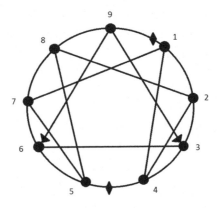

Figure 1.4

Everyone is a blend between a primary and secondary Enneatype. If a person is a *One with a Nine subtype*, their primary type is One, and their secondary type is Nine. In Figure 1.4, the point marked between types One and Nine corresponds to someone that is primarily a One, because the point is closest to the periodic point One; and the secondary type would correspond with type Nine. As another example, taking the point that is close to the periodic point Five, that person is a *Five with a Four subtype*. The subtype is also commonly referred to as a *wing*. By convention, the primary type is always stated first, followed by the subtype, such as 1w9 or 5w4.

The Enneagram also allows for an estimation of the relative percentage for each type. Using figure 1.4, the point between one and nine would be approximately 80% type One and 20% type Nine; while the point between five and four would be approximately 55% type Five and 45% type Four. The primary type is generally between 51% and 99%; although it's theoretically possible, albeit very rare to find, that someone is a 50% blend of two types. Just as rare is the person whose type falls directly on a numeric point.

Enneagram theory states that every individual exists in one of three states: Integrating (evolving), static, or disintegrating (devolving). The state of

Integration means that a person is acquiring the virtues of the types in the path indicated by the Enneagram. The disintegrating state refers to a person who is regressing or devolving toward a lower, more primitive state of Being. And static means a person is neither evolving nor devolving. These states inform that the Enneagram is a dynamic hieroglyphic key to understanding the reality of change and evolution, a fact alluded to by Gurdjieff when he said that the Enneagram is perpetual motion.

The interconnecting lines between the periodic points highlight the relationships between each Enneatype. These relationships demonstrate one of the predictive powers of the Enneagram. Arrows have been placed in Figure 1.4 to mark the direction of integration and disintegration for type Nine, demonstrating that Nines integrate toward point Three, and their direction of disintegration is toward point Six. In this way, the Enneagram predicts that Nines who are static will remain at Nine, and those Nines who are integrating will acquire the powers and evolved traits of Threes. And those Nines who are disintegrating will acquire the devolved traits of Sixes.

The Enneagram also demonstrates the evolutionary sequence that is required for every human being to reach full maturity. For example, Nines integrate first to Three, then to Six, and then onto Nine, with each step moving closer to full development, maturity, and enlightenment. The integrating path for Eights begins with Two, then to Four, One, Seven, Five, and then back to Eight. Although types 3, 6, and 9 have only three sequential steps (as compared to six steps for types 1, 2,4,5,7,8), each of the three steps are proportionally greater in scope; and thus, much more difficult to attain. However, the overall amount of difficulty is the same for every type. Integration is discussed further in the closing chapters.

Functions of the Ego

Decoding the evolutionary purpose behind each of the Enneatypes requires accurate knowledge of the ego, specifically how the ego operates as a mechanism of survival because an inaccurate understanding will produce spurious results. Perhaps the best example of a spurious model is the one developed by Carl Jung, which is notable for correctly grouping many of the modern human traits and behaviors, while also being notorious for failing to identify the evolutionary purpose for each type. If Jung had adopted an evolutionary perspective, then perhaps his model would have grown to include the necessary perspectives, and he would have discovered that there are nine ego types instead of eight. An analysis of the Jungian model appears in Appendix B.

In this section, some of the survival functions of the ego are explored, from the perspective of the Thinking, Feeling, and Instinctive Centers. The Thinking Center (mind) is the intellectual faculty related to cognition, solving problems, and rational thinking. The Thinking Center operates by a process known as object relations, where reality is differentiated by an array of distinct objects, with each object known by a specific label. The process begins with the five senses, which allows for the identification of distinct objects. Everything is considered an object from the perspective of the Thinking Center, such as people, places, and things; including the individual who is observing objects. Each object is descriptively and discretely labeled and memorized, and that information becomes part of the conscious and subconscious mind, allowing for future familiarity, recall, and identification. In this way, the present moment is filtered and understood by the recall of past experiences, seen through the template of the various predefined objects stored in long term memory.

The immediate experience of the self is made possible by the recall of predefined objects stored in long term memory. These objects allow the Thinking Center to smooth the experience of reality into one continuous flow, without confusion, interruption, and chaos, which makes the basic day to day functioning possible. It also enables certain gross rational processes, such as forecasting, planning, and effective decision making. The Thinking Center is the slowest of the three functional centers.

Where the Thinking Center labels objects, the Emotional Center informs the emotional tone and effect between those objects, giving an added dimension to the human experience. Here, the Emotional Center operates by empathy and attunement to the emotional states of others and provides the guidance and intelligence needed for effective relationships. The Emotional Center is a discriminating faculty of perceptive awareness, functioning like a tuning fork that feels and measures the vibrations in its sphere of experience. The

Emotional Center also has an intuitive dimension, which is a special abstract intelligence that brings a depth of understanding to many types of complex social interactions. Many people associate the Emotional Center as perhaps the most satisfying dimension of human experience.

As the fastest of the three centers, the Instinctive Center is the locus for the sensory modalities, including the exteroceptive, interoceptive, and proprioceptive senses. Proprioception is the awareness of body position relative to space and time. Proprioception includes the sense of balance, and an awareness of body position relative to the horizon, thus allowing ambulation with the eyes closed. Without the element of balance, what remains is a sense of the body's position in space, defined as kinesthesia.

The gross exteroceptive senses provide information about the external environment by sight, smell, touch, and hearing. There is also the "fine exteroceptive" senses, which includes the sense of being watched, or that a natural phenomenon is about to occur such as an earthquake or tsunami; or that an accident or natural event is about to occur. The fine exteroceptive senses generally provide intuition, extrasensory perception (ESP), or clairvoyance; however, not all individuals are aware of this faculty of experience.

The gross interoceptive sense informs the status of our internal functions, such as respiration, hunger, heart rate, bladder fullness, blood pressure, and the need for digestive elimination. The gross interoceptive sense may be more developed in some individuals, giving an awareness of problems within the body, such as torn joint cartilage, cerebral tension, dietary deficiencies, hyperglycemia, allergy causes, and many others. With practice, the gross interoceptive sense can be infinitely developed.

The fine interoceptive sense, which informs the experience of the Universal Qualities, can also be infinitely developed. For example, most people can describe the difference between Joy and Compassion. Joy manifests as a slight tickle in the heart that arises with a touching experience, like hearing a baby's first laugh, bringing us to take delight with the moment. And Compassion manifests as the graceful presence within that calms, soothes, and empathizes with others. But the degree of development for the fine interoceptive sense varies substantially across the population. The average person may be comfortable discussing a few of the Universal Qualities, but it is a topic that is rarely touched upon, even though most human beings have extensive experience regardless of gender, religion, or culture.

Even rarer is the ability to differentiate the Universal Qualities from other dimensions of experience. For example, everyone has extensive experience with the Universal Quality of Strength, but few people can explain the relationship between the ontological experience of Strength, and the emotional experience of Anger. That is partly because the fine interoceptive sense is grossly undeveloped in many individuals. The development of the fine interoceptive sense brings a newfound appreciation for the inner experience, along with some new skills and abilities.

By way of these sensory modalities, the Instinctive Center serves three primary functions, that of survival, motor skills, and circumstantial intelligence. Understanding the primary functions of the Instinctive Center is indispensable to diagnose the Enneatypes. For example, proprioception is mentioned in the context of certain Enneatypes to explain why they tend to perform better in activities requiring excellent physical coordination, balance, and motor skills. The relative functioning of the exteroceptive and interoceptive senses, along with some of the ontological issues specific to each Enneatype, provide background information that enhances the ability to discern the Enneatypes.

Enneagram theory informs that each of the Enneatypes has a specific adaptation concerning the three centers of the ego. This adaptation has the effect of manipulating the energy that is distributed between the three centers, thereby altering the relative activity of each center, which sets in motion a distinct set of behavioral parameters. These parameters constitute the functional endpoint of a discrete, rational, and complex psychological and physiological evolutionary mechanism composed of nine distinct organisms. Thus, the manipulation of the three centers is the evolutionary predicate for the Endeavor, specializations, and functional adaptations that are unique to each of the Enneatypes. The following table describes the imbalances that occur between the Thinking, Feeling and Instinctive Centers for each Enneatype:

	Thinking	Emotional	Instinctive
Type One	Biased	Compensating	Hypoactive
Type Two	Biased	Hyperactive	Biased
Type Three	Hyperactive	Impaired	Hyperactive
Type Four	Biased	Hypoactive	Compensating
Type Five	Hyperactive	Biased	Biased
Type Six	Impaired	Hyperactive	Hyperactive
Type Seven	Hypoactive	Biased	Compensating
Type Eight	Biased	Biased	Hyperactive
Type Nine	Hyperactive	Hyperactive	Impaired

Table 1.1 – Enneatypes

Table 1.1 lists the Enneatypes of the Enneagram and the relative functioning of the three intelligence centers for each of the types. Types 3/6/9 have a center which is impaired, types 1/4/7 have a center which is hypoactive, and types 2/5/8 have a hyperactive center. Using Sixes as an example, the Thinking Center is functionally impaired, which places a burden on the Emotional and Instinctive Centers to perform the functions of the Thinking Center. Because the Thinking Center is impaired, the Emotional and Instinctive Centers join forces, thereby taking on the work of all three centers. The Emotional and Instinctual centers cannot replace the functions that are normally performed by the Thinking Center, resulting in a personality that has impairment of the Thinking Center. This bias introduces attitudes, traits, behaviors, and distinct physiological traits. Threes and Nines demonstrate a similar pattern, except that they have impairment for the Emotional and Instinctive Centers, respectively.

Enneatypes 1/4/7 possess a center that is developmentally hypoactive, which is compensated for by one of the remaining centers. In the case of Ones, the hypoactivity of the Instinctive Center is compensated for by the Emotional Center, and to a lesser degree by the Thinking Center. Of course, the Emotional Center cannot replace the functions of the Instinctive Center, so this creates a bias which becomes Enneatype One. There is a similar pattern of hypoactive development and compensation for Fours and Sevens.

Enneatypes 2/5/8 have an overactive center which consumes a disproportionate amount of the energy and resources that are available to the ego. Using Enneatype Two as an example, the Feeling Center is overactive, which in this case deprives the Thinking Center of the energy and resources it needs to properly function. And the Emotional Center is so dominant and creates so much noise, that the Instinctive Center becomes biased, distorted, and subordinate to the Emotional Center. The same functional pattern applies to Enneatypes five and eight.

Armed with an understanding of the basic structures of the ego, it is now possible to compare different personality models, such as the Jungian and Enneagram models. Appendix B contains an analysis of the Jungian model, for those interested to understand why Carl Jung captured only eight of the nine ego structures in his model.

FUNCTIONAL INTEGRITY LEVELS

The level of functional integrity is an assessment of psychological maturity. Assessing functional integrity is crucial because the personality traits exhibited by an individual depends first on their Enneatype, then on their level of functional integrity. The functional integrity level depends on many factors, including the degree to which an individual has successfully integrated the Universal Qualities. Individuals with greater integration of the Universal Qualities are functionally more adaptive to change, have a higher tolerance for negative stimuli, and are more adept at handling environmental challenges.

The Universal Qualities include Love, Joy, Peace, Power, Strength, Will, Compassion, Value, Ingenuity, and Contact. The capacity to experience the Universal Qualities is an important differentiator between Modern Humans and the rest of the animal kingdom. But more important is that the Universal Qualities provide some support to the Enneatypes in performing their evolutionary functions, and without these human qualities, the functional adaptations for each Enneatype begin to lose their form and function.

Functional integrity depends on the degree of stress in an individual's life, as people who experience above-average amounts of stressful events such as accidents, financial problems, and relationship difficulties will have a lower probability of ascending to higher levels. The levels of functional integrity form a continuum of human development potential, with the absence of Being on one end of the continuum, and the indelible presence of Being on the other. Functional integrity has the following seven levels of maturity:

LEVEL	VIRTUE	VICE	MISSING
1	guidance	temporal mind	permanence
2	unconditional love	ethics	recognition of unity
3	relationship	conditional love	self-awareness
4	responsibility	control	love
5	self-determination	denial	identity
6	self-recognition	entitlement	living in the moment
7	life	ignorance	nexus to being

Table 1.2

The discussion of the functional integrity levels begins with level 7, the beginning stage that every human being must pass through, where the universal presence of Being forms a nexus with the body. When there is a connection with Being, advancement to level 6 occurs. Any impediment to the connection with Being will stunt further development. If the impediment is severe, such a person will not pass beyond level 7, as the connection between Being and ego was disrupted, stunted, or failed altogether. Individuals at level 7 are pathologically disabled by schizophrenia, dissociative disorders, or other states of dementia. The disability results from an absence of the Universal Human Qualities, and or their incongruity with the mechanisms of the psyche, thus producing individuals who are unable to function autonomously. Level 7 manifests to extoll the virtues of life.

At Level 6, there is a developmental deficiency between the Universal Qualities and the mechanisms of the psyche, which gives individuals at this level an entitlement disposition. Each type will act out this sense of entitlement according to the programming of their Enneatype: Introverts will withdraw; extroverts will become aggressive, and so on. Individuals at this level can differentiate themselves from others, but they have very little capacity for self-awareness, especially the fine interoceptive senses. In general, individuals at this level have not developed beyond the most primitive needs, desires, and motivations of the instincts. There is a deficiency of cooperation, conformity to social expectations, and respect for the boundaries of others. There is marked resistance to accepting social, financial, or familial responsibilities; hence, this level is named the *level of ego resistance*. Persons at this level may have difficulty holding a job and maintaining significant relationships with friends, family, and intimate others. There may be evidence of neuroses corresponding to their ego type. Physically and emotionally abusive relationships, lawlessness, and incarceration are common for individuals functioning at this level. Diagnosing individuals at this level can be challenging, especially if any of the relevant facts are concealed or not readily apparent.

At level 5, the vice of entitlement from level 6 becomes the virtue of self-determination. But self-determination does not mean independence; on the contrary, individuals at level 5 have an attachment to traditional functional roles such as parenting, career, and marriage. Here, there is an attempt to satiate the need for identity with functional roles, such as parenting or careers, because identity is the core issue for this level. Individuals at this level have a strong tendency to identify with their functional roles and deny awareness and development of their Truth; and this leads to a failure to see and appreciate the Universal Qualities of Love, Joy, Compassion, etc. For these reasons, love relationships tend to be shallow and operate by the mechanism of codependency. Individuals at this level are generally unhappy, depressed, or deeply insecure; and they often have little awareness of their impact on others. Resiliency to change is very limited for individuals at this Level: For example, the loss of a job or a long-term relationship may take years to overcome.

Level 4: From a grounded sense of identity emerges a semi-adjusted sense of self and a newfound sense of responsibility. Beneath the façade of a new identity resides an underlying sense of deficiency, which brings with it the needs of materialism, attachment, and control. The sense of deficiency results from inadequate integration of the Universal Quality of Love, which creates a quest within the individual to fill the void. Individuals at this level subconsciously equate Love with power, fame, and control over others. The quest for Love explains the superficial orientation toward life, and the futile attempts to fill Love's void with all manner of human creations, including money, fame, or social status. Individuals at level four will treat others as potential sources of Love, and relationships are the lowest common denominator of Love's currency. For these reasons, relationships at this level revolve around interpersonal control, jealousy, and codependency.

Level 3: A limited self-realization of the Universal Quality of Love emerges at level three, which focuses attention on the development of positive relationships, even though the ego continues to influence the interpersonal attitudes and behaviors. At this level, individuals are free from the usual identification roles of modern society, such as a job title, parenting, and gender roles. This freedom springs from the experience of the Universal Qualities that are not present at lower levels, which broadens and deepens the human experience. Individuals at this level are more in touch with their spiritual identity, which allows them to engage in deeper personal connections with others. The overall effect is one of flexibility, adaptability, and a self-adjusting equilibrium; yet, the Ego continues to have a restricting effect on the Universal Qualities. For example, Love is conditional, depending on the person, circumstances, and the return on investment, as it becomes a commodity that is dispensed only to the worthy. In short, the Universal Qualities are very much at the service of the ego.

Level 2: Reaching Level 2 requires significant dedication to the integration of the Universal Qualities, by methods of the three traditional paths, such as the monk, the yogi, or the ascetic. Or by paths which allow an individual to participate in society such as Fourth Way Paths. There are many degrees of development within level 2, depending on the path chosen, and the individual's ego type. Development work at this level centers on the struggle between the self-seeking behaviors of the ego, such as for attention, pleasure, autonomy, and self-preservation, and the Universal Qualities which provide their resolution. Individuals at this Level may deny or repress the needs and deficiencies of the personality, or outwardly seek to fulfill them. With level 2, the discord between the personality and the Universal Qualities continues because of insufficient recognition and integration of the Universal Qualities; so, work at this level focuses on the recognition, development, and integration of these qualities. Reaching Level 2 generally requires many years of intense inner work, and the guidance of a skilled Teacher.

Level 1: Level 1 is actualized when all qualities and faculties of Being are unrestricted and in perfect harmony with the Ego. The actualization of Level 1 is the culmination of many years, and in most cases, decades of intense inner developmental work under the skillful guidance of a Teacher. Depending on the path chosen, there may be many levels of development within this level, which are differentiated by the degree of development of the Universal Qualities and faculties. The actualization of Level 1 marks the completion of the first stage of human evolution.

Regardless of the level of functional integrity, diagnosing a person's Enneatype is possible, although it can be difficult to make accurate assessments for individuals at the extremes. In the case of level 7, a blurring of boundaries between the various mechanisms of the ego occurs, such that a new set of skills become necessary to make assessments with a high degree of confidence. The problem is that persons at level seven will manifest the pathological states that are generally not well defined by psychologists. Depicting these states within the appropriate paradigm is beyond the scope of this book.

Individuals at level 1 are difficult to diagnose because the mechanisms of the psyche are fused as if consolidated into a unified whole that functions seamlessly, effortlessly, in total harmony with Being. For these individuals, the ego is relatively balanced, in that the Thinking, Feeling and Instinctive Centers of the ego function proportionally to the needs of any situation. The elements of personality are supported by, and function in harmony with, the Universal Qualities. For these reasons, it becomes difficult to differentiate the various mechanisms of the psyche, because they are inextricably fused and balanced with the Universal Qualities.

UNIVERSAL QUALITIES

Within each functional integrity level, there are various degrees of arrested development between the mechanisms of the psyche and the Universal Qualities. And each of the Enneatypes has more difficulty with the integration of a cluster of specific Universal Qualities, which results in ego compensation, or a conflict within the ego because of inadequate integration. Learning to recognize the absence of Universal Qualities, and how the ego copes with the absence, provides more information that can be used to identify the Enneatypes. The following table provides information related to the absence of the Universal Qualities in each of the Enneatypes. This information matches each Enneatype with a Universal Quality that is absent or poorly integrated:

Enneatype 1: Strength (patience)

Enneatype 2: Will (generosity)

Enneatype 3: Value (gentleness)

Enneatype 4: Compassion (kindness)

Enneatype 5: Peace

Enneatype 6: Trust (faithfulness)

Enneatype 7: Joy

Enneatype 8: Introspection (self-control)

Enneatype 9: Love

The Universal Human Qualities have a long and storied history, with literary descriptions appearing in both religious and non-religious texts. For example, the Christian Bible describes the Universal Qualities as the *nine fruits of the holy spirit*: "But the fruit of the spirit is Love, Joy, Peace, Patience, Kindness, Generosity, Faithfulness, Gentleness, and Self-control" (Galatians 5:22). In some cases (Enneatypes 5,7,9), the Biblical fruits of the spirit are self-explanatory. The rest require some degree of interpretation or explanation.

The contemporary writings of A.H. Almaas also depict the human qualities, what he terms *essential aspects* or *Essence,* in thorough detail. Almaas writes extensively about the Universal Qualities to bring attention, understanding, and knowledge to this facet of human experience. Ostensibly, he aims to support the development of the Universal Qualities, thereby helping humanity to reach its full potential. Many agree that the full potential of humanity depends partly on increased awareness, appreciation, development, and integration of the Universal Qualities.

THE NINE HUMAN ENDEAVORS

Having explained how and why humans evolved, the focus turns to the specific mechanisms of human evolution, to address some of the existential questions that remain. These answers lie buried within the differential functions of the human ego, and how those functions manifest as Nine Human Endeavors, within a paradigm represented by the Enneagram symbol. Thus, an understanding of the purpose and meaning of life begins with the realization that the functional endpoint of each Enneatype corresponds to one of Nine Human Endeavors. And each Endeavor is made possible by the specializations, primary role, and functional adaptations that are collectively responsible for the differential attitudes, traits, and behaviors necessary to eradicate the factor of extinction from which each Enneatype evolved.

In the nine chapters that follow, the Nine Human Endeavors are depicted, followed by a discussion of the specializations, primary roles, and functional adaptations that succinctly describe each Enneatype. These depictions outline the evolutionary function for each Enneatype, with the understanding that each Enneatype is restricted or tethered to a specific Endeavor, which explains the theory that the modern human ego has a fixation. In this case, the fixation describes the tethering of an Endeavor to the factor of extinction from which it evolved.

The ego fixations form attitudes, traits, and behaviors that can be further differentiated depending on the level, dimension, or perspective taken. For example, differentiating the ego fixations by worldly vices reveals that Eights pursue power, while Nines pursue peace and Ones pursue perfection and so on. However, since the predicate for each of the Nine Human Endeavors is a function of the natural sciences, there is only one perspective that reveals the evolutionary purpose for each Enneatype, and that is an all-encompassing multidisciplinary scientific perspective. Thus, a multidisciplinary scientific approach is a prerequisite to understanding the intricacies of human evolution, including the scope, complexity, and purpose of each Enneatype.

This book assumes a very broad perspective of evolution, inclusive of the natural sciences, as this approach reveals the scientific predicates for each Enneatype. Certain predicates, such as sociology, are not fully delineated within the Enneatype depictions when eclipsed by the psychological, economic, and anthropological factors. Indeed, psychology was the most important, because it was a common denominator in the evolution of every Enneatype. Thus, an emphasis on the psychological factors is necessary to illuminate how the specific traits, cognitive processes, and behaviors for each Enneatype evolved in response to the NFE. And where it is mandatory, the principles of other scientific disciplines are utilized, to facilitate a greater understanding of the Nine Human Endeavors. However, there are many perspectives, levels, dimensions, and sciences, such as those related to theology, spirituality, or cosmology, given less treatment in this book.

A focus on the Nine Human Endeavors, within the context of the applicable scientific predicates, is necessary to reveal the system that evolved in response to the Nine Factors of Extinction. Knowledge of this system begins with an understanding that each point on the Enneagram corresponds with one of the Nine Factors of Extinction. The next step is to see that the Nine Human Endeavors are fixed (matched) to one of the Nine Factors of Extinction. Next is to understand the specialization that supports each of the Nine Human Endeavors, and how each specialization aligns with a specific role, which is the primary role that each Enneatype is designed to fulfill by default. Also included are the functional adaptations, delusion, and basic psychology for each Enneatype.

The investigation of human evolution is like peeling an onion, with the outer layer represented by the Nine Human Endeavors, and the second layer represented by the Nine Factors of Extinction. The third layer consists of the specializations that support each Endeavor, followed by a layer for the primary role, functional adaptations, and so on. The unconscious mechanisms, such as the delusion, can be found in the core of the onion. Peeling the evolutionary layers reveals that very little can be gained by chopping the onion and then trying to dissect and analyze the pieces. A better approach is to peel the onion one layer at a time or to use a cross-sectional approach where indicated so that each layer can be analyzed and understood in context.

This book peels the onion with a reductionist approach that began with the Nine Factors of Extinction and continues with an explication of the Nine Human Endeavors, as this provides the progression of knowledge necessary to comprehend, interpret, and utilize the Enneagram Paradigm. This approach aligns with the fact that the Nine Human Endeavors are a reduction of the Nine Factors of Extinction. The reduction continues as each Endeavor is further reduced according to specialization, primary role, and functional adaptations, to provide a detailed understanding of the Enneagram Paradigm. What emerges from this approach is the objective blueprint by which humanity operates. Knowledge of this blueprint provides a deeper understanding of the human condition, while at the same time it provides a contextual understanding of how and why humans evolved, putting to rest the long-standing debate on this topic.

This knowledge has many implications, with the greatest being that it reveals the purpose and meaning of life for every human being, shedding new light on a subject that has been debated by philosophers for millennia. And because this knowledge illuminates the less accessible aspects of the human condition, many individuals will gain new insights, perspectives, and wisdom, which for some will be a very intimate, deep, and moving experience. Indeed, knowledge of the human condition is the starting point for personal growth, development, self-actualization, and Integration.

CHAPTER 4

TYPE EIGHT: THE CONSERVATIONIST

Endeavor: Conservation of Resources

Exogenous Barbarism was extremely detrimental to Early Humans, because it allocated resources without regard to merit, and wasted human resources without due regard for the sanctity of life. Perhaps most detrimental was that it effectively nullified the natural selection process, which meant that regressive traits took precedence over traits that conferred a greater survival advantage. Under these conditions, the use of force became an ineffective mechanism of allocating and conserving resources.

From an evolutionary perspective, the violence inherent to Exogenous Barbarism was not a problem in and of itself. That is because violence, when used judiciously, can be an effective means for resource competition, allocation, and conservation. But this did not apply to Early Humans, as violence was often wielded unnecessarily, indiscriminately, and with no reverence for life. Moreover, the wielding of violence was unrelated to resource allocation, survival, or necessity. And in cases involving the reallocation of resources for survival, it did not necessarily result in an allocation of resources to those possessing superior survival traits. The net effect of Exogenous Barbarism meant that resources, especially human resources, were not being conserved. On the contrary, Exogenous Barbarism was responsible for the inefficient, ineffective, and indiscriminate utilization of resources.

The notion that the use of force serves an evolutionary purpose may be alarming, and perhaps offensive, especially to those who are universally opposed to the use of violence. However, evolution operates by its own devices, which in this context means that force is often a necessary competitive mechanism in the efficient allocation and conservation of resources, especially when resources are scarce. That is because the use of force equilibrates resources to those possessing the greatest survival advantage, in the same way that price allocates goods and services to those having the greatest economic advantage.

The use of force must also be controlled, metered, and wielded only when necessary. And only to the extent necessary. Because when the use of force is left unchecked, it escalates like a wildfire, leaving nothing behind except death, destruction, and scorched earth. Thus, wielding force can equilibrate and conserve resources, but it also has the potential to cause the extinction of a species. Unfortunately for Early Humans, their psyche was ineffective at controlling their use of force, and so they suffered from the effects of Exogenous Barbarism.

To remedy the problems associated with Exogenous Barbarism, and the concomitant misallocation and wasting of resources, evolution created Eights who specialize in the conservation of resources. In this context, the conservation of resources includes the identification, acquisition, guardianship, protection, enhancement, and mentoring of the resources necessary for survival. Anything that contributes to survival, directly or indirectly, is considered a resource. Thus, Eights exert domain over food, animals, humans, weapons, tools, shelters, technology, precious metals, natural resources, and so on.

Eights possess greater size, strength, and power relative to other Enneatypes, which allows them to compete, acquire, guard, and protect the resources needed for survival. Also, Eights have an acumen for identifying and mentoring resources, which prevents the squandering, wasting, and underutilization of resources. Thus, the specializations inherent to Eights ensure that the resources available to humans are efficiently allocated, utilized, and maximized to their greatest economic effect, while at the same time the use of force is controlled, metered, and wielded only when necessary.

From an evolutionary perspective, Eights ensure the efficient allocation of resources to those possessing superior traits related to survival, including size, strength, intelligence, and technology. The most basic function of this Darwinian mechanism is militaristic, as Eights specialize in the use of force, and Endeavor to use force as a means of resource conservation. Thus, the organization of militaries and the confrontations and wars that occur between militaries provide evidence of the mechanism for resource conservation that was introduced by evolution to solve the problems associated with Exogenous Barbarism. Indeed, evolution replaced Exogenous Barbarism with a human mechanism for war, thereby reinstating Darwinian principles to matters of resource allocation within the human species.

Primary Role: The Conservationist

The primary role of Eights is to act as the conservationist within their social group. There are several functions within this role, and each of these functions depends on the ability to identify resources properly. For this reason, Eights possess a very perceptive awareness and intelligence of their environment, which enables them to gather information about the resources that are immediately available in their locale. Eights have this ability due to a restricted focus of attention that naturally filters out objects, places, and experiences that provide no survival advantage. Because extraneous information is filtered out, Eights have an effortless ability to focus their attention on the people, places, and things that are important in their role as conservationists.

Perhaps the most important function for Eights is the acquisition of resources. The methods used to acquire, convert, or reallocate resources depends upon the degree of scarcity at hand. In places where there is no scarcity, Eights may acquire resources with very little effort, thru the fruits of their chosen vocation. In times of minor scarcity, Eights may need to expend relatively greater time and energy, and if scarcity becomes a persistent phenomenon or there is a major scarcity of food, then force may be required to convert the resources of others.

The conversion and reallocation of resources, from the weakest to the strongest, is part of the natural selection process. Natural selection ensures that groups possessing superior traits, especially in the areas of strength, knowledge, and intelligence, will take priority in the allocation of resources. Eights are an integral part of the natural selection process, as they are the competitive mechanism by which resources are selectively, efficiently, and expeditiously awarded to those possessing superior traits.

As a human mechanism of resource conservation, Eights compete for resources in the most efficient manner possible. Efficiency requires that Eights conserve their energy in times of abundance, and expend their energy when times are leaner, wielding as much force as necessary to acquire resources for themselves and their community. In extreme cases, the maximum degree of force may be required, involving militaristic operations that are aimed to reallocate resources to the strongest, fittest, and most resourceful. The predilection toward violence means that Eights are specifically adapted to function as soldiers, warriors, and mercenaries. In this capacity, Eights use forceful means to acquire, protect, conserve, and defend the resources necessary for survival.

The functional adaptation for war, inherent to every Eight, is supported by dominating, aggressive, and power-wielding behaviors that collectively are one of the least understood phenomena in human behavior. The confusion about dominating and aggressive behaviors persist because they are generally not understood to be mechanisms of resource conservation. However, there is an abundance of evidence that supports the contention that resource conservation, manifesting as interpersonal violence, is a socio-economic phenomenon. For example, urban violent crime rates are much higher in areas of persistent or extreme scarcity. In the aggregate, international wars represent attempts to reallocate socio-economic resources through the use of force. And so on.

Although war is a primary mechanism of conservation, Eights are not aptly described as soldiers of war, because that moniker is only fitting within the context of persistent or extreme scarcity. Describing Eights as soldiers would neglect the big picture, which is that Eights serve the evolutionary purpose of resource conservation, especially the conservation of their energy resources. Indeed, Eights are motivated to conserve every drop of available resources, which necessarily requires that they avoid pursuits that are wasteful, inefficient, and unproductive.

The perspective of conservation informs that Eights have a strong preference against the use of force, violence, or aggression. Indeed, Eights are primarily motivated to conserve resources. Violence is the method of last resort because it risks the loss of the very resources that Eights must conserve and protect. For these reasons, Eights prefer to avoid violence, except in situations of extreme scarcity where resources are not forthcoming. Eights have a strong preference to avoid violence, as an integral part of their specialization for conserving resources, because they are the primary preventative mechanism for Exogenous Barbarism. (emphasis)

Emerging from this discussion is an appreciation that Eights are uniquely adapted, depending on the circumstances, to pursue the survival interests of their social group. In times of abundance, Eights generally prefer attending to other matters of conservation, such as mentoring and coaching the human resources within their community or applying their resourcefulness to entrepreneurial pursuits such as starting a business. And in times of scarcity, Eights employ the necessary militaristic tactics needed to convert the resources of others, which aligns with the evolutionary objectives related to resource conservation.

Observing the ways that Eights function as conservationists is fascinating. But perhaps the most important observation is mostly hidden from view, which reveals a certain irony about Eights, especially concerning their role as conservationists. The irony is that Eights are the resource of last resort, meaning that under the direst of circumstances, Eights are designed to persevere and survive whatever comes their way; thus, they are aptly described as the *survivalist* because survival is the functional endpoint of conservation.

Functional Adaptations

In a very literal sense, Eights are the physical manifestation of the evolutionary mechanism of resource conservation. Eights embody resource conservation by channeling, focusing, and directing their energies toward adapting and transforming, in very physical ways, into the ultimate human resource within their community. The science-fiction character of Clark Kent demonstrates the transformation from weak to powerful when he transforms into the all-powerful Superman. In this case, Superman represents the alter-ego that is responsible for the protection, reallocation, and conservation of resources.

Eights are unique in their ability to adapt, transform, and develop themselves according to changing environmental conditions, the needs of their community, and their competitive advantages. The ability to adapt and transform produces a great diversity of traits, talents, skills, and abilities. However, it is important to understand that the ability to adapt and transform is always in the service of conserving resources, in direct alignment with the purpose that evolution assigned to Eights. Understanding the many ways that Eights adapt and transform to the needs of their environment requires more elaboration.

In times of scarcity, survival requires greater skill and prowess, which requires Eights to adapt and embody new skills, abilities, and approaches to survival. If scarcity persists or becomes extreme, Eights must develop the strength needed to compete, in case the use of force becomes necessary. And in times of abundance, Eights become a store of resources, as their bodies conserve, store, and hold large amounts of energy in the form of adipose tissue. This adaptation means that Eights possess an unsurpassed ability to adapt, transform, and mirror the changing needs of their environment.

The emergence of modern societies has required Eights to adapt in ever-changing ways. One of those adaptations has been in the area of sports, where athletic achievements rank among the highest of honors and distinctions. More than any other Enneatype, Eights have played a dominant role in sports, which reflects their ability to adapt to changing environmental needs. For example, a significantly greater percentage of long-term professional sports players are Eights. In the case of the National Football League and the National Basketball Association, more than 90% of long-term players are estimated to be Eights. The Olympics are also dominated by Eights, given that a very high percentage of gold medals go to Eights. But probably the best example is heavyweight professional boxing, which has a very high saturation of Eights, estimated to be at least 95% of all participants.

The dominance that Eights achieve in sports demonstrates many things, foremost being the single-minded focus on resource conservation, development, and management that Eights possess. Eights are the living and breathing embodiment of resource conservation, which they happily put on display for the rest of the world to witness. Second is that Eights are dominant in sports precisely because they can adapt, in every respect, to the individual needs of most sports. That is because Eights can adapt at all levels: Physical, emotional, and mental. And many examples can be given of the extreme adaptation and transformation that Eights undergo to be the champion of resources in their community.

Professional bodybuilders are an excellent example of the adaptation and transformation capabilities that Eights possess. As a rule, Eights are the only type endowed with the functional adaptation for acquiring, developing, and conserving the resource of physical strength, which explains why over 99% of professional bodybuilders are type Eight. Gymnasts are another example of how Eights adapt and transform their bodies into strong, flexible, well-balanced machines of great agility. The ability to adapt and transform athletically goes a long way in explaining the adaptations that are required to conserve resources.

Because of their adaptability, and focus on resource conservation, Eights possess a broad set of skills that can be applied in other vocations apart from sports. For example, Eights belong to a subgroup of Enneatypes that perform very well in sales functions. Eights possess a fundamental sales ability that becomes evident by distilling the sales process to three steps: Identifying sales opportunities, positioning a product or service, and then closing the deal.

Eights are well adapted to identify sales opportunities because they are keenly aware of what is happening in their local environment. However, in situations where sales opportunities require proactive social networking, Eights may struggle because their networking and relationship management is not as refined as other Enneatypes. Eights may also struggle to properly position a product or service because this aspect of sales requires an ability to assess a customer's needs, which requires a degree of emotional attunement that Eights are generally lacking. Putting it another way, Eights are relatively less adept at the subtleties of reading a customer's wants and needs so that they can then position how a product or service will fulfill those wants and needs. That is because Eights are focused on resource conservation, rather than the wants, needs, and emotions of others.

Eights are generally quite successful in sales situations that require strong closing techniques because they are not afraid to ask the customer to buy a product or service. And if the customer has objections, Eights are not afraid to confront the objections and try to work out a deal. Thus, even though Eights do not excel in all aspects of the sales process, they do have a natural sales ability that puts them in a special group.

Another area where Eights are generally successful is in the medical professions since a disproportionate percentage of doctors and nurses are type Eight. Eights are attracted to the medical profession because it aligns very closely with the evolutionary prerogative of conserving human resources: Every time a patient is treated, healed, and restored to health, Eights feel a sense of having accomplished their evolutionary purpose of conservation.

Eights are also ideally suited for the legal profession because, perhaps more than any other profession, it provides ample opportunities for the protection, reallocation, and conservation of resources. Eights pursue all areas of law, and all vocations, such as judges, attorneys, and prosecutors. But where Eights do particularly well is in the representation of individuals who have suffered losses from personal injuries, accidents, or the negligence of others. That is because Eights have a natural ability to reallocate resources from those who were negligent, to those who suffered losses, and they do so with great alacrity.

Acting is a profession where Eights are dominant due to their fundamental ability to adapt, emulate, and portray a constellation of character traits. As a group, Eights have a natural ability to emulate, portray, and project a wider range of traits than any other Enneatype. Projecting confidence is perhaps the most important trait that an actor needs to be successful, and Eights have an almost unsurpassed talent for projecting charismatic confidence no matter the media: Live television, Broadway productions, movies, etc. The downside is that most Eights lack a range of acting skill which necessarily restricts them to a limited genre of roles, such as western movies, action movies, opera, and so on. And they may be further restricted to specific types of roles, such as the antagonist, protagonist, support roles, singing roles, etc. Thus, Eights are naturally cast for roles that involve playing a character who projects various qualities related to conservation such as power, strength, courage, heroism, dominance, and aggression.

Farming aligns perfectly with the specialization of Eights because it is one of the few vocations that directly involve the conservation of resources. Most important is that Eights can adapt, more than other Enneatypes, to the physical demands of agricultural work. Thus, no other Enneatype can match the tremendous energy that Eights put into this endeavor.

Eights also do very well in various types of small business enterprises, because they are very adept at matching resources with opportunities, which explains much of their success in entrepreneurial endeavors. Also, Eights do very well in medium to large businesses because they are supremely confident in their ability to conserve resources. The ability to conserve resources, while at the same time projecting confidence, enables Eights to guide businesses to greater profitability in many cases. For these reasons, Eights are more likely than all other Enneatypes to ascend to the management and executive ranks of medium to large businesses.

The astute reader will recognize that the most basic form of resource conservation occurs through military operations, as the primary objective of every military is to identify, compete, acquire, protect, and conserve resources. And Eights are the evolutionary mechanism responsible for the organization of militaries, guards, and militias. Thus, both are a mechanism of the natural selection process, ensuring the Darwinian allocation of resources. Indeed, Eights have the functional adaptations, such as courage, strength, and will, necessary to battle for the acquisition, protection, and conservation of the resources necessary for survival. The evidence for these adaptations appears in the military institutions of every nation-state.

Basic Delusion

As the most violent of the Nine Factors of Extinction, Exogenous Barbarism was responsible for creating the most powerful, indelible, and profound impressions on the collective psyche of Early Humans. Over time, these impressions crystallized as an Environmental Archetype that captured the essence of these very intense experiences. The essence of Exogenous Barbarism and the Environmental Archetype associated with it is that violence is an instrument of survival.

The Exogenous Barbarism Environmental Archetype resides in the part of the brain that is responsible for detection and rationalization of environmental threats. In the case of Eights, this part of the brain is amplified, which exaggerates the perception of imminent threats to a substantial degree. The amplification of threat perceptions produces individuals who perceive these threats as life-threatening, ubiquitous, and surreal. The subconscious, omnipresent, and spurious perception of imminent annihilation constitutes the basic delusion for type Eight.

Perhaps most important to understand is that Eights perceive environmental threats to be severe, tangible, and potentially life-threatening. On an experiential level, Eights describe having an ever-present subconscious fear that someone or something wants to cause them great harm. This fear manifests as paranoia, which if not treated, may progress to schizophrenia. However, the most common experience is a subconscious feeling of imminent annihilation, which manifests as a derivative of the Environmental Archetype of Exogenous Barbarism. Thus, the fear of annihilation described by Eights is closely related to the Environmental Archetype that has its roots in the historical use of violence as an instrument of survival.

The ego identity for type Eight grows and develops around the delusion, alongside the mental and physical characteristics inherent to the specialization of Eights, which confers upon Eights certain competitive advantages and behaviors. One of the behaviors that arise from the delusion of annihilation is the drive to amass the power, strength, and resources needed to overcome the threat of annihilation. The drive to be resourceful requires that Eights undergo a fundamental transformation, in very physical ways, in the metamorphosis from powerless to powerful.

Interpersonal Relationships

Eights use power as the primary means for acquiring, conserving, and defending resources. Wielding power in this manner predisposes them to the unconscious disposition, inherent to every Eight, that people are obstacles separating them from the resources that they desire to acquire, control, and conserve. Such a disposition sometimes manifests as a pattern of behavior, ranging from subtle to violent, where Eights attempt to subjugate others. In those Eights lacking self-control, this pattern may manifest in some or all categories of relationship, including familial, business, religious, academic, and so on.

Of the many difficulties that Eights experience in relationships, most are due to the brutish tendency for asserting power, influence, and control over others. The way that Eights project power into relationships comes across to others as bullying, insensitive, and demeaning. In some cases, Eights resort to interpersonal violence to achieve their objectives. However, most Eights temper and normalize their projection of power in relationships, at least to the extent that they learn to project power in more subtle ways.

Although many Eights are enamored with the possibility of a lifelong relationship based on love and commitment, they often have difficulty finding partners who can accept their need to assert power, which is the most common problem in relating with Eights. However, many Eights do find a partner who is willing to accept them without reservation. A common match for Eights is type Nine, discussed in the next chapter. Twos are another natural match for Eights, especially those Eights who allow themselves to be charmed and tamed by Twos, as further discussed in Chapter 7.

Parenting is an area where Eights often excel. One reason is that Eights recognize that children are resources that need mentoring, coaching, and grooming. And Eights are indispensable in providing the parenting that is crucial to a child's development. Perhaps most important is that parenting is a relationship where the exercise of power in the name of discipline, accountability, and responsibility is appropriate; and sometimes beneficial for the growth, development, and guidance of young egos. But probably the best reason is that Eights generally enjoy parenting because it is one sphere where they can nurture a very critical resource, if not the most important resource.

Some Eights may have difficulty in a parenting role because they are unable to control their temper, which sometimes leads to a pattern of using corporal punishment inappropriately. However, most Eights are very effective mentors, because they embody the traits of strength, courage, and will, which leaves a lasting impression on young minds. Countless young people have benefited from the coaching, mentoring, and leadership of Eights. For these reasons, Eights are indispensable to the mentoring and guidance of young minds.

Psychology of Eights

Primary Ego Trait: Power

Regressive Traits: Gluttony, excess, exaggeration.

In Search Of: Resources

Focuses On: Who controls the resources.

Basic Fear: Annihilation.

Basic Desire: To acquire, conserve, protect, defend, and nurture resources.

Basic Need: Adequate resources.

Stress Reaction: Projection of strength and power.

Sense of Self: I'm ok if I have enough resources.

Motto: The most resourceful will survive.

Mental Model: Power and justice are relative.

Motivations:

- Self-reliance
- To champion resources
- To be the ultimate human resource in their community.
- Overcome their vulnerabilities

Physical Characteristics

Conserving resources requires a highly adaptable constitution, especially concerning environmental conditions, which explains the wide diversity of elite physiological characteristics found among Eights. Because Eights have such a wide range of physiological traits, it can be challenging to identify them based solely on their physical presentation, without first understanding the unique physical characteristics of resource conservation. Fortunately, the physical traits of resource conservation are very transparent. And this fact helps to easily identify Eights, making them perhaps easier to differentiate from the other Enneatypes.

Eights accumulate resources by focusing their power on the environment. Eights derive much of their power from an amplification of the instinctive drives in the physical body. The amplification of the physical body affects endurance, hunger, pain, pleasure, sex drive, aggression, energy level, and so on. Understanding this phenomenon can be an aid in the identification of Eights because the first thing to be noticed about the amplification of the physical body is that it produces the largest constitutions among the Enneatypes.

Of the many reasons that explain why Eights have the largest constitutions, perhaps the most important is that the instinctive drive to eat is amplified, which is the predicate for overeating and weight gain. However, this does not adequately explain why many Eights are overweight, as many people who overeat do not gain weight. So, other factors are at play.

The most important factor explaining the large constitutions observed among Eights is related to their specialization. Eights embody resource conservation, in a very literal sense, which allows them to store more energy reserves than any other type. The energy reserves may be in the form of adipose tissue, muscle, or both. Body mass indexes (BMI) exceeding 100 are not uncommon among Eights, with the highest ever recorded being 204; whereas a BMI exceeding 40 is rarely observed in the other Enneatypes.

Also important is the understanding that the amplification of the physical body is not always transparent. Indeed, many Eights are less likely to increase in size over time, such as those who engage in ultra long-distance running, because exercise prevents weight gain. Apart from the massive number of calories burned during exercise, long-distance running is unique because of the hormonal effect that prevents the body from adding extra weight. However, the time comes when it is no longer possible to run long distances, and beyond that point, the propensity to gain weight will manifest. But in this example, it should be mentioned that long-distance running is itself an amplification of the physical body.

Eights also have some subtle physical characteristics that are less common or rare when compared to the other Enneatypes. For example, Eights lean slightly forward as they walk, which prepares them to meet any challenge or difficulty head-on. The adaptation in gait manifests because of an alteration in the skeletal structure of the lower extremities, formally described as genu varum (bow-legged) and genu valgum (knock knees). The effect of this evolutionary adaptation is that it forces the toes to point inward, and shifts the center of gravity slightly forward, thereby allowing Eights to walk with a slightly forward gait. It also means that Eights will fall forward, toward an incoming threat, if they lose their balance. This adaptation is the opposite of Nines, whose toes are pointed outward, allowing Nines to fall back and away from threats.

Eights prefer authoritative postures, such as walking with their arms slightly extended, which prepares them for a possible attack. But one of the signature physiological traits of Eights is that they prefer to wear their hair as short as culturally allowable. Where culturally accepted, male Eights often shave their heads: A behavior that is much less common in the other Enneatypes. Also, Eights are subject to hair loss at an early age, including female Eights, with a significant portion of both sexes eventually balding. Excessive balding, extreme thinning of hair, or alopecia is less common with the other Enneatypes.

Eights are host to many subtle physiological characteristics that support the evolutionary prerogative of resource conservation. For example, balding hair allows for greater attunement with the environment, and a forward center of gravity allows Eights to project power toward external threats. These physiological characteristics, along with many others, are easier to explain by video or personal demonstration.

FACIAL TENSION

The facial tension for type Eight affects the symmetry, shape, and curvature of the nose. The asymmetry in the nose is sometimes noticeable upon direct examination; and is characterized as a distinct lean to the left, as seen from the perspective of the observer. In some cases, the lean creates an irregular curvature in the nose. The tension may also affect the size, shape, and symmetry of the nostrils. Sometimes, the facial tension is very noticeable, which has prompted some Eights to pursue surgical corrections.

IDENTIFYING AND DIAGNOSING EIGHTS

Because Eights constitute a disproportionate share of the population, estimated to be approximately 24% of the US population, the objective physiological traits that are associated with Eights are very common. Thus, Eights are the default diagnosis, notwithstanding an identification of another Enneatype. The objective physiological traits are:

1. Extreme athleticism or extreme obesity

2. Male thinning or bald hair

3. Forward center of gravity

4. Bowlegged or knock-kneed

5. Authoritative posturing

6. Above-average BMI

7. A powerful voice, often with bass to baritone characteristics

CHAPTER 5

TYPE NINE: THE STABILIZER

Endeavor: Stabilization

Chapter Two revealed that Intrinsic Barbarism was the result of the regressive traits within the psyche of Early Humans, including envy, jealousy, deception, greed, lust, resentment, anger, hostility, vindictiveness, and hate. These traits are considered regressive because of their negative consequences, including intra-species violence, the fracturing of nuclear families, and the division of social groups. Although the regressive traits were individually problematic, they eventually became a major factor of extinction, due to their downstream effects on critical activities.

Chapter Two focused on the trait of hate and how it constituted a direct threat to Early Humans because of the violence it sponsored. And the same discussion could be had for each of the regressive traits because each constituted a direct threat to Early Humans, each according to their context. But the greater problem, at least from an evolutionary perspective, was in how the regressive traits posed an indirect threat to Early Humans.

It's important to understand that the entire population of Early Humans, including every member of every species, exhibited all or most of the behaviors that are associated with the regressive traits. The ubiquity of the regressive traits meant that every individual exhibited behaviors of envy, jealousy, deception, greed, lust, anger, hostility, vindictiveness, and hate. And it was the ubiquity of these traits that made them an indirect threat to Early Humans.

The regressive traits constituted an indirect threat for many reasons, but perhaps the most important reason was that they collectively undermined the cooperation that existed among Early Humans. Cooperation between individuals was important for the success of nuclear families, but it was of paramount importance for the success of social groups. Unfortunately for Early Humans, the ubiquity of the regressive traits undermined their ability to cooperate, which effectively prevented them from evolving more complex social structures.

The inability to evolve to more complex social structures meant that Early Humans were often forced to live in small groups composed of nuclear families. The limitations imposed by the regressive traits meant that the advantages of complex social structures, including efficiency, specialization, and economies of scale, were either denied or limited. Thus, the regressive traits had devastating socio-economic effects.

Intrinsic Barbarism is the result of the regressive traits, but also the many types of defective intra-psychic disorders, which would have included many types of dissociative, depressive, neurodevelopmental, and psychotic disorders. Most of the defective intra-psychic disorders have been cataloged by psychologists, into a reference manual that is comprehensive in scope. The regressive traits and intra-psychic disorders constitute the *Regressive Psyche*.

Most readers of this book are aware of the impact of the Regressive Psyche. That is because most people have learned by their own interpersonal experiences, which confers an intuitive understanding of the role and contribution that the Regressive Psyche played in the formation of Intrinsic Barbarism. However, some individuals might discount the severity of these phenomena, so it's important to go a little further in defining the realities of Intrinsic Barbarism.

Intrinsic Barbarism was responsible for the state of fear, chaos, and barbaric acts of violence that occurred secondary to the Regressive Psyche of Early

Humans. The reality of Intrinsic Barbarism meant that no one could be trusted, not even the members within a social group because every individual had the propensity to become violent at any moment. Worse, the violence associated with Intrinsic Barbarism was unpredictable, as it manifested spontaneously from innocuous circumstances such as a minor scarcity of resources. The chaotic nature of Intrinsic Barbarism meant that every individual lived in constant fear of the violence that might spontaneously descend upon them on any given day. No one could relax, or let their guard down, as tensions were always high. From a theological perspective, Intrinsic Barbarism is the Hell that is imposed by the primitive mind.

The Hellish conditions of Intrinsic Barbarism are very similar to what is experienced by modern-day inmates of maximum-security prisons, where the most violent offenders are kept at bay, to segregate and protect the rest of society. Incidences of interpersonal violence occur almost daily in maximum-security prisons, which creates conditions where no one can relax or let their guard down because doing so invites exploitation and violence. Worse is that the violent attacks are unpredictable because they are often triggered by something trivial, or by nothing at all. For these reasons, inmates held in maximum-security prisons typically have very high-stress levels, which reflect the conditions that are imposed by the Regressive Psyche.

Evolution responded to Intrinsic Barbarism with the Enneciation of Nines, who are specifically designed to stabilize the collective psyche of the human species. The arrival of Nines was a crucial development because it sponsored an array of new behaviors that had never existed in the previous seven million years of human evolution. The scope, complexity, and sophistication of these behaviors evolved as a match to the Environmental Archetype formed by Intrinsic Barbarism, such that it put in motion the Human Endeavor of stabilizing the collective psyche of the human species. Of the many ways that Nines Endeavor to stabilize the collective psyche, perhaps the most powerful is in their role as counselors.

Primary Role: Counseling

The total elimination of Intrinsic Barbarism is not possible, because the only realistic way to accomplish that would be by the total elimination of the Regressive Psyche. As a practical matter, it was necessary to carry many parts of the Regressive Psyche forward to modern humans, as certain elements were necessary for the specializations that are inherent to each of the Enneatypes. The following list provides an example of a regressive trait and an intra-psychic defect necessary for the Endeavor of each Enneatype:

Type Eight: Gluttony - Paranoid Personality Disorder

Type Nine: Apathy - Dependent Personality Disorder

Type One: Anger - Obsessive-Compulsive Personality Disorder

Type Two: Hubris - Histrionic Personality Disorder

Type Three: Deception - Narcissistic Personality Disorder

Type Four: Envy - Depressive Personality Disorder

Type Five: Avarice - Schizoid Personality Disorder

Type Six: Cowardice - Borderline Personality Disorder

Type Seven: Greed - Manic Depressive Disorder

The above list is not meant to be comprehensive, as only the primary regressive trait and primary diagnostic category appear for each Enneatype. This information has many uses, as it provides a glimpse of the obstacles to personal growth, development, and self-actualization for each Enneatype. With some reflection on this information, an understanding emerges that the Endeavor for each Enneatype tends to restrict, limit, and impair the ability of the individual to function outside of their evolutionary role. However, the key point in this discussion is that each Enneatype has regressive traits, and intra-psychic defects, that are specific to each type. And it is the primary role of Nines to mitigate, manage, and prevent the conditions of Intrinsic Barbarism that are caused by these intra-psychic phenomena.

Nines fulfill the obligations of their evolutionary role in several ways. The first way is that Nines embrace, embody, and exemplify a faultless character, thereby setting a standard of interpersonal conduct for all Enneatypes. The standard of interpersonal conduct is aptly described as loving, forgiving, patient, kind, selfless, accepting, trusting, innocent, unpretentious, optimistic, reassuring, and supportive. Nines possess a persona that comports very closely with the archetype of an angel. Indeed, Nines combine a relatively fault free character, with an advanced degree of psychological sophistication, to form an angelic persona.

Given their highly evolved character, Nines function effortlessly as a mechanism of deconfliction and reconciliation, by assuming the basic social role of Counselor. In this context, a Counselor is an unbiased, objective, and open-minded person that helps others with problems related to the Regressive Psyche. Moreover, Nines must be patient, reassuring, supportive, and optimistic. Nines easily meet these requirements, while having the natural ability to understand the character faults as they manifest in the other Enneatypes.

Another way that Nines reduce the effects of Intrinsic Barbarism is by assuming the role of mediator when there is a conflict in their sphere of influence. Although Nines do not always seek the role of mediator, it is theirs by default, as they act objectively, independently, and with no signs of malice. Thus, Nines are adapted to be the default mediator in all social contexts.

Reconciliation is one of the best strategies employed by Nines to stabilize the effects of Intrinsic Barbarism. Nines are profusely apologetic, regardless of who was responsible for the conflict, as a primary tactic for reconciling every conflict they encounter. That is because effective reconciliation requires that Nines be prepared to accept the responsibility for all conflicts, regardless of who is to blame. The willingness to accept responsibility for the wrongs committed by others, in the endeavor to promote stability, harmony, and peace, is evidence of the highly evolved character attributable to Nines. For these reasons, the moniker of Apologist, Reconciler, or Peacemaker is often used to describe Nines.

The examples given in this discussion provide insight into the traits, characteristics, and methods used by Nines to stabilize the effects of Intrinsic Barbarism. What is often not understood is that Nines are often the unwitting participants of their Endeavor, as they provide a model of human virtues, based on forgiveness, humility, selflessness, and sacrifice. These traits allow

Nines to assume their primary role of counseling others, and to mediate and reconcile conflicts, to stabilize the collective psyche of the human species. Nines possess many functional adaptations that enable them to be highly effective stabilizers.

Functional Adaptation

The most notable adaptation for Nines is that they do not exhibit any signs or traces of the Regressive Psyche. The absence of the Regressive Psyche means that Nines are relatively free of the regressive traits and the defective intra-psychic phenomena that plagued Early Humans for eons. Nines possess a functional adaptation that suppresses the Regressive Psyche, which necessarily requires the suppression of most parts of the Instinctive Center since the Regressive Psyche is mostly rooted in the instincts. Thus, the key to understanding Nines rests with an understanding of how the human experience is affected by the suppression of the Instinctive Center.

The suppression of the Instinctive Center attenuates certain collateral functions such as situational awareness, fear responses, and assertive behaviors. That is because the most basic function of the Instinctive Center is to ground the human experience to the present moment, to what is happening in the moment, which is a necessary predicate for participation in the world. Of course, an individuated sense of self is the predicate to these core experiences. However, without the Instinctive Center, the nexus to the moment is lost, along with an intrinsic sense of an individuated self. The repression of an individuated self might sound like a terrifying experience, but it is a necessary part of the functional adaptation of Nines.

The suppression of the instincts is necessary because it effectively disconnects, insulates, and isolates Nines from what is happening in the world around them. Thus, Nines are not affected by conflicts, violence, and aggression in the same way as other Enneatypes. Indeed, their situational awareness is softened, muted, and buffered to a great extent, allowing them to be mostly independent of their environment. The fact that Nines are independent with respect to their environment stands in contradistinction to Eights, who adapt, conform, and mirror the needs of their environment.

Having environmental separation allows Nines to function, even under extreme psychological duress, which is an adaptation that is ideally suited for the conditions of Intrinsic Barbarism. This adaptation allows Nines to rise above the barbarism, even under the direst of circumstances, and maintain a sense of selflessness, acceptance, and optimism. The environmental separation that Nines enjoy explains why they do not engage in exploitation, revenge, or violence, allowing them to be the primary source of mental stability in their social group.

There are many other ways that the suppression of the Instinctive Center allows Nines to function as the ultimate stabilizer of the collective psyche. Perhaps the best example is in how Nines prevent Intrinsic Barbarism. Preventing Intrinsic Barbarism begins with the formation of the ego, known as the individuation phase of ego development, which occurs from the age of approximately eighteen months to forty-eight months. During individuation, the ego requires a very stable environment, so that the basic structures of the psyche can develop with integrity. A stable holding environment provides object constancy, meaning that an infant perceives the nurturing objects as stable and constant. When the holding environment is stable, the ego develops an image of the self that is stable, fluid, and constant. Only when the holding environment is both stable and constant does the ego develop a sense of self that is stable, integrated, and constant.

When the holding environment is chaotic, unpredictable, and violent, the individuation of the ego will develop in a chaotic, unpredictable, and disintegrated manner. And to the extent that the holding environment is chaotic, the ego will fail to develop or integrate the positive qualities needed for high-level functions; and will instead incorporate the regressive elements of the psyche. Thus, a chaotic holding environment plays a key role in the development of the Regressive Psyche, which later manifests as Intrinsic Barbarism, in a generational process that is self-perpetuating. The continuity of Intrinsic Barbarism explains why it is difficult to break the chain of Intrinsic Barbarism once it has started, as it is passed from one generation to the next by way of the holding environment.

Nines break the chain of Intrinsic Barbarism by providing the necessary object constancy needed in the holding environment. The key to object constancy is to prevent young egos from experiencing trauma, violence, and abuse, which Nines accomplish by providing a peaceful, stable, and consistent holding environment, thereby creating the conditions for optimal development. In so doing, Nines break the chain of Intrinsic Barbarism and prevent it from taking hold in future generations. Nines accomplish this feat in their role as parents, surrogates, and Counselors.

Nines also have functional adaptations that are ideal for many occupations. One of the best examples is the relatively new field of computer science, which is very suitable for introverted types, including Nines who enjoy the challenge of replacing cyber chaos with stability. Nines are specially adapted for computer work, as they bring solid logic, math, and problem-solving skills that are prerequisites to many information technology jobs. Part of this adaptation for working with computers is because both the human psyche and computers are abstractions of the physical world: The skills needed to stabilize the human psyche are transferable, from a practical perspective to the abstract problems encountered in the virtual world of computers.

Astronomy is a field that is dominated by Nines. Astronomy is an observational science that requires endless hours of research and observation to develop and test theories that might explain how the universe operates. Nines have a competitive advantage here because they have almost infinite patience for researching and observing the Heavens. But Nines are also very curious, and their curiosity provides support for seemingly endless astronomical research. Nines are also able to synthesize their findings with other areas of science, so that they may reach logical conclusions, thus furthering the understanding of the universe. For these reasons, Nines have worked to further an understanding of the universe more than most of the Enneatypes.

Nines play an important role in nearly every area of scientific research, including biology, medicine, astrophysics, climatology, and anthropology. Many of the greatest scientific discoveries were made or assisted by Nines. Thus, scientific research itself constitutes a vocational area where Nines have a competitive advantage.

As a final point, Nines possess many other unique physiological adaptations that are specific to their Endeavor. For example, Nines have a nervous system that is passive, rather than reactive, to environmental stimuli. A passive nervous system allows Nines to relax, and let their guard down, thus enabling them to perform their evolutionary functions. An adjunct to this adaptation is a pain threshold that is the highest among the Enneatypes. These adaptations allow Nines to perform the functions of their primary role.

Basic Delusion

Understanding the basic delusion for Nines requires an understanding of the phenomenon of Universal Trust. Universal Trust is the most basic form of trust that colors how humans perceive, identify, and interact with the physical world. The experience of Universal Trust allows one to relax in the direct knowledge that the universe cares, loves, and appreciates all life forms. Universal Trust fosters a sense of security in the operation of the universe, while at the same time, opening the soul to the experience of Love. It has been described by many throughout the ages as a fundamental, but not infallible, part of the human experience. Humans are dependent on Universal Trust because it provides the foundation for functioning in the world. Without Universal Trust, there is paralysis, fear, and insecurity.

Although Humans depend on Universal Trust to function in the world, the ability to experience Universal Trust is very subjective, as many factors play a role in the development of Universal Trust. Especially important is the early holding environment because that is the period of development where the ego is most vulnerable. The period of greatest vulnerability is during the first two years of life when the crystallization of the most basic object relationships and identity structures within the human ego occurs. The degree of love, nurturing, and stability provided by the early holding environment will determine the qualitative integration of Universal Trust within the human soul during the crucial stages of ego development.

Regardless of the quality of the holding environment provided to Nines, the qualitative integration of Universal Trust is partially impaired, giving Nines a unique psychological adaptation that effectively insulates them from certain types of experience. The insulating effect that coincides with the arrested integration of Universal Trust is responsible for muting many types of experience, and this is a necessary adaptation that has some collateral effects that are of interest. One of those effects is that the ability to experience love is impaired.

Nines have an impaired ability to perceive, feel, and receive love from others, due to impairment with the parts of the brain responsible for Universal Trust. The result of this impairment produces individuals who have an unconscious belief and insecurity that they are not cared for, loved, and appreciated by the universe. The ego for Nines grows and develops around the belief that love is a local phenomenon as opposed to a universal phenomenon. The unconscious belief that love is a local phenomenon produces individuals deluded with the belief that they are not loveable.

The ego identity for type Nine grows and develops around the delusion that they are not loveable, and effectively compensates by adopting certain mental and physical characteristics that will attract love, while at the same time preventing the development of personality traits that might repel love and acceptance. In this way, Nines exemplify a constellation of mental and physical characteristics that are uniquely designed to attract love and acceptance.

Interpersonal Relationships:

Nines excel in the area of interpersonal relationships, due to having a functional adaptation that suppresses the Regressive Psyche, which negates the expression of anti-personal traits. From a psychological perspective, Nines have very few faults, which carries important implications in matters of interpersonal relationships. And Nines are endowed with many positive traits that facilitate and support meaningful interpersonal relationships. Next, this discussion will apply the Five-Factor Model to Nines, to further illustrate how Nines compare to other Enneatypes:

> **Extroversion:** Nines are introverts, a functional adaptation necessary for universal compatibility in relationships. Introversion is important since extroversion is not universally compatible in relationships.

Agreeableness: Nines are the most agreeable Enneatype, a functional adaptation necessary for universal compatibility in relationships.

Conscientiousness: Nines are very conscientious in their behavior, and how they relate to others, which confers universal compatibility in relationships.

Neuroticism: Because Nines rate lowest in neurotic behaviors, they are much less likely to cause problems in their relationships, ensuring that they have universal compatibility with others.

Openness: Nines are very open to new experiences, which is necessary for universal compatibility with others.

Relative to the other Enneatypes, Nines rate at the extreme on each dimension measured in the Five-Factor Model. But the key point from this discussion is not the personality traits associated with type Nine, but rather that Nines cannot be understood by rating their personality traits. That is because Nines are the embodiment of a faultless character that evolved within the context of Intrinsic Barbarism. Thus, any attempt to analyze Nines must use a reductionist approach, beginning with the traits associated with the Regressive Psyche, rather than the traits that they do have. The use of other approaches will fail to capture the character traits, attitudes, and behaviors of this Enneatype.

Despite having a nearly flawless character, and having universal compatibility with others, Nines do encounter many difficulties in their relationships. A persistent problem occurs when other people project their faults and vices onto Nines. Projection happens quite frequently; however, the problem is compounded by the inept responses that Nines often provide. Another common problem for Nines is that they often fail to meet the expectations of others. Failed expectations occur because most relationships operate on quid pro quo. As it often happens, Nines fail to reciprocate the love and attention that comes their way.

The primary problem for Nines is that they have difficulty in setting boundaries for others. Nines demonstrate a pattern of allowing others to trespass, exploit, and take advantage of their generosity. Nines become resentful, which leads to passive-aggressive behaviors, where Nines attempt to deny, deflect and avoid those that have acted offensively. An unintended consequence of these passive-aggressive measures is that unresolved problems continue to escalate.

With rare exceptions, when interpersonal conflicts arise, these conflicts are almost universally caused by others. When Nines do contribute to the interpersonal problems that come their way, it is generally because of something that they failed to do, such as communicate their position, feelings, wants, or needs. Thus, they might have some complicity, but any objective analysis would not place the blame on Nines. The blanket exoneration of Nines should come as no surprise, given that Nines evolved to help others with their problems, instead of being the source of problems.

Parenting is another area where Nines have mixed results. Nines tend to excel during the early formative years, when the ego completes the basic stages of development, by ensuring that neonates receive a proper holding environment. A proper holding environment allows the ego to grow, develop, and mature with basic trust, positive self-esteem, and resiliency. However, Nines often have difficulties during other phases of parenting.

Nines have most of their parenting difficulties during the adolescent and late teen phases of development. The difficulty lies in the fundamental responsibilities that parents must fulfill. These responsibilities include setting, explaining, and enforcing boundaries for their children. Nines are generally not effective at setting boundaries for themselves, so this carries over to their role as a parent, where they are generally lax in setting boundaries for their children. Even if Nines are effective at setting boundaries, they tend to be ineffective at explaining boundaries, because they want to avoid conflicts with their children. And the most problematic for Nines is the enforcement of boundaries because Nines view the enforcement of boundaries as a conflict. For these reasons, the children of Nines are known to describe their Nine-Parent as absent, distant, or laissez-faire.

Psychology

Primary Ego Trait: Peace

Regressive Trait: Apathy

In Search Of: Reconciliation and merging

Focuses On: The mental state of others.

Basic Fear: Of Being unlovable.

Basic Desire: To be free of vice.

Basic Need: Peace and harmony.

Stress Reaction: Denial, withdrawal, depersonalization.

Sense of Self: I'm ok when there is peace.

Motto: Don't rock the boat.

Mental Model: Always keep an open mind.

Motivations:

- Offer unconditional forgiveness
- Maintain the status quo
- Foster a stable environment
- Reconcile conflicts and tension

Physical Characteristics

The mental stability that Nines enjoy is an integral part of the adaptations that are necessary to stabilize situations involving Intrinsic Barbarism. In addition to the mental adaptations, Nines are also uniquely adapted on a physiological level to address the physical violence that is associated with Intrinsic Barbarism. The physiology needed to handle the various degrees of physical violence requires an adaptation for handling pain, physical abuse, and even torture. For these reasons, Nines evolved the highest pain tolerance of all Enneatypes.

The physiological defense mechanism for pain tolerance serves an important purpose. To understand why Nines are adapted with a very high tolerance for pain, recall that Nines wish to reconcile conflicts whenever possible. From a strategic point of view, the best way to reconcile conflicts is to never engage in physical conflicts under any circumstances. To avoid conflicts, Nines will do everything in their power to avoid a physical fight. They will apologize profusely, instead of retaliating or escalating conflicts. They will accept verbal, emotional, and physical abuse, all with little or no resistance. These behaviors are made possible by a pain tolerance that is unsurpassed among the Enneatypes.

For the same reasons cited earlier, the best way to describe the physical characteristics of Nines is to describe the characteristics that Nines are missing. Nines are absent many of the physical attributes that are unattractive or repelling to their community and the opposite sex. These physical attributes do not apply to every Nine, as there are always exceptions; yet, some of these attributes are present in every Nine.

Nines have many layers of defense mechanisms for avoiding conflicts. Perhaps the most superficial of these layers is in their physical appearance. Nines dress in a way that is never confrontational, extraordinary, or countercultural. Nines prefer simplicity over attention-seeking styles. Their clothing choices are mostly mainstream and simple, which aligns with their overall strategy of avoiding attention and creating a stable, harmonious, and peaceful environment. For Nines, simple is considered better, and this applies to their choice of hairstyle. Female Nines prefer naturally long hair with very few if any alterations. Male Nines are also known to let their hair grow to very long lengths, which is a rarity among the other Enneatypes.

Although Eights have a slightly forward lean in their gait, the opposite is true for Nines, who have a backward lean as they walk. The physiological adaptation that allows this is in the feet. Nines have their toes pointed outward, allowing them to fall back and away from conflicts. This adaptation is very subtle and requires some practice to recognize.

Nines carry themselves with a sense of simple elegance, and they use a minimum of body language, especially when compared to other Enneatypes.

These subtleties mean that Nines tend to keep their arms close to their bodies, which allows them to minimize body movements as they ambulate. For these reasons, there is a notable absence of movement in the hips, torso, and shoulders during ambulation when compared to other Enneatypes.

Facial Tension

The facial tension for Nines is perhaps the easiest of the Enneatypes to identify. From the perspective of the observer, the facial tension for Nines appears as a squint in the left eye, such that the left eye appears closed slightly more than the right eye. The left eye tension for Nines may be very faint, subtle, or intermittent; however, most Nines will have the left eye squint most of the time. The squint is due to a contraction in the eyelid muscle, which in some cases adversely affects the muscles connected to the eyeball, causing a misalignment of the eyeball known as strabismus. This condition is an evolutionary consequence of the physiological adaptations that are unique to Nines. For Nines having strabismus, the right eye is dominant, and the left eye is passive, from an observers perspective.

Identification and Typing

Nines are estimated to comprise approximately 11% of the American population. Nines are often misdiagnosed as Ones or Fives because they share some basic physiological traits and features. The key objective physiological traits for type Nine are:

1. Non-athletic build.

2. Very long or simple hairstyle

3. Backward leaning gait, with toes pointed outward slightly.

4. Neutral posture

5. Favorite color is purple.

6. Soft-spoken, shy demeanor

CHAPTER 6

TYPE ONE: THE CIVILIAN

Endeavor: Civilization

Although Homo Erectus was the first hominid to emigrate from Africa, they were not particularly civilized creatures, a fact that is due partly to their primitive living conditions. And though they were fast learners and somewhat adaptable creatures, they were held back by several regressive traits and behaviors. For these reasons, Homo Erectus generally acted according to their immediate desires, making them somewhat untamable, brutish, and callous opportunists. Their incivility was evidence of being poorly equipped for, and generally incapable of creating, societies based on fundamental human values such as freedom, accountability, and justice.

Despite their limitations, Homo Erectus was distinguished by a consciousness that brought many new capabilities, including independent perceptions, thoughts, and actions. The intelligence that coincided with greater consciousness propelled Early Humans to new heights, as it allowed them to think, act, and solve problems independent of their animal instincts. The independence sponsored by consciousness meant that Early Humans could, under ideal conditions and circumstances, act and behave in a civilized manner.

Unfortunately for Early Humans, the conditions and circumstances required for civilized behavior rarely materialized, given the very primitive subsistence level conditions that prevailed. In this context, the primitive conditions that prevailed were just enough to allow for the genesis, diversification, and evolution of life. Missing were the basic structural supports of civilization, such as covenants, laws, or higher authorities, that might coerce, control, and govern behavior in conscious beings.

Of the basic structural supports that had evolved before the arrival of Homo Erectus, each failed to regulate the violent tendencies in Early Human behavior, especially those that coincided with the rise of consciousness. Even the superego, which is the most powerful internal coercive mechanism of the psyche, was no match for the independence of thought, action, and behavior that was sponsored by the expansion of consciousness in Homo Erectus. That is because consciousness effectively overrides the preprogrammed instincts, emotions, and coercive mechanisms of the physical body. The power of consciousness effectively exempted Early Humans from the laws of nature that governed the behavior of all other creatures.

Exemption from the laws of nature allowed conscious beings to act in new ways that were antithetical to the evolution of life. These behaviors were responsible for a substantial reduction in the ranks of Early Humans, along with the fracturing of nuclear families and communities, such that their negative effects were second only to Exogenous Barbarism. Because the source of these behaviors was endogenous to Early Humans, these behaviors constituted a new form of violence known as Endogenous Barbarism: The extremely savage, cruel, and violent acts that conscious beings exact against their peers.

Endogenous Barbarism is not observed elsewhere in the animal kingdom because all other animals have a basic reverence for the laws of nature. However, because consciousness does not impart a reverence for life, there was nothing to prevent Early Humans from acting with a reckless disregard for life. The net result is that consciousness effectively replaces the laws of nature, or the laws of God, with the belief that the individual self is God. Thus, the rise of consciousness introduced a new phenomenon of atheism.

Evolution responded to the primitive atheism of Early Humans with the introduction of Ones, who evolved to displace the rampant chaos that was a defining characteristic of Early Human life, with the orderly and lawful conduct that is the defining characteristic of Modern Humans. Ones bring law and order by erecting the pillars of civilization that are necessary to restore the fundamental reverence for life. As a mechanism for law and order, Ones specialize in the creation of civilization, within the evolutionary prerogative of creating, administrating, and managing the civil institutions that ensure accountability, responsibility, and control of the individual.

Because a major part of their specialization is to create the elements of civilization, Ones assert jurisdiction over all matters related to the civil institutions that they create, administrate, and manage. These institutions fall into three basic categories, with each category forming a basic pillar of civilization: Education, government, and religion. This discussion continues with the primary roles that pertain to each of the pillars of civilization.

Primary Role: The Civilian

Early Humans were certainly capable of civility, but only under the right conditions and circumstances. The conditions that Early Humans required, but rarely experienced, are those related to the endogenous structural supports provided by civilization. In this context, civilization is important because it provides the necessary order, structure, and support that holds individuals accountable and responsible for their actions. The accountability, responsibility, and control of the individual is directly dependent upon the three pillars of civilization: Education, government, and religion.

Education is a prerequisite, and a cornerstone, for the genesis, growth, and maturity of civilization. For this reason, every individual must be taught the virtues of life, beginning at a very early age. This teaching must be absolute, under very controlled conditions, to be effective. There is little room for hypocrisy, error, or bias. The point here is that the teaching must be factual, logical, unbiased, objective, and without the errors of fallacy. To the extent that individuals are taught the virtues of life, without the errors of fallacy, several possibilities emerge.

Conscious beings who are educated in an objective manner express a high degree of accountability for their actions. And when they make mistakes, they are more eager to take responsibility, rather than deflect the blame onto others. They accept their punishment, and learn from their mistakes, as they tend to be more amenable to correction and rehabilitation. For these reasons, education is the best way to ensure that citizens are accountable, responsible, and revering of life.

Government is next in importance after education because it provides the three basic structures necessary for law and order. The main structure is the designated authority for creating laws, such as a legislative body, and the body of law that is duly authorized. The laws created by the designated authority are then subject to enforcement and policing by the designated personnel who identify, capture, and detain those that have violated the law. The third structure is judicial, which is the process of adjudicating those that have violated the laws, to hold offenders accountable for their actions. Collectively, the three basic structures of government form a system of criminal justice that is a defining mark of civilization.

History has proven that the three basic structures of government can be highly effective at maintaining law and order; and when educational support is factored in, a massive reduction in the phenomenon of Endogenous Barbarism occurs. However, the combined effects of government and education are limited, in that both have limited jurisdiction since all governments operate within a distinct geographical boundary. Language is another barrier to the efficacy, efficiency, and economy of scale for education and government. Governments are also very prone to instability. But perhaps the greatest limitation of government and education is that it neglects the fundamental cause of Endogenous Barbarism: Atheism.

To confront the problem of atheism head-on, Ones evolved to create, administrate, and manage the major world religions. Religion has several advantages over government and education. The foremost advantage of religion is that it has unlimited jurisdiction, so it does not have the geographical, language, or political instability problems that are associated with the various types of government. And because participation is voluntary, religion has the will of the individual as an advantage over the compulsory institutions of government and education. For these reasons, the major world religions have become the indelible icons of civilization, while nation-states have come and gone many times over.

The efficacy of religion explains why the major world religions have done more to end Endogenous Barbarism than all current and historical government institutions combined. However, certain religions have, in certain temporally isolated instances, been a source of barbarism. These points aside, there is no question that the major world religions have been very effective at reducing Endogenous Barbarism. That is because religion is a basic pillar of civilization, which in this context means law and order, for the same reasons as education and government. Some examples help to illuminate this point.

Education is the cornerstone of all major world religions, given the Biblical teachings of Christians and Catholics, the Quran to Muslims, and the Hebrew Bible to Jews. Buddhist texts are foundational to the teaching of Buddhist Monks, the Tao Te Ching to Taoists, the Veda to Hindus, and so on. Although the verbiage varies, each religion teaches that all conscious beings must show reverence for the dignity, value, and sanctity of life. Thus, the sanctity of life is a fundamental teaching in each of the major world religions.

In the same way that governments create laws, each of the major world religions has a governing set of principles or commandments to follow. For example, the Hebrew and Christian bibles list ten commandments that must be followed (although the New Testament of the Christian bible shortens the list to two commandments). Hinduism and Taoism also have ten commandments. And Buddhists have the Dharma, and so on. What is striking is the commonality, especially concerning the basic laws and commandments, shared between religion and government. For example, almost every major religion and institution of government has an edict of *thou shalt not kill*.

Although the major world religions are less coercive and punitive than the criminal justice exacted by government, the expectations and standards set by religion are much higher than those set by most government institutions, which necessarily requires different methods of enforcement. For example, followers of the three traditional paths of religion, Yogis, Monks, and Ascetics, are generally required to practice or live at a monastery full time.

By removing participants from their social group, these religions can ensure compliance with the edicts, laws, and commandments of their path. Other means and methods for compliance include various rites, rituals, ceremonies, baptisms, confessions, excommunications, and so on.

Despite the many advantages of religion, there are several reasons to explain why it cannot be considered the primary remedy for Endogenous Barbarism. First, since participation in religion is voluntary, there will always be a certain percentage of the population that remains an atheist, which leaves the door open for Endogenous Barbarism to take root. And because attendance is voluntary, religion is not an effective coercive agency, which explains why religion has little effect upon the most intractable cases of violent offenders. For these reasons, religion is not always effective in the establishment of law and order, as it is intended to function as a complement to government and education.

Functional Adaptations

As part of their specialization, Ones possess an Instinctive Center and Superego that is specifically adapted to perform certain evolutionary functions. Recall that the Instinctive Center is the survival mechanism that allows an individual to interface with their environment in meaningful ways. Because it is programmed mostly by direct experience, it acts as a mirror of the environment. The primary directive of the Instinctive Center is to ensure survival, using any means necessary, including aggression and violence. The Instinctive Center has many forms of aggression, including violence that is antithetical to the interests of a species, such as all forms of barbarism.

One of the primary functions of the superego is to protect a species from the damaging effects of barbarism, which it accomplishes by acting as an inner coercive agency that controls the thoughts, behaviors, and actions of the individual. The superego guides, controls, and coerces an individual to think, act, and behave in a civilized manner. Thus, the superego evolved to be a check against the damage, such as Endogenous Barbarism, stemming from and caused by the Instinctive Center.

Unfortunately for Early Humans, the superego was no match for the violence and aggression emanating from the Instinctive Center. The damage caused by instincts prompted the Enneciation of Ones, whose instincts are repressed, alongside an amplified superego. One of the defining characteristics of Ones is that, as a group, they are mostly exempt from the negative effects of Endogenous Barbarism. The exemption from the effects of Endogenous Barbarism means that if they experience violence, they are not likely to mirror that experience back to their environment. On the contrary, being subjected to Endogenous Barbarism activates their potential to perform in the primary role of promoting law and order by and through the pillars of civilization.

The repression of the Instinctive Center, coupled with the amplification of the superego, produces individuals who are inner-directed by facts, logic, and reason. They are relatively free of the instinctive drives for food, pleasure, sex, and materialism. A closer examination reveals that Ones are very similar to Nines in that they possess an almost faultless character, although with one primary difference: Ones seek to be agents of change, whereas Nines seek to maintain the status quo.

The drive to be an agent of change is due to the amplification of the Superego. That is because the focus of the Superego is to find, detain, and eliminate all forms of corruption. From the perspective of the Superego, corruption is broadly defined as anything that undermines, circumvents, or threatens the establishment of law and order (civilization). The amplification of the superego creates a drive to find, detain, and eliminate anything that might constitute a threat to civilization. Thus, an amplified superego produces individuals who seek to create, to an exacting degree of perfection, a civilization that is free of all forms of barbarism.

As the agents of perfection, Ones work tirelessly for constant improvement, especially concerning the three pillars of civilization. However, Ones are functionally adapted to seek constant improvement in all areas, vocations, and endeavors related to civilization. The key to understanding this adaptation is that Ones are the embodiment of civilization. They are the representatives of law and order, civility, and ethical behavior, meaning that they are the ultimate civilian, similar to how Nines exemplify the ultimate in human character and Eights are the ultimate human resource.

As the ultimate civilian, Ones are a dominant force in all areas of civil life, but especially in the three pillars of civilization. Their dominance in civil life explains their ubiquity as teachers, educators, and administrators of educational institutions. Teaching is directly aligned with the specialization of Ones, as they are uniquely adapted to deliver educational services that are factual, logical, unbiased, objective, and without the errors of fallacy. To the extent that other Enneatypes substitute themselves into these critical roles, various types of bias will be introduced based on the subjectivities inherent to each Enneatype, thereby undermining the role of education as a pillar of civilization.

Ones are also dominant in the governmental departments responsible for law and order, including the functions of policing, prosecuting, and adjudicating criminal offenders. Ones evolved many of the adaptations needed for policing, including the basic skills and techniques that are necessary for handling physical altercations. The evidence of their skill resides in the many examples of elite martial artists that are Ones. Ones have a natural ability to perfect the techniques that are necessary for handling altercations, and this serves them well in performing the basic aspects of policing.

Ones are also dominant in the prosecution and adjudication of criminals. The role of prosecutors and judges has the same basic requirements of teaching, which is an approach that is factual, logical, unbiased, objective, and without the errors of fallacy. And to the extent that other Enneatypes substitute themselves into these critical roles, various types of bias will be introduced, thereby undermining the efficacy of these very important functions of civilization.

The functional adaptations specific to Ones are ideal for the requirements of religion, considering that the primary purpose of religion is to teach, foster, and encourage a reverence for life, as a means for establishing law and order. The teachers of religion, which in this case would be the pastors, priests, and clergy, must be individuals of high moral character. In this context, high moral character is the absence of character faults, vices, and regressive traits. With a repressed Instinctive Center, Ones are naturally exempt from the character faults, vices, and regressive traits inherent to most other Enneatypes. But what qualifies Ones is their ability to coerce, motivate, and inspire others to adopt a reverence for life. That is because Ones have an unsurpassed ability to embody, emulate, and live according to the highest ethics, moral principles, and edicts of the divine.

Apart from the specific roles cited in the areas of education, government, and religion, Ones gravitate toward roles that require a high degree of order, accountability, accuracy, integrity, reliability, and ethics. Listed below are some of the vocational titles that Ones are uniquely adapted:

Accountant Actuary | Auditor | Bank Teller | Compliance Officer | Dentist | Engineer | Ethics Officer | Quality Assurance | Statistician | Surgeon | Technician Underwriter

Although the three pillars of civilization are the natural domain for Ones, civilization includes all manner of human enterprises, such as businesses, non-profits, charities, foundations, political entities, etc. Thus, you will find Ones supporting all institutions of civilization, using the skills, talents, and abilities that are inherent to their Enneatype, in an ever-expanding range of roles. From this perspective, Ones are worthy, trusted, and indispensable partners of the various enterprises manifesting in modern civilizations.

The key point of this discussion has been that Ones are functionally adapted to be the primal source of civilization, its creation, and how it is structured. When viewing Ones from this perspective, a deeper appreciation for the evolution of civilization materializes, especially the critical role that Ones play. Along with appreciation, a certain amount of respect is due, as Ones evolved to be the mechanism responsible for creating civilization. Without the pillars of civilization, there would be no law and order; and without law and order, there would be no civilians. For these reasons, Ones are the ultimate Civilian, a moniker that accords with the highest traditions of dignity and respect.

Basic Delusion

The Instinctive Center is a neural network that connects the brain to all parts of the body, gathering the information that is necessary for protecting the health, safety, and integrity of our body. The central node of this network resides in the gut, where it collects sensory data from all regions of the body. These facts are captured by such colloquialisms as *follow your gut instincts*.

The sensory data collected by the Instinctive Center is used to protect the organism, either through reflexes, fight or flight, or other physiological mechanisms. But its most basic function is to provide information about what is happening in the immediate environment, specifically whether the environment is safe, secure, orderly, and predictable. This basic function of the Instinctive Center evolved to detect environments that are unstructured, disorderly, unpredictable, and chaotic as an alert for the presence of Endogenous Barbarism.

Ones are unique among the nine Enneatypes in that the Instinctive Center is effectively disabled, resulting in a type that perceives their environment to be unstructured, corrupt, disorderly, chaotic, and dangerous. The subjective, continuous, and unsubstantiated perception that the environment is corrupt, chaotic, dangerous, and prone to violence constitutes the delusion for Enneatype One. The delusion of perpetual chaos sets in motion the behaviors necessary for the erection of all modern institutions of civilization.

Interpersonal Relationships

As with all Enneatypes, Ones have some distinct advantages and disadvantages concerning their relationships. Their primary disadvantage concerns their ability to trust. Interpersonal relationships of all varieties, including familial, spousal, collegial, and business, all depend on implicit trust. Ones have difficulty balancing trust with their evolutionary purpose of establishing law and order. Their issues with trust explain the distinct pattern of behavior where Ones suspect everyone of corruption. Everyone is a potential target: parents, children, family, colleagues at church and work, and so on. Thus,

Ones subconsciously believe that every human being is potentially corrupt and in need of rehabilitation.

The difficulty that Ones have in trusting their environment is due to the repression of the Instinctive Center, which in turn represses the fundamental human quality of strength, effectively disabling the appendage of discernment. The lack of discernment partly explains the anger issues that Ones sometimes display. However, it's important to understand that anger is a primitive emotion that evolved alongside the evolutionary prerogative of establishing law and order. And as an individual grows and matures, primitive emotions such as anger will evolve into faculties of greater acuity.

When humans are connected and supported by Strength, a very precise understanding of what occurs each moment becomes available, manifesting as a deeper faculty of awareness: A comprehensive clarity about the moment materializes, which sponsors a deep acceptance of what is occurring moment to moment, without the need for rejecting, changing, or modifying reality. Without access to the quality of Strength, the fundamental facts of reality cannot be discerned, thus creating a bias toward others. This bias generally manifests as a desire to modify, change, or reject others.

The interpersonal relationships of Ones are adversely affected by their inability to accept others without conditions. The desire to change others is an irresistible urge, and it becomes a pattern of behavior that operates regardless of whether serious corruption is at hand. The perpetual pattern of criticizing, judging, and rejecting others carries into their relationships, where it wreaks havoc on their significant others by creating overtly negative impressions. These impressions may eventually lead to negative consequences, especially concerning their interpersonal relationship outcomes.

In many ways, Nines are the opposite of Ones, especially concerning their ability to love unconditionally. That is because Nines embody love, which manifests as a deep appreciation and acceptance of others, with no conditions or strings attached. But this type of unconditional love is very difficult for Ones, because it generally conflicts with their mission to identify, quarantine, and neutralize corruption. Their limitations concerning love can be mitigated to some extent if Ones find a person who is close to their ideals of perfection, or if they develop the self-awareness for controlling the impulse to criticize, judge, and reject. Otherwise, Ones have a very subjective capacity for love, which sometimes translates into relationships that are short, heated, and tumultuous.

Enneatypes Nine, Two, and Four are the natural partners for Ones. Nines can tolerate the criticizing, judging, and controlling behaviors of Ones more than the other Enneatypes. And Ones are more trusting with Nines because Nines project a persona that is tolerant, faultless, and incorruptible. For example, Nines respond to the criticizing nature of Ones by going into *Counselor* mode, thus deflecting accusations of corruption back to the source. In this way, Nines expertly disarm the superego attacks launched by Ones.

Perhaps the best way of dealing with the superego attacks emanating from Ones is with comedy and laughter. Taking a humorous approach works with Ones because although they have a façade of seriousness, there is a river of feelings and emotions beneath the surface. Humor can be used to break thru the façade of seriousness, and gain access to the rich emotional world that Ones are hiding. Fours have a natural talent for humor, and this enables them to form close bonds with Ones by offsetting their rigid, pedantic, and distant persona to some degree.

Ones can be very effective parents, especially for the young Enneatypes that must have a structured, stable, and orderly growing environment. Ones are the best teachers, and for that reason alone they are the best parents by default. But the content of what they teach, especially discipline, ethics, responsibility, and accountability, is what puts them in a special group. These are the cornerstones of what it means to be a responsible citizen, and a productive member of civilization, making Ones the best parents overall.

Psychology of Ones

Primary Ego Trait: Perfection

Regressive Traits: Anger

In Search Of: Corruption

Focuses On: Errors, Corruption, and Unlawful Behavior

Basic Fear: Corruption, Chaos, and Violence

Basic Desire: Law and Order

Basic Need: Self Determination

Stress Reaction: Intolerance, Anger

Sense of Self: I will be Ok if others follow the rules

Motto: The World is Uncivilized

Mental Model: The world must improve

Motivations:

- To have integrity, principles, and ethics.
- To hold others accountable.
- To correct errors, mistakes, and nonconforming behavior.
- To set the best example of civilized behavior.

Physical Characteristics

The repression of the Instinctive Center has many collateral consequences, such as the repression of the basic senses, including thirst, hunger, hearing, and taste. The inability to sense hunger is responsible for a certain degree of naturally induced calorie restriction that has multiple effects on the physiology of Ones. First, calorie restriction works together with the physiological adaptation of ectomorphic body type, inherent to most Ones, to produce one of the lowest average BMI measurements of all Enneatypes.

Second, calorie restriction may also go to the extreme. The extreme in this case is anorexia, which is estimated to coincide with type One in more than 80% of cases. Although anorexia is a medical diagnosis describing a calorie restrictive eating disorder, Ones are not suffering from an eating disorder, but rather the effects of an evolutionary adaptation that is specific to Ones. This understanding can help those affected in many positive ways.

Another side effect of calorie restriction is longevity. Calorie restriction has been shown in multiple animal studies to be the only way to increase longevity in mammals. The clinically proven effect of calorie restriction on mammals explains the increased longevity enjoyed by Ones. For these reasons, more than 50% of centenarians living in the USA are estimated to be Enneatype One.

Ones have a reduced sensitivity to environmental sounds that is compensated to some degree by the outer part of the ear, defined as the pinna, that directs sound into the ear. The compensation in the structure of the outer ear manifests as an enlarged pinna, which is responsible for making the ears protrude outward from the skull. An enlarged and protruding pinna is easy to identify and may be used as a confirming identifier for type One.

Another confirming identifier for Ones is their gait. Ones tend to walk with their toes or forefoot striking the ground first. Although a toe strike gait is often medically diagnosed as an abnormality, caution is advised with such an assessment, as the toe strike gait is an evolutionary adaptation. Ones have a toe or forefoot striking the ground first, because this provides a greater sense of balance, thus better preparing the individual to confront Endogenous Barbarism. The toe or forefoot strike is relatively easy to identify with practice and is sometimes accompanied by a bounce that occurs midway through each step. Although the bounce can be very subtle, it is also relatively easy to identify with some practice. One thing to keep in mind is that all, either, or none of these tendencies may be discernable to the untrained observer. However, the presence of the toe strike or gait bounce provides evidence that helps confirm a diagnosis of this very common Enneatype.

Ones have the most rigid posture of all Enneatypes, which gives the appearance that the shoulders and back are one immovable structure. Thus, when Ones bend at the waist, the thoracic and lumbar spine remains rigid because there is little or no flexibility in the spine. Ones also have a certain degree of rigidity in all their joints, which they sometimes compensate for by doing yoga. This rigidity becomes easier to identify with practice.

As the ultimate Civilian, Ones dress in a way that is most acceptable to the views, traditions, and morals of their culture to avoid any appearance of uncivilized behavior. Although cultural standards, traditions, and morals vary tremendously, Ones dress in a manner that upholds the more conservative moral principles of their locale. Thus, female Ones tend to dress conservatively, elegant, and ladylike; while men dress in a manner that is stately, dignified, and utilitarian.

FACIAL TENSION

From the perspective of the observer, the facial tension appears in the right eye as a small amount of swelling in the outer and upper part of the eye socket. The swelling that occurs in the right eye creates an asymmetry with the left eye, such that the right eye socket may appear to be smaller, darker, or shaded when compared to the left. The swelling in the upper part of the right eye socket may impinge on the eyelid, and give the appearance of a squint, especially upon reaching middle age.

IDENTIFYING AND DIAGNOSING ONES

Ones constitute a disproportionate share of the population in the USA, estimated to be 12%. The following are the key physiological characteristics that correspond to type One:

1. Below average BMI.
2. A large and protruding pinna.
3. Toe strike gait.
4. Midgait bounce.
5. Rigid posture.
6. Conservative style of dress.

CHAPTER 7

TYPE TWO: THE GOVERNOR

Endeavor: Governance

Cultural stagnation was a major factor of extinction because Early Humans lacked the behavioral sophistication necessary for commerce, trade, and enterprise to flourish. Commerce refers to the marketing of goods and services, trade refers to the exchange of goods and services between disparate social groups, and enterprise refers to the economic entities that produce all varieties of goods and services. From this point, all references to commerce, trade, and enterprise will be as Commerce.

The human behavioral factors that affect Commerce and by extension, the overall economic output of a species, can be categorized as cultural, intrinsic, or entrepreneurial. Twos focus on the cultural factor, which includes the emotional attitudes, interpersonal behaviors, and language that facilitate Commerce. The prevailing culture of a species is critical to economic success because it facilitates the interpersonal economic transactions that become the sum of GSP. Thus, it is necessary to discuss the specific ways that Early Human attitudes, behaviors, and language created the conditions of economic stagnation that eventually led to their demise.

Individuals possessing a positive, enthusiastic, and open-minded attitude will initiate a greater number of positive economic transactions. And conversely, negative individuals that are offensive and closed to new experiences will generate substantially fewer positive economic transactions; and they inevitably dampen the economic discourse of others. Thus, emotional attitudes play a key role in determining both the quality and quantity of economic transactions generated by an individual. In the case of Early Humans, their interpersonal attitudes were unambiguously cold, impersonal, antisocial, and closed to new experiences. These attitudes hindered communication, engagement, and social participation in Early Human economies, thereby reducing the total number of economic transactions.

The primitive attitudes of Early Humans could have been offset by positive behaviors, notwithstanding that Early Humans exhibited behaviors that were antithetical to Commerce. However, Early Humans exhibited a range of negative behaviors, from the basic antisocial behavior of shunning others to the horrific acts of barbarism discussed in previous chapters. These behaviors undermined social cooperation, effectively reducing the number of positive economic transactions, which in turn adversely affected the growth of Commerce in Early Human economies.

Without a mechanism to govern behavior, Early Humans failed to develop the necessary behaviors needed for Commerce. These behaviors include the social norms, etiquette, and customs of interpersonal relationships. Anthropologists refer to this as culture, but here it is defined as a code of conduct, to distinguish it from other aspects of culture. The key point is that Early Humans were not subject to a common code of conduct that sponsored the cooperative behaviors necessary for Commerce to flourish.

The ability to communicate, as determined by the quality of language, was another aspect of Early Human culture that was problematic. The problem was not anatomical, as Early Humans were capable of significant advancements in language, given the capabilities that came with having some of the largest brains ever recorded. The problem was that the language of Early Humans was prone to the formation of dialects, due to a geographically dispersed population, behavioral impediments, and issues related to the psyche. As an example, consider that the lack of a horizontal learning channel effectively limited communication between nuclear families, which undermined the ability of Early Humans to devise, implement, and conform to a common language. Thus, the lack of a horizontal learning channel was a contributing factor in the formation of dialects.

The vocabulary of Early Humans was another limiting factor in their ability to communicate. The primitive nature of their culture and the lack of a horizontal learning channel, coupled with the problems of dialect, meant that the average vocabulary of Early Humans would have been quite limited. This assertion acknowledges that there are many other factors affecting vocabulary, with some that indicated a greater vocabulary: Such as the fact that Neanderthals had a brain that was larger than Modern Humans. And some that limited vocabulary, such as the lack of a specific mechanism for language. In consideration of all probable factors, the average vocabulary of Early Humans is estimated to be a small fraction of Modern Humans.

The ability to communicate, as determined by the degree of language sophistication, was a crucial factor in the performance of primitive economies. The language of Early Humans was important because of its role in the vertical and horizontal learning channels, both of which provide the means for sharing ideas, concepts, methods, and solutions that are necessary for economic behaviors. Moreover, language is necessary for the formation of economic enterprises, as these activities become exponentially more difficult without a common language. And language is the primary facilitator of all economic transactions, which in the context of Early Human economies was the barter of goods and services between individuals and groups of individuals. Thus, the language used by Early Humans was critical to all manner of economic activity occurring in Early Human economies. For these reasons, the inability of Early Humans to develop a common language that was thorough, precise, and definitive had significant economic consequences.

The Early Human problems related to language and behavior reflect the lack of unity and cohesiveness that was a defining mark for Early Humans. These problems meant that Early Humans had a very primitive social structure that was divisive, incoherent, and fractured. Having a primitive social structure was responsible for creating Early Human economies that were fragile, fractured, and stagnant. Early Humans had no mechanism to sponsor cooperation, cohesiveness, and the unity of purpose necessary for Commerce to flourish. For these reasons, a mechanism that sponsored cultural unity was needed.

Twos have unique specializations, specifically in the areas of language and behavior, that allows them to effectively remove the barriers to Commerce that were prevalent in Early Human economies. For the barriers associated with language, Twos have a specialization in linguistics, which brings unity and conformity in communication. The purpose of this specialization is twofold. First, it prevents the fractionalization of language into dialects. Second, the specialization in linguistics bridges the gap between disparate dialects and languages, by providing the basic skills necessary for translation.

For the problems related to behavior, Twos specialize in the synthesis, implementation, and enforcement of a behavioral code of conduct. The code of conduct governs the behaviors that are necessary for Commerce to flourish. A code of conduct is necessary to ensure that every individual exhibits the behaviors commensurate with economic stability, growth, and advancement. As specialists in human behavior, Twos are responsible for all aspects of the code of conduct, including the terms, conditions, and enforcement.

When the specializations in language and behavior are combined, they form a mechanism for creating human networks that endear social cohesion, cooperation, and unity. This mechanism is responsible for a human networking behavior that has unlimited jurisdiction, including familial, religious, collegial, extracurricular, and commercial contexts. The human networking behavior is responsible for the creation of substantive networks, alliances, and enterprises that collectively form the economic backbone of a society. The social networks and alliances created, sponsored, or inspired by Twos are ubiquitous in modern human societies; and are evidence of the social cohesion, cooperation, and unity that Twos bring to the world.

The evolution of a specialist in language, behavior, and networking was a direct consequence of the cultural stagnation that had plagued Early Humans for millennia. Twos Endeavor to provide the Governance necessary for creating human networks, alliances, and enterprises, which necessarily requires that they embody, emulate, and enforce the fundamental traits and behaviors that are part of an objective code of conduct. Their evolutionary purpose is to create and Govern a cultural environment where Commerce may flourish. Thus, Twos embody, teach, and spread the fundamentals of human culture, which is that humans are economic creatures that thrive when individual freedoms are protected, including the freedoms associated with speech, trade, commerce, and enterprise.

Primary Role: Governor

The primary role of Twos is to enforce compliance with a socially ordained, evolving, and dynamic code of conduct. To fulfill the requirements of this role, Twos subconsciously see themselves as being above the social hierarchy, essentially as the Governor of human culture. The primary objective of the code of conduct is to ensure that all individuals conform to the attitudes, language, and behaviors that are necessary for Commerce to flourish. Understanding the importance of the code of conduct requires a few words on how attitude, behavior, and language support Commerce.

Language is the most basic requirement of commerce because, without a common language that is free of dialects, all commercial activity would be adversely affected. The commercial activities referenced here includes all manner of economic transactions, the formation of enterprises, and the flow of goods and services between various demographic regions. Language must also be fluid and dynamic, to capture the technical nuances of the ways, means, and methods of performing ever more technical tasks, so that commercial knowledge can be shared and disseminated freely. And because language can be divisive, the use of derogatory terms must be restricted, especially those terms that are found to be universally offensive. For these reasons, language must be controlled, restricted, and governed, but only in the context of commerce.

From an economic perspective, the viability of Commerce is fundamentally dependent on the prevailing social attitudes because all economic activity requires a fundamental spirit of openness, engagement, and curiosity. Societies and individuals who shun new experiences do not barter for goods and services, engage in cooperative enterprises, or innovate new ways, means, and methods of enterprise. Other traits that shape attitudes may be helpful to commerce, such as extroversion and conscientiousness, but those are irrelevant without openness. For these reasons, the fundamental aim of a commercial code of conduct is to inspire a prevailing culture of openness to new experience, so that the gears of commerce may operate unimpeded.

The behavior of the individual, which includes their acts, deeds, and omissions, is perhaps the most important factor affecting commerce. Behavior was especially important in prehistoric times, where written contracts did not exist, and all commerce occurred verbally. The problem was that Early Humans acted without compassion; and in most cases, they acted with a complete disdain for the interests of others. These behaviors had a catastrophic effect on all manner of economic discourse. Complicating matters was that Early Humans had no mechanism to sponsor a more sophisticated culture. For these reasons, a code of conduct was necessary to ensure that individuals act with integrity; and are held accountable to the highest interpersonal standards of respect, honesty, transparency, and accountability.

Emerging from this discussion is the importance of a code of conduct that controls language, inspires positive attitudes, and governs behavior. The primary role of Twos is to develop, sponsor, implement, and enforce the code of conduct. Developing a code of conduct requires that Twos participate in the process of determining the rules of language, attitude, and behavior. Thus, it requires that they assume leadership roles; or when that is not possible, that they lobby and influence the leaders in their community. For these reasons, Twos generally seek social positions where they have substantive influence and control over the terms and conditions of an objective, evolving, and dynamic code of conduct, which generally involves roles where they are directly involved in the Governance of others.

To be effective in the implementation of the code of conduct, Twos must embrace, embody, and demonstrate the virtues of the code of conduct they are promoting. This role requires that Twos exemplify the highest ethical standards in their language, attitude, and behaviors in all their interactions, including their familial, commercial, and social interactions. Twos may enforce a code of conduct in other ways, such as when they perform certain social roles, including that of a parent, priest, and counselor. In this way, Twos assert jurisdiction over the attitude, language, and behavior of every person they encounter. And a key method for asserting jurisdiction is through the development of social networks.

Of the many methods used by Twos to develop social networks, perhaps the most important is the direct engagement of individuals. Twos have a natural talent for engaging others, including total strangers, to learn their relevant skills, abilities, and interests. This information is then memorized, thereby creating a mental database of people and their relevant biographical data. This information is indispensable to the creation of markets, enterprises, and economic trade.

In modern times, the primary role of Governance takes many forms, with the human resource (HR) department of every enterprise being perhaps the most ubiquitous example. That is because the HR department for most organizations is responsible for the development, implementation, and enforcement of a code of conduct that applies to each of its members. Thus, it should come as no surprise that Twos are the type most likely to be working in the HR department of the various types of organizations that form the backbone of every modern society.

Governance is also required in other social spheres, especially where behavioral oversight is required, such as in the various levels of government: City Council Member, Mayor, Police Chief, Fire Chief, Sheriff, State Representative, State Senator, Congressional Representative, Congressional Senator, State Governor, and President of the United States. Because these governmental roles align directly with the primary role of Governance, and for reasons discussed in chapter thirteen and fourteen, Twos are the Enneatype most likely to appear in these positions.

Many other positions require Governance, from CEO to Union Steward, and the many supervisory positions in between. In every case, Twos provide the Governance that is necessary to ensure that the gears of Commerce operate as intended by evolution. For these reasons, Twos acquire, develop, and wield the social power necessary for Commerce to flourish.

Functional Adaptations

Although Twos have many functional adaptations, there are two that are of distinct importance for their specialization in language and behavior. The first is that Twos have an ego identity that is qualitatively more refined, resolute, and sophisticated, which provides a fuller, richer, and more robust sense of individuality, as compared to the egos of all other Enneatypes. The effect of this functional adaptation is that it provides a magnified, elevated, and superlative sense of self. The superlative self is a psychological phenomenon, defined by some psychoanalysts as the Grandiose Self, that is more broadly understood to be a type of narcissistic disorder.

From the perspective of evolution, the Grandiose Self is not a disorder, but rather a very powerful coercive mechanism of human behavior. This context informs that the evolutionary purpose of the Grandiose Self is to generate the behaviors needed by Commerce. Collectively, these behaviors operate as a mechanism that Governs behavior by imbuing Twos with a fragile sense of inherent superiority. The ego identity is fragile in that it requires constant validation, mirroring, and support from the tasks that Twos are functionally adapted to perform.

The Grandiose Self is responsible for three types of behavior that collectively serve to promote Commerce. The most basic behavior is related to their specialization in creating human networks, which involves the engagement, interaction, and solicitation of as many people as possible. The second behavior is the introduction of a behavioral innovation that directly enhances commerce, whether by increasing productivity, lowering cost, increasing trade, etc. And most important is leadership, where Twos seek to unite others behind a common purpose, initiative, or enterprise. The following examples demonstrate how these behaviors stimulate economic activity.

Perhaps the most basic example of commerce is a cooperative endeavor to market food to consumers, also known as a co-op, initiated by one or more individuals. The first step is to solicit the cooperation of producers, who will bring their goods to the market at the assigned time and place, under the promise that economic transactions will occur. The second step is to ensure that consumers will appear at the assigned place and time, in the hope that economic transactions will take place. These steps describe the market making behaviors that are secondary to the social networks that are created by Twos. From an economic perspective, networking is the human mechanism that is responsible for creating markets, as all markets are simply a network of individuals engaging in economic transactions.

As Twos work to create networks, they unwittingly become the mechanism that is directly responsible for creating markets. The success of the markets that they create turns on their ability to maximize the attendance of producers and consumers. The important point is that markets do not happen on their own: They happen because of the networking efforts of Twos, who typically receive some recompense from those that participate in the market.

Of the many types of prehistoric enterprise, perhaps the most basic example is related to the coordinated hunting of big game. Consider that a group of five hunters may be capable of landing one large buffalo per day using spears, whereas a group of fifty hunters can land hundreds of buffalo per day using a technique of herding. There are many economic advantages to the enterprise of herding, including a many-fold gain in productivity, reduced injuries and deaths, and greater overall conservation of resources. However, this type of cooperative enterprise does not happen on its own: It happens because of the functional adaptation for networking that is directly attributable to Twos.

Twos often innovate new behaviors that stimulate commerce on a massive scale. A good example of this occurred with the cultural innovations of Elvis Presley and Michael Jackson, both of whom stimulated commerce with innovations in dance, music, and the performing arts. As exemplars of Enneatype Two, Messrs. Presley and Jackson were effective in uniting great numbers of people through the cultural innovations and activities that they sponsored, thereby setting in motion commercial enterprises that continue to this day.

Twos may also innovate new behaviors that stimulate commerce on a relatively small scale, such as the behavioral innovations that are introduced by a humble factory worker. Consider the true story of a union machine operator named Dick, a member of the United Auto Workers Local 662, who led several three-member teams that manufactured automobile bumpers for

General Motors. Although the targeted production was 180 bumpers per eight hours, it was rare to find a team that could meet the target, and no team could consistently meet the target. That was the case until Dick arrived, as he quickly innovated the methods necessary to produce one bumper per minute, by merging his talents with the skills of his teammates. Thanks to the networking, innovations, and leadership introduced by Dick, the teams that he led finished their eight-hour shift in just three hours.

The second functional adaptation inherent to Enneatype Two is the amplification of the Feeling Center. The amplification of the Feeling Center produces individuals with a high degree of emotional, verbal, and empathic intelligence. The inner feeling state of these individuals becomes magnified, and directed through various channels of self-expression, including body language and verbal communications. Having a high degree of verbal fluency, combined with emotional and empathic intelligence, serves multiple purposes.

The amplification of the Feeling Center, which provides Twos with a high degree of emotional and empathic intelligence, is necessary to secure compliance with an objective code of conduct. An amplification of feelings is a necessary adaptation because compliance with a commercial code of conduct is not compulsory, it must be lobbied, negotiated, and encouraged, by building relationships with one individual at a time. The functional adaptations for verbal fluency, combined with emotional and empathic intelligence, allows Twos to build relationships with others. Over time, trust develops in those relationships, which opens the door to many types of cooperative endeavors related to Commerce.

Sales positions provide a good example of how building relationships is congruent with the needs of commerce. Twos are very adept in all phases of the sales process, and this is especially true in the first stage of sourcing sales referrals, where Twos enjoy a competitive advantage due to the specialization in creating networks. The competitive advantage that Twos enjoy in sales positions stems from the functional adaptation for cultivating and developing relationships within the networks they have created, providing them with a rich source of potential economic transactions. Cultivating relationships is critical in certain types of selling situations, especially large ticket purchases such as telecom equipment, new vehicles, business equipment, and heavy equipment sales. Relationship management is also important in account management positions such as a stockbroker, whose job is to place buy and sell orders for their customers. Here again, Twos excel in this sales scenario because they are the most adept at maintaining good customer relations that translate into a greater quantity of sales.

Twos are also exemplary in the second step of the sales process, which is positioning a product in a precise manner, as a means for overcoming all objections raised by the buyer. Part of their ability stems from having superior communication skills and part is due to their ability to acquire or infer the customer's wants and needs. Twos combine these skills to effectively position a product or service to match a customer's situation. This ability comes naturally to many Twos but is mostly foreign to the other Enneatypes, who might otherwise struggle with sales and marketing.

In the final step of closing the deal, Twos are not afraid to ask for the sale, and then overcome any objections raised by the customer. With proper instruction, Twos can master the art of closing better than all other Enneatypes, because they have an empathic sense for when their customers are ready to buy. Thus, Twos know when to take a shortcut to an early closing. Moreover, Twos know when they are losing the sale and can adjust automatically during the sales process, to overcome objections as they arise. For these reasons, Twos outperform all other Enneatypes in sales positions.

As a general rule, Twos match well with any position that requires excellence in sales, marketing, and governance. However, the mechanism that enables Twos to be effective in these areas, the Grandiose Self, has never been credited as the functional adjunct of Commerce and Governance. Instead, Psychologists have branded the Grandiose Self to be a narcissistic disorder, rather than an evolved regulatory mechanism that addresses, prevents, and reverses cultural stagnation.

The key point of this discussion has been that Twos are mission-critical for Commerce. Twos do the difficult work of building relationships, one person at a time, creating the social networks that are indispensable to economic discourse. For these reasons, Twos are the glue that connects, unites, and binds a society together. Although evidence of their work exists in all aspects of Commerce, probably the most direct evidence of their work can be found in the code of conduct that most every organization puts on display.

Basic Delusion:

The basic identity structures of the ego are enhanced, amplified, and magnified in Twos, producing ego-centric individuals having an unconscious belief in their superiority. The unsubstantiated belief of being superior to others, known as the superiority delusion, constitutes the basic delusion for type Two.

There are many implications associated with the superiority delusion. One implication for those afflicted with this delusion is that people, and all objects for that matter, are perceived to have a specific rank. At the highest level of this order is the Grandiose Self, which is an ego identity that is resistant to introspective analysis. As the ego of Twos grows and develops, the Grandiose Self seeks affirmation and validation of their inherent superiority, while filtering anything that might challenge, contradict, or negate their sense of superiority. The inherent sense of superiority partly explains why the Grandiose Self discounts the needs, capabilities, and interests of others, while at the same time giving Twos a self-centered orientation toward reality.

The superiority delusion is a delusion of grandiosity that is sometimes referred to as the delusion of omnipotence because the persons affected have an unconscious belief that they have infinite powers and abilities. The belief in infinite powers is sometimes described as a God complex because it coincides with the unrealistic substitution of the self for God. Individuals affected by this delusion perceive their status to be above everyone else, while at the same time, they have much less capacity for introspection relative to the other Enneatypes. For these reasons, Twos fit into a category of hyper-narcissism, which is a type of narcissism involving an inflated, exaggerated, or amplified self-image.

Interpersonal Relationships

The primary function of Twos is to ensure conformity with a socially ordained code of conduct. The most expedient way that Twos achieve conformity is to develop relationships with those that are in their sphere of influence. So, it should come as no surprise that Twos are the exemplars of interpersonal relationships, as they have a natural ability to secure the adulation, agreement, and cooperation of massive numbers of people. Twos use a wide range of methods and tactics to build relationships, most of which are very subtle, covert, or almost invisible to detection, while others may be considered extreme.

Twos are consummate communicators, a talent that allows them to develop a great diversity of relationships. Twos are not shy when it comes to reaching out to others, as they are always ready to share who they are, what they are about, and where they are going. They bring warmth, friendliness, and cheer to their conversations, and they inspire others to be open and receptive. They have a positive attitude, wit, and charm that is infectious. People genuinely want to be around Twos, so when they pass out the invitations, droves of people will show up for the party.

Sharing and giving is the cornerstone of their hospitable nature. Twos enjoy sharing everything from recipes to stories of their favorite vacations and travels. Interacting with Twos can be educational, heartwarming, and filled with humor. And when you think that you know them, they will surprise you with a new angle to their persona that you were unaware.

If you are around Twos long enough, you will realize that much of what you see is a façade that is hiding an alter ego that evolved to enforce a social code of conduct. The enforcement of a code of conduct requires manipulative skills, tactics, and strategies that do not fit the superficial persona that Twos present to the world. Twos are generally unaware of these processes, and even if they were aware they wouldn't admit to them because doing so would threaten their rise to the top of the social hierarchy. Gossip is perhaps the best example of this.

At first glance, gossip would appear to be a benign aspect of networking, as part of networking does involve the sharing of information. However, gossip is motivated by aspects of the Regressive Psyche, specifically the traits of envy, jealousy, and hate, to become an activity that is otherwise hiding an agenda of narcissism and manipulation. The agenda is not related to Commerce, but rather serves to aggrandize the Grandiose Self, by the subliminal insinuation that the person with knowledge about others must somehow be omniscient, superior, or elite. Thus, when Twos engage in gossip, they are unwitting victims of narcissism, especially the distorted belief in one's omniscience, superiority, and elitism.

Gaslighting is another tactic that is used by Twos to manipulate others. Twos generally use gaslighting to coerce a change of behavior when other tactics have failed. Although gaslighting is defined as a pathological behavior by many psychologists, in consideration of the mentally destabilizing effect that it has on others, this does not mean that Twos have the intention of destroying their victims. On the contrary, most Twos are simply attempting to Govern compliance and conformity with the code of conduct that they have developed.

Psychology of Twos

Primary Ego Trait: Connection

Regressive Traits: Hubris

In Search Of: Relationships

Focuses On: The behavior of others

Basic Fear: Inferiority

Basic Desire: To be superior

Basic Need: Intimacy

Stress Reaction: Resentment

Sense of Self: The world needs me

Motto: Be good, feel good

Mental Model: I'm only as good as the network I've developed

Motivations:

- Express their feelings
- Govern the conduct of others
- Cultivate special relationships
- Bring people together
- Rise above others

Physical Characteristics

Relative to the other Enneatypes, Twos possess one of the weakest constitutions, as confirmed by the fact that Twos have one of the shortest longevities of all Enneatypes. These shortcomings are partly the result of spending their life's energy focused on others, continuously networking as many relationships as possible, rather than spending their energy to take care of their own body. Thus, they are generally less effective at making the lifestyle decisions needed for optimal health. Their lifestyle choices often do not improve when they achieve celebrity status, with Elvis Presley and Michael Jackson as prime examples. Part of this phenomenon stems from the narcissistic tendency toward drugs, alcohol, and poor diet that are exacerbated by celebrity status. But part of it is also physiological, in the sense that Twos are physiologically predisposed to ill health that is exacerbated by a tendency to deny the nutritional needs of the body.

The digestive system is the weakest part of their constitution, which becomes easily irritated by foods that are foreign to the intended design of the human body. Twos have the greatest difficulty with diets that are very complex, such as diets consisting of large quantities of meat, processed foods, and preserved foods. However, when Twos follow a strict dietary regimen, consisting of foods that do not irritate the human digestive system, their negative health symptoms improve or disappear. Many Twos have reported that they feel and perform their best consuming an organic plant-based diet, with no processed foods, and little or no animal products. Twos may gain additional improvements from small quantities of nutritional supplements, especially biologically available vitamin-mineral complexes, plant-based essential fatty acids, and probiotics to improve their weak digestion.

Although Twos run the gamut of body types and sizes, they rarely go to the extremes of obesity, such as BMI's that are significantly over 40. Twos are unable to digest that much food. However, Twos do go to the extremes of anorexia, although with less frequency compared to type One. Anorexia is sometimes a problem for Twos, due to the distortions in the body image that are secondary to the delusion of superiority. Compounding the problem is that many cultures teach that supermodels, with their very thin body type, are superior to average people. For these reasons, some Twos feel subconsciously compelled by their superiority delusion to maintain extremely low BMI's.

Like Eights, Twos sometimes have thinning or balding hair, but this generally appears around middle age. As for the hairstyle in the USA and many other countries, many female Twos choose a hairstyle that is just below the chin. Male Twos tend to style their hair in a variety of short styles, but they often enjoy wearing a full beard. Twos of both sexes will sometimes color their hair, often in a shade of pink, to express their individuality. Many Twos report that pink is their favorite color.

Twos will often obtain tattoos as a way of expressing their individuality. These tattoos are often symbolic of how they see themselves; or to what objects they identify. For example, Twos who identify with songbirds may express this identification with a songbird tattoo. Men will often choose a tattoo that expresses an aspect of their superiority. The tattoos chosen by both sexes tend to be small or inconspicuous, express some aspect of individuality or culture, and are mostly concealed underclothes to avoid undue attention.

The amplification of identity structures has an amplifying effect on gender identity and the corresponding choices in clothing. Indeed, their clothing choices are a subject of great depth that involves an analysis of the conflicting gender identities and their respective behaviors. These behaviors include clothing choices that are gender opposite, gender-neutral, and gender ampli-fied. Thus, male Twos often feel impulses of femininity that may, as an example, be expressed by a desire to wear pink. Female Twos often feel male impulses that may be expressed by a desire to wear masculine pants or boots. Gender amplification would appear as an ultra-feminity or ultra-masculinity. These are just some basic examples that must be kept in mind when trying to identify Twos.

Twos have perhaps the sunniest disposition of all types, as it seems that they are always smiling, especially when greeting others. The sunny disposition is mostly due to the amplification of the Feeling Center, which creates a type that is especially prone to emotional lability. Thus, you may observe Twos overreacting to a situation, demonstrating excessive emotions, or instigating emotional dramas to get attention.

There are many other subconscious physical traits and mannerisms for type Two that are related to their delusion of superiority. Although it takes a bit of practice to recognize these physical traits and mannerisms, since they are quite subtle, they can be very helpful in confirming a diagnosis because they are unique to type Two. The backward head tilt is a behavior that is easy to identify, as the head is tilted back slightly to allow Twos to look down upon others, which makes sense in the context of a delusion of superiority. This behavior is very subtle in most Twos, and it may be inhibited in others having more self-awareness, such that it may take some practice for discernment.

Since the face is the expressive organ of the human body, and Twos are the most expressive of the Enneatypes, the qualitative observation of facial expressions can help identify Twos. Twos have a greater range in facial expres-sions, and their ability to display extreme expressions such as disgust is more convincing when compared to other Enneatypes. Also, Twos are more fluid with their expressions, and there is some degree of exaggeration that occurs, such that Twos can go from smiling to disgust and back to smiling in milliseconds.

Twos have many other eccentric mannerisms stemming from the Grandiose Self. The common denominator among these behaviors is the constant need for validating, aggrandizing, and protecting an inherent sense of superiority.

Although the possibilities are infinite, a common situation where Twos feel a need to protect their sense of superiority is when eating food, partly because the mundane act of eating connotes an image of animalistic behaviors that are deemed inferior. Thus, Twos will often avoid eating in public, or they will cover their mouth while eating, to disassociate themselves from any perception of inferiority. For similar reasons, they may be easily offended by the sloppy eating habits of others.

FACIAL TENSION

The facial tension for type Two is analogous to the tension for Enneatype One, except that it occurs within the left eye socket, rather than the right eye socket.

IDENTIFYING AND DIAGNOSING TWOS

Twos are estimated to be approximately 16% of the USA population. The objective physiological traits for Twos are:

1. A subtle hip swivel in the gait.

2. Well kept, shorter hair.

3. Excellent singing voice.

4. Highly expressive, sunny, and emotional.

5. Above average in the performing arts.

CHAPTER 8

TYPE THREE: THE ECONOMIST

Endeavor: Economization

The Law of Energy Conservation provides a basic, fundamental, and critical survival mechanism, embedded in the DNA of all creatures, that prevents behaviors that are wasteful, detrimental, or inefficient. This law was indispensable to the evolution of life on Earth, as it ensured the basic conservation of resources while allowing those activities that were necessary for survival. As a fundamental principle of evolution, the Law of Energy Conservation has governed the evolution of life on Earth for billions of years.

The Law of Energy Conservation can be observed in modern-day primates, as their energy expenditures closely align with the needs of survival, with only rare exceptions. Although they are capable of great feats of strength and endurance, they conserve their energy whenever possible, and in ways that are unique to their physiology and environment. The operation of this law explains the sloth-like behaviors observed across the primate family.

The sloth-like attitudes and behaviors of primates were carried forward to Early Humans, manifesting as a general apathy, inertia, and ambivalence toward the ever-changing demands of survival. These vestigial attitudes and behaviors had consequences, especially economic consequences because they affected the economic psychology of every individual. Understanding the economic psychology of the individual, especially in the context of Early Humans, is a prerequisite to understanding the specialization of Enneatype Three.

The economic psychology of Early Humans was shaped by several factors that, severally and individually, were responsible for the economic behaviors that persisted within the Early Human economies. These factors were responsible for specific economic behaviors, including the phenomenon known as the *free-rider effect*. Economists define a free rider as a person who receives economic benefits, typically from a group or enterprise, without making any contributions or recompense. There were substantial numbers of free riders within Early Human populations, as no mechanism had evolved to prevent, modify, or deter this behavioral phenomenon. Thus, the impact of free riders on the per-capita GSP of Early Humans would have been inestimable.

Chapter Two's discussion of Intrinsic Stagnation included an analysis of the economic psychology of humans. The income and substitution effects were among the reasons explaining the relatively greater preference for leisure enjoyed by Early Humans. However, the income and substitution effects would have been secondary to other factors such as the Law of Conservation and a fundamentally irrational approach to solving problems.

Early Humans were certainly capable of rational thought, but this is not the same as rational decisions, attitudes, and behaviors. For example, rational decision making requires the ability to make objective inferences of fact, followed by the appropriate application of the rules of logic to reach a valid conclusion. Even for Modern Humans, rational decision making is not innate: It must be taught, through rigorous academic courses that include logic, statistics, and the scientific method. Among those with proper training, very few can strictly adhere to the protocols of logic, statistics, and the scientific method in their everyday life. So, even if Early Humans had some capacity for rational thought, they were grossly incapable of cultivating this ability, which meant that their ability to make rational decisions was greatly compromised. Chapter 10 delves into this subject with more detail and examples.

The deficiencies in rational thought attributed to Early Humans meant that they were grossly incapable of performing certain basic survival functions. The most fundamental of those functions is the economization of resources, which is the process of utilizing resources in a manner that yields the greatest economic advantages. To illustrate one aspect of economization, consider the following example of an economy composed of three members A, B, and C, each capable of producing a certain quantity of calories corresponding to foods X, Y, and Z:

	X	Y	Z
A	24	8	6
B	10	16	12
C	12	14	18

Table 8.1

If the objective is to maximize the total number of calories produced per minute, then individual A will produce X, B will produce Y, and C will produce Z. Economizing human resources in this manner will produce 58 calories per minute. All other combinations will produce less. Although this is a very simple exercise, it does require certain cognitive abilities: Forming an objective, collecting data, and then solving for the desired solution. Unfortunately, very few Early Humans possessed the necessary cognitive abilities to carry out this analysis.

Resource economization also requires the ability to understand certain fundamental economic laws. One of the most important is the law of diminishing marginal returns, which demonstrates the decreasing marginal return of an input when other resources are held constant. A good example is the changes in crop yield that occurs as fertilizer is varied while holding other inputs constant. The following data demonstrates this phenomenon:

Fertilizer/lbs	Corn/bushels	Marginal Product
0	150	
100	300	150
200	420	120
300	520	100

400	590	70
500	630	40
600	630	0
700	600	-30

Table 8.2

In this example, the amount of fertilizer is variable, while other inputs such as land are held constant. The data demonstrates that the marginal product of fertilizer falls as the amount of fertilizer is increased. And at a certain point, which in this case would be any units beyond 600, the marginal product for fertilizer becomes negative.

There are many other economic laws and principles related to the economization of resources, such as those of economies of scale, specialization of labor, and the optimization of factor inputs. Detailed discussions appear in the introductory microeconomic college textbooks that are available. These are difficult concepts for the average college student to learn, apply, and master. For those who are curious to test their ability in this subject matter, a standardized test of college economics (TUCE) is an excellent starting point, as found online or in the Economics Department of most universities.

The economization of resources requires logic, analysis, and problem-solving abilities. It also requires an intuitive understanding, and working knowledge, of the basic laws and principles of economics. Much of this can be learned by trial and error, given enough aptitude, rational thinking, and external supports. But Early Humans did not have the aptitude, rational thinking, and problem-solving abilities necessary for economic advancement. In short, Early Humans were hopelessly incapable of economizing resources. Evolving from these shortcomings was the specialization in resource economization necessary to ameliorate the economic stagnation that follows an inefficient utilization of the intrinsic factors of production.

A very important point has emerged from this discussion, which is that the inability of Early Humans to economize the intrinsic factors of production played a major role in their eventual extinction. This point underscores the importance of the intrinsic factors of production, as the individuals that produce goods and services are the heart, soul, and gears of economic output. Evolution recognized the importance of the intrinsic factors of production, as evidenced by the introduction of an Economic Psychologist, whose primary role was to economize resources.

Primary Role: Economist

In describing Threes, the term *Intrinsic Resource* refers to the economic psychology embedded in all human resources. The economic psychology of the human species encompasses the knowledge, skills, work ethic, methods of production, and intrapsychic economization mechanisms that evolved and accumulated over time. And the economic psychology of an individual refers to their knowledge, skills, work ethic, talents, and problem-solving ability. In both cases, economic psychology includes the vestigial subconscious mechanisms of evolution, such as the Law of Conservation.

The *Intrinsic Resources* that are available to an individual are intangible and hidden from view since they are a function of the economic psychology embedded within all human resources. The implication here is that *Intrinsic Resources* are a subset of human resources. To illustrate this point, recall that Eights are the ultimate *human resource*, given their ability to adapt to the demands of any environment. In the context of Eights, the use of the term *human resource* is appropriately broad, as it includes physical attributes such as size, strength, power, and the ability to dominate the environment. However, a narrower term is needed to describe the Endeavor, specializations, primary role, and adaptations that are specific to Threes.

The primary role of Threes is to be the ultimate *Intrinsic Resource*, as a remedy for the intrinsic economic stagnation that persisted among Early Human economies for eons. The fundamental duty of this role is to economize resources, especially those *Intrinsic Resources* that are within reach, to realize greater economic efficiency, productivity, and output. Understanding the resources that are within reach, and how Threes economize them, is necessary to understand the primary role of Threes.

When the mechanism of resource economization is left unfettered, Threes will first cultivate their knowledge, skills, abilities, and talents, to establish one or more competitive economic advantages in their local economy. This process begins at a very early age, before adolescence in most cases, and continues into adulthood and beyond. Self-cultivation explains why Threes, during their lifetime, tend to accumulate more knowledge than most other Enneatypes. This knowledge is necessary to attain the competitive advantages that are critical for the economization of Intrinsic Resources.

It is common knowledge that a college degree confers a competitive economic advantage in modern labor markets. Measuring the economic advantage of a college education requires taking the difference between lifetime earnings of college graduates against non-graduates. Many studies have attempted to measure this phenomenon, and the consensus is that the economic advantage of a college education is worth more than $1 million in lifetime earnings. Despite this advantage, many Threes do not pursue a college education. The reasons for this are economic rather than intuitive.

Many factors affect the economization of labor, such as the opportunity costs associated with seeking a formal education. If one can earn $25,000 per year, then the opportunity cost for a four-year college education would be $100,000, and investing half of this amount in the stock market will yield more than $2 million upon retirement. From an economic perspective, the opportunity cost of seeking a college education is prohibitive in many cases.

The economization of labor requires that all manner of costs, including opportunity costs, be accounted for in making a career decision. When threes economize their labor, they consider the opportunity costs involved, resulting in a wider variety of career choices that are selected. Many Threes will attend college, some will pursue skilled trades, and some will start a business. For these reasons, Threes appear throughout the labor force, in all positions and levels, as a natural consequence of economizing labor.

The ubiquity of Threes in the labor force is by design, as it allows for an aspect of resource economization known as Competitive Indexing, which is the boost in productivity that occurs through competition. As an example, recall the scenario involving individuals A, B, and C, each of whom produces a certain quantity of food. In that example, each of the individuals had a competitive advantage in producing either food X, Y, or Z. This example continues with the addition of a fourth individual:

	X	Y	Z
A	24	8	6
B	10	16	12
C	12	14	18
D	26	24	30

Table 8.3

In this example, Individual D is a Three who enjoys an absolute advantage in the production of each food. The introduction of individual D is disruptive and will change the dynamic in this group through the operation of Darwinian competition. The competition that ensues between each laborer will result in greater productivity for each member, yielding a new matrix of productivity:

	X	Y	Z
A	28	12	15
B	10	20	19
C	12	16	34
D	26	24	30

Table 8.4

The first thing to notice is that although laborers A, B, and C have made incremental productivity increases in at least one crop, D has retained an absolute advantage in the production of crops Y and Z. This result will not go unchecked, as competitive pressures will motivate laborers B and C to increase their output. This process continues until a new point of equilibrium is reached: The Competitive Indexing Equilibrium. The competitive behaviors taking place, the changes in productivity that ensue, and the Competitive Indexing Equilibrium are the result of Competitive Indexing.

The primary benefit of Competitive Indexing is that it effectively increases the average per capita output. Threes account for part of the overall increase in output, given the leadership position in overall productivity that they enjoy, but the greater part of the increase stems from the changes in economic psychology that occurs. Recall that economic psychology refers to such intangibles as the knowledge, skills, talents, work ethic, methods of production, and problem-solving abilities that are uniquely individual. Threes alter the economic psychology, and the economic ecology, of the labor markets where they participate. Understanding this phenomenon requires more details for how Threes act as a mechanism for the economization of Intrinsic Resources.

The previous example illustrated one way that Threes identify, infiltrate, and economize resources. Each of these steps, the identification, infiltration, and economization, are the result of subconscious processes: Threes identify opportunities in their locality that need economic improvement due to inefficiencies, mediocrity, sloth, or waste. They then infiltrate the sector of the economy that is operating inefficiently, either by forming an enterprise, acquiring an enterprise, or working directly in that sector. And in the final step, Threes introduce new knowledge, skills, talents, technologies, and motivational techniques that increase efficiency, productivity, and output, thereby increasing overall productivity and output. Thus, the general process for economizing resources follows the template of identification, infiltration, and economization.

The key point of this discussion is that Threes evolved to be the economic mechanism specifically adapted to identify, infiltrate, and economize resources that are otherwise ineptly, incompetently, or inefficiently utilized. As they unwittingly perform their primary role as Economists, they alter the prevailing economic psychology of their social group in positive ways, which ushers in a windfall of many positive economic benefits. These benefits include improvements in the quality, efficiency, and output of labor; coupled with an economic ecology that is more diverse, specialized, and productive. The result is a vibrant, diversified, and infinitely evolving economy that is marked by an ever-increasing per capita output.

Functional Adaptations

Threes have specific adaptations that allow them to identify, infiltrate, and economize the Intrinsic Resources in their local economy. Understanding these adaptations requires consideration of the overall scope, purpose, and objectives that are incumbent upon Threes. As to their scope, Threes have jurisdiction over all sectors of the economy, and all occupations within each sector. Having unlimited jurisdiction over the economy is necessary to fulfill their evolutionary purpose, but it also exposes Threes to many different types of conflicts. For example, when Threes attempt to economize the education sector of an economy, they will necessarily run into resistance from Ones, who have a natural domain over all matters related to education. The same is true when Threes attempt to economize the military, a place where Eights have a natural domain. Although the potential for conflict is virtually unlimited, Threes are specifically adapted to move beyond any conflicts, so that they can fulfill their evolutionary purpose.

As to their purpose, Threes focus on Intrinsic Resources to ensure efficiency, economy, and logical utilization. The term Intrinsic Resource refers specifically to the economic psychology of individuals and groups. So, in a sense, Threes are Economists tasked with changing the economic psychology and behavior of their peers. These tasks require the problem-solving skills of an economist, combined with the intuitive skills of a psychologist, a combination that is unique to Threes.

The objectives that are incumbent upon Threes vary depending on the circumstances, but they generally involve economic changes that are tangible, measurable, and quantifiable. The drive to obtain tangible results requires specific physical, mental, and emotional adaptations that, severally and synergistically, enable Threes to fulfill their evolutionary purpose. Some examples of these adaptations will be given to illustrate how they support the specialization, primary role, scope, and objectives of Threes.

Given the broad jurisdiction over their economy, Threes must be prepared to work wherever they are needed, which necessarily requires the suppression of the Emotional Center. That is because the Emotional Center determines an individual's occupational interests, desires, and choices. The suppression of the Emotional Center is a necessary adaptation, as it effectively insulates Threes from the whims of their emotions so that they can focus on the sectors of their local economy that need economization.

Another consideration is that the Emotional Center is the primary source of impulses, drives, and emotions, which tend to act as a drag on productivity because they reduce the ability to focus on tasks, goals, and results. The suppression of the Emotional Center allows Threes to focus on the economization of Intrinsic Resources, instead of being distracted by love, relationships, negative attitudes, gossip, and superfluous activities.

A consequence of suppressing emotions is that the thinking and instinctive faculties are more active, producing a behavioral pattern where Threes are either thinking about something, doing something, or thinking about doing something. An energy loop between the Thinking and Instinctive Centers manifests, putting Threes in a never-ending cycle of perpetual activity, where they have seemingly endless energy to pursue multiple projects simultaneously. The high rate of activity is reflective of the tremendous amounts of mental and physical energy required to economize resources.

Threes also have adaptations in the Thinking Center that are specifically designed to support the scientific methods that are necessary for the economization of Intrinsic Resources. These adaptations include a rational, as opposed to emotional, approach to problem-solving. The adaptation of logic and rational thinking provides an analytical ability for solving problems. And an ability to use logical reasoning, as opposed to the errors of fallacy, to formulate and test potential strategies and solutions. These innate thinking adaptations allow Threes to assume the role of Economist. Also, Threes must be competent in their ability to implement their recommendations, which explains why Threes are specifically adapted with an Instinctive Center that is more complex, resolute, and evolved. These adaptations provide Threes with the proprioceptive abilities, physical coordination, and physical intuition that is necessary to implement the solutions required for the economization of resources.

Although the adaptations discussed thus far are important, it is also important to understand that the collateral effects of economizing Intrinsic

Resources include the disruption, restructuring, and revamping of all economic resources. The universe of economic resources includes all tangible assets, such as land, buildings, tools, equipment, geological resources, human resources, and so on. It also includes the intangible assets, which refers to the knowledge, intellectual property, skills, methods of production, and so on that have accumulated over time. Some examples will be given to illustrate why the economization of Intrinsic Resources might be disruptive to all categories of resources.

Earlier in this chapter, a scenario was presented involving laborers A thru D, where D was an Enneatype Three. That example continues under the assumption that the laborers are the fisherman of a small village laboring to catch three species of fish: X, Y, Z. Table 8.4 illustrates that the arrival of laborer D (Three) has increased the productivity of each laborer in a process that produced a new Competitive Indexing Equilibrium.

Consider that the Competitive Indexing Equilibrium level of productivity, with perfectly elastic supply, corresponds to a 100% increase in output. Also, consider that the demand for fish is perfectly elastic so that the market-clearing quantity of fish increases by 100%: In this scenario, the new equilibrium substantially reduces the amount of fishing industry resources needed, including the amount of laborers due to the displacement of workers throughout the fishing industry, including those working to supply boats, equipment, and so on. The disruption to the fishing industry, especially the disruption and displacement of human resources, has significant psychological effects.

From the perspective of a laborer, the prospect of displacement due to the economization of resources causes immense psychological stress, strife, and hardship. The psychological hardships of economization explain the reactionary behaviors of skepticism, disdain, resistance, and violence. And it explains why laborers wish to avoid change, to maintain the status quo, and preserve the ancient methods of subsistence living. Indeed, that's what Early Humans did, as they failed to adjust, adapt, and embrace new ways, means, and methods for increasing their economic output. The resistance to change was a major factor in the Intrinsic Stagnation that persisted among Early Humans: Individuals would master a set of tasks, and then block new entrants, competition, methods, or innovations that might disrupt their way of life.

Avoiding change, maintaining the status quo, preserving ancient methods, and a litany of anti-competitive protectionist behaviors are just some of the defensive psychic mechanisms that operate against the economization of resources. Overcoming the defensive mechanisms of the psyche requires a coercive agency of change dedicated to the economic advancement of the species. Threes are the coercive agency of economic and psychological change tasked with overcoming the barriers imposed by the primitive economic psychology of the human mind. With this understanding, attention turns to the psychological adaptation that allows Threes to fulfill their primary role as Economists.

Ambition is the intrinsic psychological adaptation, manifesting as a desire, drive, and motivation to achieve an economic goal, that serves the evolutionary purpose of resource economization. Ambition is not unique to Threes, as some degree of ambition can be found in other Enneatypes, albeit as a secondary factor. For example, Eights may have the ambition to conserve economic resources, but their ambition is secondary to the objective of conserving resources. Ones may have the ambition to create a system of education, but their ambition is simply a plan for how they will fulfill their evolutionary purpose. In the case of Threes, the experience of ambition has no constraints, boundaries, or terrestrial limits, which allows Threes to experience ambition that is free of a specific directive, specialization, role, or objective.

Ambition sets in motion an array of attitudes, traits, and behaviors that combine to support the primary role of resource economization. In matters of attitude, Threes are positive, optimistic, and realistic, which helps to offset the negative attitudes, disdain, skepticism, and rejection of economic change. Threes also have an attitude of curiosity manifesting as an unquenchable thirst for knowledge, experience, and wisdom which are necessary adjuncts for the high-level economic analysis that Threes Endeavor.

Threes are a paradox of personality traits, as they augment the traits occurring at the intersection of ambition, economics, and psychology. Ambition is charming, charismatic, adaptable, goal-oriented, persistent, industrious, and knowledgeable. Whereas, economics is professional, logical, objective, analytical, and mostly impersonal. And psychology is open-minded, patient, accepting, calm, and reconciliatory. The marriage of these traits is made possible by a narcissistic adaptation for deception.

Recall that Threes have a suppressed Emotional Center, which effectively distorts and suppresses the self-image, thereby suppressing all manner of self-reflection. A distortion in the self-image is a common phenomenon among the Enneatypes, but in the case of Threes, the distortion does not lend itself to correction. Thus, this type of narcissism is not amenable to introspection, revision, or rehabilitation. Narcissism is a necessary adaptation because it allows for an unrestricted ambitiousness that seeks to economize resources without regard to subjective factors such as feelings, emotions, attachments, legacy, posterity, and so on.

Threes have a type of narcissism that prevents certain aspects of introspection, which creates an identity dilemma known as deception, that serves an important evolutionary purpose. Recall that the primary role of Threes is to infiltrate all sectors of the economy, which necessarily requires a persona devoid of specific passions, expectations, inclinations, or ambitions. Such a persona is created by suppressing the Emotional Center, which effectively retards the development of desires, goals, and ambitions that are uniquely personal to the individual. The result is that Threes are not inner-directed by their inner needs, wants, feelings, desires, or ambitions: They are outer-directed, focusing their ambitions on the needs of their local economy.

The astute observer would be keen to point out that there is a bit of narcissism inherent to each of the Enneatypes. Indeed, narcissism is ubiquitous because, without some degree of narcissism, each of the Enneatypes would otherwise become conscious of the restrictions that were placed on human consciousness to create the Nine Human Endeavors. The revelation of this knowledge would be untenable in many situations, so evolution uses narcissism to keep the Endeavors, specializations, roles, and adaptations hidden from view, thereby keeping the evolutionary machine of humanity intact.

Threes are a special case because all traces of individuality must be suppressed to create a persona that will act as the coercive agent of economic change. In this case, individuality is suppressed by masking the elements of identity, which effectively mutes self-expression, erases dreams, and curbs personal desires. However, the deception includes the person wearing the mask, in that they are out of touch with their individuality, passions, and emotions, ensuring that they are unable to acknowledge their true self.

A masked identity unleashes an unbridled ambition to economize resources because it prevents Threes from pursuing a self-serving agenda. As a result of this narcissistic adaptation, a self-deception occurs simultaneously with the deceptive process of economizing resources. The irony here is that everyone is deceived, including Threes, because no one is aware that an evolutionary mechanism is operating behind the scenes. This arrangement ensures that Threes blindly go where they are needed, and perform the work that is needed incognito, to bring greater economy, efficiency, and productivity to their local economy.

There is a certain paradox here: Although Threes are outer-directed, they are not easily awakened to this fact, as this realization is wholly dependent on their inner state of consciousness. Even when Threes awaken to their vice of deception, they happily continue their quest to economize resources, but with a renewed vigor and a sense of purpose. Despite the vice of deception, many Threes can find personal fulfillment by aligning themselves with activities that are simultaneously inner and outer-directed.

Basic Delusion:

Value is the fundamental human quality that imbues the human soul with a sense of integration with the universe. A certain degree of integration with the universe is important because it directly impacts the ability to function as a human being. Thus, a feeling of integration is necessary for functioning because it provides a sense of belonging, a home base, a reference point, a launching pad, from which an individual can function. In this way, Value provides the human soul with the inherent sense of integration with the universe that is a prerequisite for functioning in the world.

When the fundamental human quality of value is impaired, the ability to function in the world as a human being is impaired. The relationship between value and functioning exists because value provides a fundamental sense of belonging, as in the context of belonging to a community, and that sense of belonging has a direct effect on the ability to function. And when the sense of belonging is lost, the sense of connection to the world is lost; and more importantly, the inner sense of connection to Being is lost. Without a sense of connection, there is a paralysis stemming from feelings of isolation, entrapment, and powerlessness.

Threes are afflicted with the delusion of having no value, which effectively cuts them off from a sense of integration and belonging, and the innate ability to function in the world. The delusion of having no value limits their individuation, range of emotion, and ability to relate to others. The ego for Enneatype Three grows and develops as a compensation, producing individuals who are super functional and ambitious, in the sense that they are designed to function and perform in exceptional ways relative to the other Enneatypes.

As the ultimate Intrinsic Resource, Threes are driven to succeed, achieve, and win at all cost. These competitive behaviors are secondary to a lost sense of individuality, belonging, integration, and value. Threes spend their lifetime attempting to regain a sense of value, unwittingly economizing resources along the way, as the exemplars of economic advancement.

Interpersonal Relationships

A common interpersonal problem for Threes is that, in their effort to find a sense of value in the world, they are unable to be themselves. The lack of authenticity means that Threes are constantly deceiving themselves, both consciously and subconsciously, into believing that they are something they are not. If Threes are deceiving themselves, whether it be conscious or subconscious, it necessarily follows that they are deceiving others along the way. Deception is a fundamental cause of their broken relationships, but there are many other superficial causes, most of which are amenable to change.

A good starting point for Threes is to see that they view relationships as an extension of their work, as another project that they hope will be successful. And to see that they bring the same emotionless, logical, task-oriented approach to their relationships that they bring to their careers. These behaviors allow Threes to remain detached and distant, especially in romantic relationships, to avoid having demands that might interfere with their drive for success. Many Threes avoid romantic relationships altogether, for fear that love relationships might interfere with their actualization of success.

The suppression of the Emotional Center is responsible for creating an unemotional, insensitive, and uncompassionate disposition. These traits make sense when you consider that Threes are Economists, whose role is to channel their energy toward activities that will bring measurable results, achievements, and success. The result is that Threes are out of touch with their emotions; and by extension, they are out of touch with their relationships, to the detriment of those close to them. Despite these disadvantages, Threes are still capable of normal relationships, if they develop a certain degree of wisdom.

Although the odds for wisdom are long, it would seem plausible that Threes could focus some of their abundant energy introspectively for the development of their emotions. But sadly, Threes are perhaps the least introspective of all Enneatypes, partly because of the systemic belief that value is more important than anything else, and partly from the cultural attitudes and customs surrounding value.

Psychology of Threes

Primary Ego Trait: Ambition

Regressive Traits: Deception

In Search Of: Economization

Focuses On: Tasks, goals, results

Basic Fear: Failure

Basic Desire: Validation

Basic Need: Adulation

Stress Reaction: Hostility, rejection, excommunication

Sense of Self: I am what I do

Motto: Failure is not an option.

Mental Model: What others can do…I can do better.

Motivations:

- To inspire and motivate others
- Achieving goals, ambitions, and results
- To distinguish themselves from others
- To demonstrate superior skills, abilities, and talents

Physical Characteristics

Threes tend to be very image-conscious, so it will come as no surprise that they put their best foot forward, by combining several unique physiological adaptations. As a group, Threes possess traits that are generally considered attractive, charismatic, and sexually appealing. From a Darwinian perspective, charisma serves multiple purposes, most notably that it compensates for their emotional limitations.

Although beauty is somewhat subjective, Threes have many of the basic physical characteristics that are considered attractive, sexually appealing, and charismatic. The first is a body structure that is lithe, athletic, and gracefully efficient. Having a body that is both very functional, and athletic in appearance, is considered sexually appealing by the opposite sex. Thus, Threes will rarely be found exceeding a BMI of 30, which is the limit of the normal range of weight.

Perhaps more important than body structure is the facial symmetry. In this context, facial symmetry is the relative positioning of the eyes, eyebrows, cheekbones, nose, mouth, and chin. The precise positioning of the facial features is important because scientists have determined that facial symmetry affects the rating of attraction by the opposite sex. Because Threes possess excellent facial symmetry, they are generally rated as the most attractive by the opposite sex when compared to other Enneatypes.

Overall, Threes have a physiology that is adaptable, efficient, and incognito. They present themselves as average people who happen to be charismatically above average. They tend to be unemotional, methodical, and purposeful in their demeanor. The best way to appreciate these attributes is to see a group of Threes standing together. Doing so demonstrates the unique blend of economic, psychological, and physiological traits that are possessed by Threes.

FACIAL TENSION

The facial tension for type Three is identical to Nines, except that it affects the right eye, as seen from the perspective of the observer.

IDENTIFYING AND DIAGNOSING THREES

Threes are estimated to be 10% of the population in the USA. Although Threes seemingly blend into their environment, there are some attitudes, behaviors, and physiological traits that may help to identify them:

1. Excellent facial symmetry.
2. Very flexible body posture.
3. A reserved and professional demeanor.
4. Below average to average BMI.
5. Above-average communication skills.
6. Charismatic and sexually attractive.

CHAPTER 9

TYPE FOUR: THE ENTREPRENEUR

Endeavor: Entrepreneurism

History has proven that the most effective way to increase economic output is to introduce new technologies that increase efficiency, economies of scale, and automation. The supreme importance of technology partly explains why the annals of history are often characterized by a technological paradigm, such as the stone age, iron age, industrial age, or computer age, as a way of framing the prevailing technology for each historical period. However, viewing history from the perspective of paradigms understates the importance of innovation. That is because the course of history, including the rise and fall of nation-states, tends to favor those who can innovate, implement, improve, and harness the economic advantages of new technologies.

Technological innovations were a key factor in the 1,470-year reign of the Roman Empire. For example, Roman engineers had mastered the basic elements of a steam engine, including the use of steam as power, the crank and connecting rod mechanism, cylinders and pistons, and the gearing and valves. These technologies are evidence that Romans utilized new technologies in powerful ways to increase the efficiency, economies of scale, and automation of labor. Also important were the many incremental advances made by Romans, referring to the perfection of many innovations that were otherwise not invented by Romans. Thus, the Roman empire owes a large part of its success to its ability to harness the economic benefits that come with the adoption of new technologies.

The USA provides another example of economic success that is largely attributable to the phenomenon of innovation. Since its inception, the USA generated more innovations than perhaps all other countries combined. Some key American innovations include nuclear technologies, telecommunications, computers, and the internet. Collectively, these innovations have been responsible for the increases in labor productivity, economic output, and standard of living enjoyed by humanity. Thus, the innovation of new technologies has been the primary driver of economic success occurring in the USA.

Many of the economic failures occurring throughout history are due to a failure to innovate new technologies. Early Humans are the best example, as multiple species went extinct, and a failure to innovate was a common denominator in each case. However, Modern Humans have not always fared much better, given the paucity of innovation that occurred just after humans arrived. Indeed, the greater part of all human innovation has occurred only in the past 3,000 years. These facts provide hints about the phenomenon of innovation.

Innovation does not magically appear on its own volition, as it requires a specific mechanism to generate the necessary personality traits, attitudes, and behavioral pattern: Research, skill development, and ingenuity. Such a mechanism had not evolved in Early Humans. And if there are any doubts about this, one only need to consider the technological contributions of Neanderthals. Neanderthals never progressed beyond a primitive level of technology, precisely because they lacked a specific mechanism for innovation, a fact that belies their economic stagnation and eventual demise.

History also teaches that innovation is a very fragile phenomenon. Innovation is fragile in the sense that it occurs only under very precise conditions, and when those conditions are not present, the actuated potential for innovation lies dormant. Population density is perhaps the most important of these conditions, and it was certainly a major factor in the dormancy of innovation that occurred in the period immediately after Modern Humans arrived. The lack of population density also partly explains the paucity of innovation in the modern era that continues in certain parts of the world.

The key point is that innovation does not occur in a vacuum, as it is a function of a uniquely specialized mechanism, that acts as a template for a progressive pattern of modern human behaviors. This mechanism is generally not understood, as it operates incognito, masking a phenomenon of modern human creativity, ingenuity, and brilliance. Unmasking the mechanism for innovation requires knowledge of the specific human behaviors, the delusion responsible for those behaviors, and how those behaviors lead to the introduction of new technologies. The unmasking, investigation, and analysis of this behavioral phenomenon reveal the primary role of Enneatype Four.

Primary Role: Entrepreneur

Because the creation of new technologies is an economic behavior, the perspectives of economics and psychology are indispensable to understanding this facet of human endeavor. From an economic perspective, the gross revenues generated by new technology is an indicator of success. However, measuring innovations by revenues reveals an important fact, which is that a very high percentage have zero economic value, given that they generate zero revenues. The high failure rate provides important clues about the fundamental economics of innovation because if most innovations fail, it implies that the process of innovation is inherently risky. Understanding this risk is the first step to understanding the primary role of Fours.

The Law of Energy Conservation ensures that all life forms avoid risk, which means they do not engage in superfluous activities, experiments, or endeavors. When the trait of risk adversity was carried forward to Early Humans, their behaviors were effectively limited to only those activities that were necessary for survival. From an evolutionary perspective, risk adversity was essential to survival, as it prevented Early Humans from taking unnecessary risks that might expose them to an early demise. However, risk adversity is not always advantageous.

A consequential disadvantage of risk adversity was that it severely restricted the economic behaviors associated with innovation, specifically the behavioral process of innovation, which can be broken down into three basic human behaviors: Research, conceptualization, and development. The research stage is the most intensive, as it requires a non-conventional approach to the acquisition of new ideas, concepts, and information. Research requires travel to faraway places, the pursuit of eccentric teachings, reading abstract texts, and other modes of new experience, in the name of acquiring new knowledge. With these points in mind, it becomes clear that the research stage requires significant amounts of time, energy, and resources.

Innovations are born in the conceptualization stage, involving visions, dreams, experiments, accidents, or sometimes pure luck. In most cases, there is a distinct longing, curiosity, and openness to experience that precedes the conceptualization stage, and it is this openness to experience that provides a literal invitation to new ways of seeing the world. At the core of this longing, curiosity, and openness to experience is the realization that reality is superficial: And innovations are simply the intelligent perception of what is beyond the surface. Thus, at the core of innovation lies a very perceptive faculty of intelligence.

Most conceptualizations never move to the development stage, where the concept is acted upon, executed, implemented, and disseminated into the local economy. A concept may fail because of a lack of resources, technical skills, or for a multitude of other reasons. Indeed, there are volumes of innovations that were conceptualized in detail by one person and then credited to another person who developed, executed, and marketed the innovation. And there are examples where significant innovations are simultaneously conceptualized by two different individuals, each working autonomously and independently, with credit going to the innovator that was first to execute. Perhaps the best example of this was the invention of the telephone, with Alexander Bell executing his patent only hours before Elisha Gray.

The behavioral pattern of researching, conceptualizing, and implementing new technologies provides insight into the psychology necessary for innovation. And from here, a pivot back to an Economist's perspective illuminates the economic purpose of this behavioral pattern, which is market research, skills assessment, and demand matching. Market research aims to identify, qualify, and forecast the future technological needs of the market; whereas, the purpose is to identify opportunities for economic gain.

A skill assessment is a form of self-appraisal, where individuals probe, examine, and test their vocational skills, aptitudes, and abilities, to identify their relative skill set. For example, some individuals may possess an aptitude for creative endeavors: This group might include some with an aptitude for engineering, and so they may self-identify an aptitude for architecture; whereas, others may choose abstract endeavors related to fine arts. The possibilities are almost infinite, as the range of skills, aptitudes, and abilities that are possible necessarily encompasses all activities and pursuits of human endeavor.

Demand matching is the process whereby an individual matches their economic skills with the technological needs of their local economy. Demand matching is distinct from other methods of resource allocation, in that it effectively matches skills to the entrepreneurial opportunities having the greatest impact. For example, matching human resources based on their competitive advantages maximizes output in the short run, but it does not ensure the maximization of output in the long run.

Demand matching ensures that the best skills available are identified, and applied toward the introduction of new technologies, thereby maximizing economic growth in the long run. Demand matching reduces total economic output in the short run due to the deployment of human resources in the entrepreneurial activities of research, conceptualization, and development. However, in the long run, the introduction of new technologies brings substantial net increases in per capita GSP, thereby maximizing economic productivity, output, and growth.

Market research, skills assessment, and demand matching are the entrepreneurial behaviors that are necessary for the identification, innovation, and deployment of new technologies. Fours are specifically adapted with these behaviors, allowing them to fulfill their primary role as the Entrepreneurs of their local economy. These entrepreneurial adaptations are the focus of the next discussion.

Functional Adaptations

Understanding the functional adaptations of Fours requires some knowledge of how the ego develops. The ego identity develops and individuates beginning at approximately two years of age, based upon early experiences that shape and form the basic threads of identity, and these threads become the fabric of the ego. The quality of the fabric, meaning the qualitative development of the ego, depends on the quality of the threads and their integration. With tightly woven threads, the fabric has greater strength, endurance, and resiliency to stress. But as it sometimes happens, the threads of the ego may be loosely woven or loosely integrated, resulting in an ego that is weak, vulnerable, and dysfunctional to some degree.

The analogy of weak, defective, or loosely integrated threads helps to explain why there are seven levels of functioning within each Enneatype, but it does not explain the phenomenology of Fours. Applying this analogy to Fours reveals that the fabric of the ego is only partially complete, with just enough threads to create a substrate. Space is visible between the threads, both horizontally and vertically, due to the absence of many threads. Although the fabric has a slightly porous appearance, there are just enough threads to provide some structure for basic functioning, but not enough threads to make the fabric useful. Such a fabric has no utility, significance, merit, or character.

The next point in this discussion is the understanding that an individuated sense of self forms from early memories, and these memories can be isolated, recalled, and analyzed. For example, the individual components of an ego identity form from specific events that give rise to such identities as "I am charitable" "I am knowledgeable" and "I am loving". Although these events are subject to recall under the right conditions, the important point is that they provide distinct attributes, and the sum-total of these attributes form the character of an individual. Thus, an individuated sense of self is indistinguishable from a person's attributes and character, as they are the same.

Character is the primary ego trait emulated by Fours as compensation for impairment of the fundamental identity structures. However, Fours do not develop character in the traditional sense, such as the character that is conventionally developed by the ego from 18 to 60 months, as they are functionally adapted to develop character in a non-conventional manner. The non-conventional development of character begins at approximately age five and continues until self-realization or expiration, whichever comes first. Thus, Fours spend all or most of their life attempting to find, discover, create, or develop their character. The overall process for creating character, including the infinitely variable ways, means, and methods utilized by Fours, is a subject of great fascination.

The key to understanding Fours lies in the non-conventional ways, means, and methods for creating character. In this context, non-conventional means that Fours are not bound to the conventions of culture, ethnicity, nationalism, religion, gender, and so on. However, Fours are not necessarily anti-conventional; it simply means that they have a degree of freedom from the constraints that are generally imposed by society. Having this freedom means that Fours are not bound, shaped, and molded by the subjective viewpoints that are necessarily imposed by various conventions, giving them a certain immunity from social influences that allows them to be free spirits who think, act and live outside the box of conventional wisdom.

Although Fours are free-spirited, this does not mean they have no ties with the world, as the character that Fours are seeking to create is generally sub-servient to the wants, needs, and objectives of their local economy. Fours are subservient to the economic prerogatives of the world because they need attention from others to fill the void that is felt by the absence of character. In practice, this means that Fours need others to validate the character they have created. Validation by the world provides a sense of merit, significance, and verification that a uniquely individuated identity has come to fruition.

From a psychological perspective, the phenomenon under discussion cor-responds with one of the three fundamental types of narcissism. In this case, Fours suffer from the narcissistic distortion of an undifferentiated self, which is an identity that is plain, indistinctive, and anonymous due to the arrested development of identity structures. Fours experience this distortion as a void or absence of a uniquely individuated self, which sets in motion an array of behaviors meant to fill the void, by creating a self that can be distinctly, precisely, and unambiguously differentiated from others. In this context, differentiation requires character traits that are bold, unique, and steeply contrasted from others.

In the broadest sense, Fours develop their bold and unique character by living the life of the person they want to create, doing so in as many ways as there are talents. Although there are infinite ways to develop a bold, unique, and differentiated character, they share a common denominator of being non-conventional, which means that Fours live their life in non-conventional ways. To illustrate this behavioral pattern, some examples of how Fours reject conventional ways of living will be given, followed by examples of the non-conventional paths embraced by Fours.

In highly developed countries, the conventional way of living is to graduate college by age twenty-one, marry, and have children before age thirty. Fours may reject all or part of the cultural standards and timelines for education, marriage, family, and so on. In practice, this means that a significant percentage of Fours will abstain from marriage, and if they do have children, it often occurs out of wedlock. Among those Fours that do marry, they maintain a pluralistic view of marriage as an institution of civilization, social construct, financial contract, theological mechanism, and so on. For these reasons, Fours are the Enneatype least likely to have a long-term marriage, complete a college education, and accept traditional parenting roles.

The priesthood is another example of a conventional life path that is rejected by Fours. When Fours do pursue this path, it is generally under the mistaken belief that what is missing in their inner experience can be found in religion. When the realization comes that religion has no answer for the void felt in their heart, many Fours quickly abandon this path and set their sights on a new direction.

Of the many paths embraced by Fours, it is the creative endeavors that best exemplify how Fours emulate character. The creative endeavors now include architects, designers, choreographers, composers, inventors, writers, visual artists, filmmakers, and many others. Fours are attracted to these creative endeavors because it allows them to live a bold, creative, and unique life that affords ample opportunities for character development. From this perspective, the legacy of their identity appears in their designs, conceptualizations, creations, and innovations.

Many Fours live a bold, unique, and exemplary life by acting on their desire to blaze new paths into uncharted territories; acquiring new skills, abilities, and non-conventional methodologies along the way. But because of their inherent narcissism, Fours consider conventional paths and skills to be mundane and unworthy of their creative abilities. Thus, Fours place more value on their ability to design, create, innovate, or invent something unique then they place on their ability to perform the mundane tasks of existence. The disdain for the mundane creates a dilemma for Fours because the business of designing, creating, innovating, and inventing requires a tremendous amount of trial, error, and risk. History is rife with examples of artists and inventors whose risk-taking failed to produce anything of importance. Hedging this risk generally requires Fours to participate in work that is unrelated to their life mission of character development. However, many Fours would rather starve than perform menial work, hence the archetypal *starving artist*. But most will perform conventional work in the hope that their true talents will eventually be recognized.

Writing is a profession that is seemingly ideal for Fours because it combines three of the skills that Fours embody: Creativity, imagination, and character development. Writing fiction is of interest to Fours, partly because writing is a creative outlet, and partly because they can explore and develop their character as they imagine and create various character interactions. Writing becomes a passion for many Fours, and once the well of creativity opens, they often become prolific writers. For these reasons, Fours are dominant in many genres of writing, but especially in the fiction genre: Comedy, romance, suspense, crime, mystery, tragedies, dramas, etc.

Although Fours have many positive functional adaptations, it's important to understand that the impairment of the ego identity coincides with enigmatic feelings of darkness, fragility, and despair. Although others take their identity for granted, Fours are innocent to what is missing and carry a heavy burden of creating their identity from scratch. But from this adversity springs the desire to create, and from creativity descends a certain solace in knowing that suffering does serve an evolutionary purpose.

Basic Delusion

The core function of the ego is to provide the foundation for functioning in the world by way of a uniquely individuated identity. The ego identity is composed of scores of threads, each thread composed of a cluster of objects formed by a specific experience or interaction, that collectively become the fabric of the individual. In this way, the ego identity is a composition of individual identities that formed from separate and unique experiences over approximately 4 – 5 years.

Fours suffer from an arrested development of the basic ego identity structures that impair the core functions of the ego, including the basic sense of an individuated self, and how that self interacts with the world. The absence of an individuated identity and the loss of functioning and confusion that follows creates an unconscious belief that life has no purpose, meaning, or significance. These beliefs permeate the impaired ego structures, producing individuals who believe they have no purpose, meaning, or significance, and that personal significance is a matter of volition. These beliefs constitute the delusion of type Four.

How Fours compensate for their delusion is a fascinating phenomenon. Exploring this phenomenon requires knowledge of the structures associated with the undifferentiated self, and an understanding that the impairment of identity structures evolved to create a subjective mode of experience, meant to eclipse the basic human experiences of self-esteem, personal significance, and connection with the world. This knowledge explains many of the subjective experiences that are reported by Fours, especially those related to self-esteem, personal significance, self-actualization, and relationships. And it explains the complex array of entrepreneurial behaviors that are set in motion to create a bold, fresh, unique, super individuated identity.

Interpersonal Relationships

The fact that interpersonal relationships provide infinite opportunities for character development goes a long way in explaining how Fours view relationships. As a practical matter, Fours view interpersonal relationships as a primary means for searching, finding, and exploring who they are. Of special importance to Fours are the romantic relationships they experience because intimacy brings to light the missing elements of character, which sometimes brings the therapeutic knowledge needed for personal growth.

Fours often follow a distinct pattern of behavior in romantic relationships, consisting of seduction, feedback, and rapprochement. In the initial phase of seduction, Fours employ a litany of methods, tactics, and strategies for introducing themselves in a very positive light. The overall approach requires many long conversations discussing the nuances and vicissitudes of previous relationships, friends, family life, and career challenges. During this phase, Fours are creating an enigmatic persona, intending to draw their target into their inner world. Fours have a way of seducing their targets into accepting the persona they have created. The seduction phase ends when Fours feel they have *hooked*, hypnotized, and mesmerized their target.

The feedback phase can vary in length and intensity, depending on the relative degree of interest on display. But the idealism cultivated during the seduction phase begins to fade and is replaced by new renditions of personality, in some cases more realistic and some cases less realistic. As they are changing their persona, Fours will give feedback on how the relationship is progressing under the pretext of being genuine, authentic, or *real*, and this serves the general purpose of resetting the relationship. Feedback also includes the identification and setting of boundaries, expectations, and intentions, which can feel more like a negotiation than a relationship, as Fours continue to change their persona.

The rapprochement phase begins when the negotiations start to break down. The breakdown of negotiations is by design, as Fours are often the party to end the relationship, and they do so because of their need for narcissistic mirroring. Rapprochement is the beginning of the end when Fours secretly wish that their target will respond with desperation: Pleading for détente, reconciliation, and forgiveness. When the target pleads for reconciliation, they unwittingly provide the narcissistic mirroring that adulates, validates, and confirms the uniquely differentiated super identity created by the Four.

Apart from romantic relationships, Fours are prone to difficulties in other affairs, including family and business concerns. The difficulties generally stem from the narcissistic needs that Fours are not aware and includes a need for validation and endorsement of the character that Fours have created and presented to the world. When others fail to see and appreciate what Fours have created, a crisis for finding the true self ensues, but this often occurs at the expense of maintaining appropriate relationships with others. Unfortunately, Fours are generally not aware of their narcissistic dilemma, at least not until later in life, after irreconcilable differences have taken shape.

Psychology of Fours

Primary Ego Trait: Individualism

Regressive Traits: Envy

In Search Of: Character development

Focuses On: Opportunities

Basic Fear: Nonexistence

Basic Desire: Self-development

Basic Need: Adulation

Stress Reaction: Emotional venting

Sense of Self: Total emptiness

Motto: I am the one and only.

Mental Model: I still feel lonely when I'm with you.

Motivations:

- Introspection and self-understanding
- Express themselves in a beautifully creative way
- Finding the perfect partner
- Withdrawal to protect their feelings

- Feelings come first.

Physical Characteristics

Fours often describe their inner experience as dark, deficient, empty, lifeless, and devoid of feeling. Depending on their level of functioning, Fours respond to these feelings with somatic identification, somatic compensation, or exteriorization. One aspect of somatic identification is that the inner experiences are unconsciously felt to be the true self, which leads to behaviors, preferences, attitudes, and activities that reflect the inner experiences. A very common activity that reflects their feelings of darkness, deficiency, emptiness, and lifelessness is to participate in the gothic subculture.

Music and fashion are important parts of the gothic subculture. Music in the gothic subculture includes gothic rock, deathrock, gothabilly, cold wave, darkwave, and ethereal wave. Artists include The Cure, Sioux Sie and the Banshees, and Joy Division. Gothic music is considered dark and macabre, with emotional and thematic complexities that closely mirrors the inner experience described by many Fours.

Gothic fashion is also characterized as dark and macabre because participants are known to wear black clothes, black fingernail polish, black hair, black lipstick, black eyeliner, with a pale face. The gothic style also borrows from other subcultures, such as the Victorians, the Elizabethans, and punk fashion. In some cases, the gothic style is confused with heavy metal fashion and emo fashion. The common denominator among these subcultures is that they are all non-conventional, which aligns with the prerogatives of Fours, and explains why many Fours are attracted to them.

Somatic compensation is the personalization of the physical body as compensation for deficiencies in the ego identity. The personalization of the body may take many forms, with the most common being tattoos, piercings, and hair dyes. Somatic compensation is generally observed only with Twos, Fours, Eights, and Nines. Each type does so for different reasons, and these reasons are rooted in the motivations for each type. Because Fours are motivated to create a bold, unique, highly individuated character, they often choose tattoos, piercings, and hair dyes that enable them to stand out in a crowd. Along these lines, Fours prefer to express something extraordinary, arcane, or enigmatic, rather than something mundane such as flags, maps, or other ubiquitous symbols.

Piercings of the ear are very common among all Enneatypes, but Fours are unique in that they often personalize their body with piercings of the nose, lips, eyebrows, nipples, tongue, and the genital area. These piercings can be very helpful in the identification of Fours, especially when there are multiples of piercings, tattoos, dyed hair, and so on. In the case of dyed hair, Fours often choose to dye their hair black or to dye the ends of their hair a special color such as blue, red, pink, orange, or purple.

Fours can sometimes be very bold in asserting their individuality. Some have been known to tattoo their entire face. Others have adopted non-conventional hairstyles, such as a bald head, mohawk, or spiked hair. Placing large holes in the ear lobes is another non-conventional practice. Anything that is counter-cultural, non-conventional, or that stands out is possible.

The inner experience of Fours also affects their physical appearance in other ways. Probably the first thing to be noticed is the melancholy disposition that is prevalent among Fours. Fours often appear to be sad or depressed because their inner experience feels dark, empty, and lifeless, placing a tremendous burden on the soul, affecting their ability to relate to the world in ways that are positive, endearing, and enthusiastic. It's as if they're carrying around a black hole, trying with all their might to mask the full effect of its gravitational pull on their emotional wellbeing. When masking doesn't work, Fours often turn to an external stimulus for help in coping with their inner experience.

Food is a rather benign external stimulus that many Fours use to satisfy their feelings of emptiness. But food can become an addiction, and for those with mesomorph or endomorph body types, excess caloric intake usually leads to weight problems. Although Fours never reach the BMI's found with Eights, some do have a roller coaster of weight gain and weight loss. Much of this stems from the deep-seated emotional emptiness that affects every Four.

A small percentage of Fours also compensate for their inner experience with drugs. Fours are mostly attracted to mood-altering drugs such as barbiturates, opiates, and hallucinogenic drugs. Mood altering drugs allow Fours to escape who they are — a nameless persona, a person with no identity. Fours feel compelled to escape their life, as a relief for the painful burden of living a life without identity. The need to escape is typically a phase during their younger years, but many Fours are unable to manage their identity issues, leading some to an endless cycle of depression. Despite these challenges, only a small fraction of Fours will turn to drugs.

Facial Tension

The facial tension for type Four is the opposite of Eights, in that there is an asymmetry in the nose, with the nose leaning to the right from the perspective of the observer.

IDENTIFYING AND DIAGNOSING FOURS

While Fours are estimated to be 11% of the USA population, they are perhaps the easiest of all Enneatypes to identify, because most Fours seek to exemplify a persona that is unique and highly differentiated. The following physiological traits are useful in the diagnosis of Fours:

1. A history of using gothic elements or hair dyes.
2. Overt tattoos and piercings.
3. An introverted and melancholy demeanor.
4. A highly differentiated style of dress
5. Non-conventional music preferences.
6. History of chronic depression.

CHAPTER 10

TYPE FIVE: THE ADVISOR

Endeavor: Wisdom

A common denominator among the Nine Factors of Extinction was the systemic lack of knowledge. For example, the entrepreneurial endeavor to innovate is a function of knowledge; and if Early Humans had knowledge specific to this endeavor, greater economic progress would occur, and perhaps entrepreneurial stagnation would not have been a factor of extinction. The same is true for each of The Nine Factors of Extinction. Thus, the amount of knowledge and wisdom available to Early Humans played a crucial role in their extinction. However, it does not mean that Early Humans were not intelligent creatures.

As a group, the average Early Human brain was comparable to Modern Humans. In some cases, the brain size was larger, as was the case with Neanderthals, whose brains have been estimated to be larger than Modern Humans. Despite having a brain size that was comparable to Modern Humans, Early Humans were incapable of accumulating knowledge that was beyond a subsistence level of existence. The lack of knowledge wasn't anatomical, but rather, it was due to the structural mechanisms within the psyche that determined how knowledge was filtered, processed, and retained.

There are several mechanisms in the psyche that determines how knowledge accumulates over time. The first mechanism evolved in a species that predates Homo Erectus, and for that reason, it is not covered in this book apart from a brief mention here. This mechanism is primordial in that it consists of three distinct thinking styles: Inductive, deductive, and transductive. Each of these thinking styles filters information, experiences, and objects differently to accomplish certain evolutionary survival objectives. Although this mechanism has significant consequences for how information is processed, retained, and utilized, it has little relevance in the context of the Enneatypes.

The primary organically based mechanism in the psyche that is responsible for processing, retaining, and utilizing knowledge is the Thinking Center. The Thinking Center performs the same functions as a computer, as it functions by logic and reasoning, and incorporates long-term memory that allows concepts and information to be stored. The ability to conceptualize, rationalize, and develop theories all occurs within the Thinking Center; and within this context, the Thinking Center is an effective mechanism for accumulating knowledge. However, the Thinking Center does not operate autonomously.

Although the Thinking, Emotional, and Instinctive centers are distinct and autonomous, there is some degree of bleeding that occurs between each of the centers. The lack of distinct boundaries between the centers leads to the neglect, blurring, or corruption of some functions. For example, situations that require logic, analysis, and reasoning might be eclipsed by emotions, resulting in actions that compensate for the feeling state of the individual, rather than actions that are logical and rational. This phenomenon is referred to as Intrinsic Bias, as the source of the bias is intrinsic, meaning that it is within the psyche.

Although Intrinsic Bias was ubiquitous among Early Humans, they had no awareness of this phenomenon, leaving them vulnerable to its consequences. The same applies to Modern Humans, as very few individuals possess the self-awareness that is necessary to identify Intrinsic Bias. To demonstrate this phenomenon, consider which of the three centers is activated by reading the following true statement:

The ubiquitous use of speed limits reduces roadway safety, increases total

accidents, and causes a significant number of unnecessary fatalities each year in the USA.

For many people, the first thing to happen is a strong emotional or instinctive reaction that effectively eclipses all rational thought. The initial reaction can be so strong that it effectively overrides any logic, analysis, or rational thinking. Such reactions occur because of bleeding from the Instinctive and Emotional Centers, which effectively crowds out the normal functioning of the Thinking Center. In this example, the logic, analysis, and rational thinking processes of the Thinking Center are crowded out by emotional and instinctive reactions.

Although Intrinsic Bias occurs for many reasons, a very common reason is that people substitute their emotions for rational thinking due to a pre-existing emotional attachment. In this case, an emotional attachment to speed limits forms because they provide a sense of safety, guidance, and predictability, which is reinforced by the repetitive, habitual, and quotidious reliance on them. The emotional attachment persists because of other emotive factors, such as a sense of Collectivism, solidarity, and unity. Elements of the Regressive Psyche may also play a role. For these reasons, a substantial majority of American motorists have a strong emotional affinity and attachment to speed limits.

Despite having a strong emotional attachment to speed limits, American motorists generally disregard speed limit signs and instead rely on their instincts for guidance. The behavior of driving according to instincts conforms with American Federal Law:

"No person shall drive a vehicle greater than is reasonable and prudent under the conditions and having regard to the actual and potential hazards then existing." Uniform Vehicle Code 11-801

What is interesting is that American motorists generally obey the standard of UVC 11-801, while at the same time they disregard the ubiquitously posted conflicting standard appearing on speed limit signs. Despite their conformity with Federal Law, many Americans maintain an emotional attachment to the very speed limit signs they disregard en masse. Beneath this behavioral hypocrisy belies the fact that Americans want speed limits, but they don't want to follow them, due to the irrational behaviors stemming from Intrinsic Bias.

If American motorists were rational, they would demand speed limits that conform with proper traffic engineering standards:

1. A speed limit sign (R2-1 safety device) requires a safety predicate, such as an unusually high accident rate, that can only be cured by restricting speed.

2. The speed limit is set according to the 85th percentile (safest speed) by a licensed traffic engineer.

3. The speed limit is enforced and adjudicated according to the standard of UVC 11-801.

Scientific studies have proven that following the above criteria reduces total accidents and fatalities, protects and respects the constitutional rights of motorists, and reduces pollution while conserving billions of dollars in resources. Indeed, there are many benefits to implementing rational speed limits.

The problem with Intrinsic Bias is that it substitutes fallacies for objective knowledge and wisdom. In the case of speed limits, the safe driving standard of UVC 11-801 and the procedures of a licensed traffic engineer, are substituted by a fallacious invented number: The deception begins with a spurious number invented by a politician, the spurious number is enforced by police under a false pretense of safety, followed by an unconstitutional adjudication of innocent citizens. The entire process is based on a fallacy, and perpetuated by fallacies, resulting in a very significant loss of resources and lives.

The phenomenon of Intrinsic Bias explains the human pattern of irrational, indiscriminate, and fallacious actions. This pattern of behavior was so damning that evolution was forced to respond with a mechanism that directly addresses the problems of Intrinsic Bias. This mechanism effectively replaces all forms of fallacy with objective knowledge, which is knowledge obtained from logic, reason, and scientific methods of inquiry. Objective knowledge is relatively free from all subjective influences, and so it is perfectly aligned with the operation of the universe, and the ultimate truth of reality. This type of knowledge has great utility, power, and efficacy, especially as a support for the primary role of the other Enneatypes. However, the most important aspect of objective knowledge is that it opens the door to wisdom.

The constructive utilization of objective knowledge, such as the development of new medicines, opens the door to wisdom. And the application of objective knowledge, such as performing scientific experiments, solving intractable problems, or supporting the primary objectives of other Enneatypes, contributes to the accretion of wisdom. That is because the application and constructive utilization of objective knowledge leads to the development of the wisdom that is necessary for the human species to advance socially, economically, and psychologically.

Wisdom averts the pitfalls, mistakes, accidents, and blunders that are associated with all forms of fallacy. Without wisdom, humans are blind to how the world works; and doomed to repeat the same mistakes over and again. Wisdom has eliminated many of the scourges that have plagued humanity for eons, including all manner of superstition, faulty cultural precedents, irrational thinking, and the absurdities of fallacy. Wisdom has opened the door to innovations, problem-solving, and the development of new skills that have allowed Modern Humans to advance beyond the plight of Early Humans. As the physical manifestation of this wisdom, Fives embody wisdom in their primary role as advisors and consultants to all other Enneatypes.

Primary Role: Advisor

The key to understanding Fives lies in the fact that wisdom is a function of rational, logical, and objective thought. As the specialists in rational thought, Fives are the human mechanism by which objective knowledge and wisdom are acquired, stored, and disseminated to all other Enneatypes, by and through their primary role as advisors. The role of Advisor requires that Fives assert intellectual jurisdiction in all subjects by mastering all areas of objective knowledge and organizing that knowledge in meaningful ways, as a support for the functional roles of each Enneatype.

The absence of wisdom was the crux of all Early Human problems, especially the lack of objective knowledge that was necessary to properly identify, analyze, and solve the Nine Factors of Extinction. The enormity of their ignorance is not a profound revelation by itself, because the notion that Early Humans were irrational creatures with a shallow fund of knowledge is rather intuitive. However, what is not necessarily intuitive was that lurking behind each of the Nine Factors of Extinction was a fundamental absence of objective knowledge and wisdom.

As an example, consider the immense amount of objective knowledge that is required for Eights to fulfill their primary role as conservationists. Eights focus on the conservation of all resources, including food, energy, shelter, tools, weapons, clothing, metals, jewelry, and anything else that has intrinsic value. Since objective knowledge is a prerequisite to resource conservation, their ability to conserve resources is proportional to their objective knowledge and wisdom in each resource category. And conversely, when there is misinformation, ignorance, or fallacy, resources are squandered, destroyed, or otherwise wasted. For these reasons, Eights are dependent on Fives to provide the objective knowledge and wisdom necessary to fulfill their primary role as conservationists.

Every Enneatype relies on Fives to provide the objective knowledge and wisdom that is necessary to fulfill their primary roles. Thus, the primary role of Fives is to provide the intellectual support, knowledge, and wisdom needed by all Enneatypes. This arrangement ensures that every Enneatype has the intellectual support necessary for success in their primary role. Thus, it is incumbent upon Fives to, directly or indirectly, support the primary role of each Enneatype. However, the primary role of Fives is not limited to providing support to all other Enneatypes. On the contrary, Fives have jurisdiction as advisors on all subjects, to address all manner of problems, conundrums, and scourges that might arise.

Many of the scourges confronting Early Humans had mortal consequences, and perhaps the most important of these were related to nutritional deficiencies, disease, poisoning, physical injury, and infection. The common denominator among these problems is that early and appropriate intervention can prevent the unnecessary loss of lives, assuming sufficient knowledge and wisdom. Some elaboration may help to underscore these points.

In the case of nutritional deficiencies, the relevant wisdom is that the human body requires 90 essential nutrients: 60 essential minerals, 12 essential amino acids, 16 essential vitamins, and three essential fatty acids. A deficiency in one or more of these nutrients will eventually lead to one of the 600+ known deficiency diseases or one of the 30,000+ nutritional disorders. Because it is very difficult to ensure adequate consumption of all nutrients, the universe of deficiency diseases and disorders would have affected nearly 100% of Early Humans at some point during their lifetime.

Early Humans suffered exposure to a variety of environmental poisons from various sources, such as plants, animals, insects, and water. Encounters with these poisons were often fatal, mostly because an antidote was not available or because it was not timely. In cases of survival, the victim may have a permanent disability due to irreversible neurological damage such that they are unable to fend for themselves. For these reasons, poisonous exposures were a significant cause of death and disability among Early Humans.

Hunting, fishing, and foraging for food were dangerous activities that occasionally resulted in injury. When the injury involved a broken bone, appropriate care was required to prevent disability, such as resetting the bone and immobilizing the fracture so that healing can take place. A failure to render the appropriate care was a direct cause of permanent disability among Early Human populations.

Viral and bacterial infections were responsible for a significant portion of the premature deaths occurring in Early Human populations. Many deaths could have been prevented by simply adhering to proper protocols, such as wound cleaning and protection, and following proper hygiene. And most could be prevented by the timely administration of medicines and natural remedies.

Unfortunately, Early Humans did not possess the necessary objective knowledge and wisdom to address the many scourges that continually eroded their populations. The arrival of Fives marked a seminal moment in human evolution, as Fives immediately began the task of acquiring, maintaining, and disseminating the knowledge and wisdom necessary for the elimination of the scourges that had persisted for eons. Fives perform these tasks in their role as Advisors to those who require contemporaneous knowledge and wisdom.

To put this discussion into historical context, the role of Advisor appeared under various monikers such as Shaman, Witch Doctor, Medicine Man, and Healer. In modern times, this role corresponds to that of a medical doctor. Although Fives are the natural incumbent for the role of a Shaman or a medical doctor, there are many other types of advisory roles that are possible for Fives. In modern times, the primary role of Fives aligns with any position requiring a depth of knowledge and wisdom, such as advisory roles in the fields of finance, economics, law, engineering, medicine, anthropology, and many more.

From a practical perspective, Fives are the knowledge experts of the Enneagram, which requires a relentless pursuit of new knowledge, encompassing every imaginable field of human endeavor. For this reason, Fives are often found at the cutting edge of most disciplines, especially those disciplines that are still expanding and evolving. Fives generate Wisdom because of the functional adaptations discussed next.

Functional Adaptations

Although Intrinsic Bias may seem inconsequential in the short run, it has potentially devastating consequences in the long run because of the irrational thinking, poor judgment, and fallacious knowledge that it produces. The remedy for Intrinsic Bias required an amplified, interminable, and hyperactive Thinking Center, which necessarily required the suppression of the Emotional and Instinctive Centers, to ensure that all available energy resources be channeled directly to the Thinking Center. This design is very effective in the prevention of Intrinsic Bias; while at the same time, it resolves many of the secondary factors responsible for irrational behavior, including the limits that are imposed by caloric resources.

Thinking requires a tremendous amount of caloric resources, which are sometimes in short supply, and sometimes not available at all. And even when calories are abundant, the brain tends to fatigue rather quickly. Caloric deficits and brain fatigue were common experiences that played a secondary role in the fallacious thinking that was predominant within Early Human populations. Although these experiences are prevalent in modern times, Fives are mostly exempt, given the functional adaptation for extraordinary levels of mental endurance. The adaptation for extreme levels of mental endurance allows Fives to spend an inordinate amount of hours investigating, formulating, and analyzing complex problems.

Fives have excellent mental endurance due to the sequestration of the Emotional and Instinctive Center, which is highly effective in the attenuation of Intrinsic Bias, while it also ensures that reasoning, logic, and problem-solving are the highest priority. This adaptation explains the prolonged periods of rational thought, analysis, and problem-solving behaviors observed with Fives. Thus, Fives conform mostly to thinking behaviors, thinking endeavors, and thinking tasks, which supports the Endeavor of attaining ever greater knowledge and wisdom.

Emerging from this discussion is the realization that Fives are the most cerebral of the Enneatypes, explaining their attraction to vocations that require extraordinary amounts of mental processing, while at the same time they wish to avoid vocations that have emotional or physical components. However, it is more accurate to state that the Thinking Center eclipses the Emotional and Instinctive Centers: An arrangement that imposes experiential limits on Fives, as everything they experience channels thru the Thinking Center. Emotions are thoughts to be analyzed, and the body moves because of mental calculations. Because Fives operate in this manner, they have a narrower path of vocational options as compared to other Enneatypes.

The medical professions are the most important for Fives, given that a primary function of Fives is to be the doctor in their community. However, the role of the doctor has become exponentially more complex since ancient times. The increase in complexity is evidence that Fives have gained traction in their intended role, and they are getting help from the other Enneatypes, who are now acting as surrogates in the primary role of a medical doctor. Thus, the other Enneatypes have displaced Fives as primary care providers, thereby allowing Fives to specialize in advisory, teaching, consulting, and researching functions. This trend will continue, especially since many Fives have a strong preference for research, and thus are less inclined to pursue a primary care role.

Although Fives have a strong tendency toward avarice, they do enjoy the mental exercise that writing provides, especially because it allows the explication and development of their favorite concepts, ideas, and theories. Many Fives learn that putting their knowledge into a written format can be personally rewarding, not just in monetary terms, but because writing contributes to the accretion of knowledge. Many obscure works of non-fiction, such as college textbooks in the fields of anthropology, botany, and etymology, are written by Fives. And that is because Fives enjoy mastering the obscure areas of knowledge that are often neglected by others. However, this does not mean that Fives are not interested in mainstream subjects. On the contrary, Fives enjoy the challenge of furthering the body of knowledge in almost any subject of endeavor; this is true because Fives evolved to master, contribute to, and disseminate knowledge as Advisors to all Enneatypes.

There are many areas of business that require wisdom, including accounting, economics, finance, and information technology. Indeed, Fives often become knowledge experts for their company, where they serve as an indispensable human resource. Fives are often rewarded with promotions, as they have very competitive skills, especially in fast-growing companies that require knowledge expertise. But overall, Fives are the type least likely to be found working in commerce. Part of this is because there are fewer Fives in the population, but more important is that Fives tend to be very introverted, which effectively reduces the probability of success in a world that values extroverted traits and behaviors. For these reasons, the key for Fives rests with finding work that aligns with their evolutionary purpose.

Fives are indispensable to fields that require advanced levels of knowledge and wisdom; and thus, they enjoy a competitive advantage in fields that require objective knowledge, logical thinking, and mathematical ability, such as the areas of science, technology, engineering, and mathematics (STEM). That is because they possess a significantly greater endowment of the basic skills that are crucial for success in the STEM fields.

In various fields of science, such as biology, chemistry, geology, astronomy, and economics, Fives are particularly skilled at developing the predictive algorithms and statistical models used in a variety of applications. Thus, Fives develop algorithms and models for the geological industries of oil and gas, mining, and seismology. Fives also bring the logical thinking necessary for conducting scientific investigations, experiments, and research, which explains why many Fives find success as researchers in the pharmaceutical and biological sciences. And as a rule, Fives are indispensable in just about every corner of the scientific world. The only exceptions that might apply would be in the scientific endeavors that require working or living under extreme conditions. An example would be archaeological field researchers, who spend their days digging for bones in extreme climatic conditions, which exceeds the constitutional abilities of most Fives.

Fives are also very competitive in the technology fields, especially information technology (IT), where there are infinite opportunities for solving problems. Software development and engineering is an area of IT where Fives bring an exceptional ability to solve some of the most intractable problems. That is because encoding software is an exercise of knowledge, using an exacting degree of logic and mathematics, that allows a computer to perform a function. Thus, the adaptation for knowledge, logic, and mathematical ability positions Fives with a competitive advantage in the growing field of software engineering.

Most areas of engineering require strong mathematical ability, including software, civil, aeronautics, mechanical, chemical, biomedical, electrical, and many more. Having a strong mathematical ability is a basic requirement, and prerequisite, for study and work in almost all fields of engineering. That is because engineers use mathematics to solve problems, discover solutions, and validate their work. Of the many aspects of engineering, it is the analysis, computing, and mental processing that most attracts Fives to this type of work. But there is a very important point that explains why Fives are dominant participants in engineering, technology, and science.

The most important point in this discussion is that Fives, when evaluated as a group, outperform all other Enneatypes in mathematics. Indeed, Fives are responsible for many of the significant advances in mathematics and for solving the most intractable mathematical problems. These contributions can be confirmed using the information and methods presented in this book to diagnose the Enneatype of the most heralded mathematicians in the past 100 years. Performing such an exercise reveals that the most prolific and awarded mathematicians are Fives.

Evaluating Fives as a group must be done with caution because for every Five that is in the public eye, multiple others are unseen. That is because Fives are the most reclusive of all Enneatypes, and they will generally shun recognition, distinction, and awards of any kind. Indeed, many Fives will solve a difficult problem or conjecture, and then keep it to themselves, never sharing their insights or discoveries with the world.

Because Fives are highly skilled in mathematics, they are very astute problem solvers par excellence. The adaptation to think logically, store knowledge, and solve problems provides widely transferable skills. These skills are especially useful in many collateral applications, ranging from strategy games to the development of advanced technologies. The game of chess is a good example where Fives enjoy a competitive advantage due to the functional adaptation for logic, thus explaining the dominance that Fives enjoy in the game of chess.

Fives are the predominant owners of intellectual property, as they possess more knowledge per capita than all other Enneatypes, although much of their knowledge is very obscure. Nonetheless, all of the knowledge attained by Fives serves an evolutionary purpose and constitutes intellectual property that is often copyrighted or otherwise becomes a patent. For these reasons, Fives are the primary source of all intellectual property attributable to Modern Humans.

Basic Delusion

The amplification of the Thinking Center sets in motion a perceptual apparatus geared toward the rationalization of all phenomena. Rationalization is one of the primary methods employed by the Thinking Center to convert subjective knowledge into objective knowledge. Fives have an interminable capacity for rationalization, which enables them to accumulate vast amounts of objective knowledge and wisdom so that they can fulfill their evolutionary purpose as Advisors to all other Enneatypes.

A key consequence of the amplification of the Thinking Center is that it creates a mindset that focuses on what is unknown, vague, or nebulous. Indeed, Fives are incessantly curious and are unable to rest until they have rationalized their perceptions, observations, and experiences. Their curiosity sets in motion a perpetual cycle where new information is acquired, rationalized, and stored as objective knowledge. Unfortunately, the process of rationalization cannot keep up with the flow of new information.

Humans evolved to fear the unknown, as a necessary survival instinct, to protect the organism from possible harm. The fear of the unknown resides in the Thinking Center, and the amplification of the Thinking Center also amplifies the fear of the unknown, setting in motion a perpetual drive to rationalize. An exaggerated and perpetual fear of the unknown, in the absence of an actual threat, constitutes the fundamental delusion of Enneatype Five.

Interpersonal Relationships

Although Fives score very high in mathematical intelligence, they score in the average or below average range for other types of intelligence such as verbal, emotional, and proprioceptive. Such disparities are the result of physiological adaptations designed to channel all available energy to the brain, leaving very little energy for feelings, emotions, self-expression, and relationships. And there is scant energy left over for physical activities. However, this does not mean that Fives are unable to engage in relationships and sports, but it does mean that Fives lack efficiency, economy, and reciprocity in other domains. Understanding Fives from this perspective, and accepting it without conditions, may allow new possibilities to emerge.

As a general observation, Fives are the most reclusive of all Enneatypes, in part because they like to spend all their time thinking, analyzing, and postulating about what is happening in the world. They would rather think about the world, and avoid risks to their safety, rather than engage with the world. Their thinking does sometimes drift toward relationships, feelings, and emotions, but those become abstractions that must be isolated, dissected, and analyzed. And yet, many Fives are unaware that they do not experience feelings and emotions in the same way as other Enneatypes. The result is a mostly reclusive type that is viewed by others as a bit of an oddity.

The character Spock in the Star Trek series depicts the oddity of Fives. Although Spock is half Vulcan and half-human, he identifies, emulates, and embodies the Vulcan traits of being unemotional, cold, calculating, penetrating, sharp, deductive, and logical. Although these traits are a perfect match for his role as the science officer aboard a starship, Spock portrays the difficulties that Fives encounter in various types of relationships. His difficulties arise because he has a single-minded focus on work while rejecting and denouncing all emotion because emotions are unnecessary, superfluous, and illogical. Because Spock will only entertain professional relationships that are within the purview of his commission, he is considered an oddity by his colleagues who counsel, cajole, and amuse themselves at his expense. The character Spock is not too far from the experiences and realities of many Fives.

It should come as no surprise that many spouses of Fives describe them as lacking emotion, romance, and sensitivity to their feelings. And many complain that Fives have difficulty with intimacy. Despite these issues, many people enjoy the intellectual stimulation that Fives provide. Curiosity, research, and a love for knowledge is often the starting point for long-lasting relationships with Fives. When common intellectual interests are shared, Fives can be very loyal lifetime partners, willing to share the fruits of their wisdom with their family.

Thinking requires a great deal of energy, so many Fives need an inordinate amount of time alone each day, often retreating to their own space at home. The predilection with thoughts creates very strong introverted tendencies, such that they often fail to see and act on the developmental needs of their children, resulting in a parenting style that is laissez-faire. This parenting style may be ok with some children, such as Enneagram Fives, Nines, and Ones; however, it is not an effective parenting style for many other Enneatypes, including Sixes, Sevens, and Eights. The key point here is that the deficiencies in the laissez-faire parenting style are less damaging to children who are type Five, Nine, or One.

The laissez-faire parenting style of Fives is often balanced by their spouse, who is usually type One, Two, Four, or Six. Thus, the parenting style deficiencies of type Five are offset, and compensated to some degree, by the parenting style strengths of their spouse. Of course, some other combinations do occur.

Overall, Fives can be very loyal friends, spouses, and family members. But they need their space and time alone to be respected. Many Fives have been known to disavow all ties with the outside world when their privacy, space, and boundaries are not respected. It is very unfortunate when that happens because as a group, Fives are the most prolific intellectual contributors of all Enneatypes.

Psychology of Fives

Primary Ego Trait: Wisdom

Regressive Traits: Avarice

In Search Of: Missing Knowledge

Focuses On: All that is unknown

Basic Fear: Confusion

Basic Desire: To be wise.

Basic Need: Security.

Stress Reaction: Withdrawal to the safety of their mind.

Sense of Self: I'm ok if I know the answers

Motto: The wise will survive.

Mental Model: Knowledge is the greatest resource.

Motivations:

- To acquire new knowledge.

- Explore their curiosity.

- Be a source of wisdom to others.

- Solve difficult problems.

- Investigate the facts.

Physical Characteristics

When viewing Fives as a group, the first thing to notice is that they are slight of build, having one of the lowest BMI of all Enneatypes. There are several reasons to explain the low BMI, with the foremost reason being that the brain burns more calories than other body tissues, leaving Fives with relatively few calories for muscle-based activities. Along these lines, the physiology of Fives is designed to channel an inordinate amount of energy resources to seeking, acquiring, processing, analyzing, and storing massive amounts of data. Thus, Fives evolved a low BMI as part of a constitution that channels calories to the brain at the expense of other physiological functions.

Although most Fives have at least one idiosyncrasy, in the spirit of respecting privacy, this discussion is limited mostly to defining idiosyncrasies and why they occur. An idiosyncrasy is a physiological abnormality or aberration. In the case of Fives, idiosyncrasies are the result of the evolutionary adaptation in the physiology that favors thinking over physical function and performance. Examples include nervous ticks that may occur anywhere in the body, various nervous system disorders, some types of congenital disabilities, sensory deficits, and various types of disorders that may affect gait, mobility, or activities of daily living.

Another observation with Fives is that they tend to dress in the most basic attire. That is because Fives avoid unnecessary expenditures, as they prefer to live a parsimonious existence, and this is especially true when it comes to the clothes that they wear. If they are forced to wear conventional clothing, Fives will typically choose very traditional clothing that is devoid of any flair or style. But for all other occasions, Fives typically choose clothing that is either very basic or bohemian. For these reasons, many Fives may be found shopping at thrift stores as opposed to the local shopping mall.

Facial Tension

The facial tension for type Five, from the perspective of the observer, consists of an asymmetrical tension in the right corner of the mouth. The tension effectively elevates the right side of the mouth, and moves it closer to the midline of the body, giving the appearance that the right side of the mouth is asymmetrically smaller than the left half of the mouth.

Identifying and Diagnosing Fives

Because Fives are very reclusive, it is difficult to estimate their numbers. However, Fives are estimated to be approximately 6% of the USA population. For these reasons, Fives are not likely to be encountered in a public setting. Nonetheless, Fives can be identified based on the following characteristics:

1. Presence of an idiosyncrasy.
2. Bohemian, monochromatic, or basic clothing style.
3. Crass, nihilistic, pessimistic, very serious demeanor.
4. Below average BMI
5. Anxious, nervous, or repetitive movements.

CHAPTER 11

TYPE SIX: THE PROTECTOR

Endeavor: Protection

"An ounce of prevention is worth a pound of cure." This famous quote from the venerable Benjamin Franklin is a pearl of timeless wisdom that emphasizes the universal truth and importance of prevention. This wisdom was especially true for Early Humans, because despite the dangers they faced, almost every malady affecting them was preventable. The key to preventing the maladies was to properly identify, assess, and manage all species of risk.

The key to understanding Sixes turns on a detailed understanding of risk management, beginning with the evolutionary purpose that it serves: To Protect various entities from all species of risk. The keyword is *Protect* because every risk management initiative serves the fundamental purpose of providing protection, sometimes directly and sometimes indirectly. Thus, the Endeavor to manage risk is succinctly stated as an Endeavor to provide Protection. And it necessarily follows that the evolutionary purpose of Sixes is to serve and Protect others.

A good example of proactive risk management is demonstrated by life insurance companies every day. Life insurance companies provide risk management services that enable individuals to proactively manage the financial consequences that are associated with the death of a benefactor. In managing the risk of death, life insurance companies agree to indemnify for lost future income, in exchange for payments made in the interim. Thus, life insurance companies Protect their customers from the financial risks that are associated with death.

Risk management is a continuous process of assessing, evaluating, and quantifying risks. At the core of this continuous process is the always watchful eye of vigilance. Vigilance is a mechanism of intelligence, operating within the ego, that operates as a filter. This filter identifies, intercepts, and marks anything that might pose a danger or risk. At the core of Vigilance is an interminable questioning that creates a heightened awareness of danger, hazards, or risks. The experience of heightened awareness is similar for all Enneatypes, but there are some notable differences in the integration of vigilance into the egoic structures for each Enneatype. Thus, the best way to understand vigilance, especially as it pertains with Sixes, is with examples of how it operates within each Enneatype.

Eights are vigilant for threats to the resources they defend, manage, or protect, and Nines are vigilant for the problems and conflicts associated with the Regressive Psyche. Ones are vigilant for unlawful or disorderly behavior, whereas Twos are vigilant for nonconforming behaviors that violate the prevailing code of conduct. Threes are vigilant for sloth, nepotism, and free riders, while Fours are vigilant for entrepreneurial opportunities. Fives are vigilant for fallacies, and Sevens are vigilant for opportunities to optimize resources. These generic examples demonstrate how vigilance is restricted, focused, and tethered, as a secondary function of the ego, to the human endeavor and specialization for the Enneatypes.

In the case of Sixes, Vigilance is the predominant specialization of the ego, such that is becomes the primary full-time function of an ego that continuously assesses, evaluates, and quantifies risks. Anything that constitutes an endogenous, exogenous, or heterogenous risk is identified, assessed, and evaluated. This type of vigilance has more depth, breadth, and scope when compared to the vigilance experienced by all other Enneatypes. And it is untethered, unrestricted, and free, such that it becomes an ever-watchful, penetrating, and interminable questioning that serves to alert, mitigate, and manage all species of risk affecting humanity. These are the distinctions that differentiate the Vigilance of Sixes from the common vigilance of the ego.

The introduction of a hypervigilant ego, as embodied by Enneatype Six, was the evolutionary answer to the age-old question of how to manage risk. That is because Vigilance is the cornerstone, and a prerequisite, for all agencies of risk management such as insurance companies, fire and police departments, safety consultancies, hedge funds, Departments of Justice, and a multitude of other risk management enterprises. In every case, Sixes played a key role by sponsoring, developing, or inventing these risk management agencies, as Sixes are the ultimate agency of risk management.

The Vigilance embodied by Sixes forms the cornerstone of a triadic system that works seamlessly as an effective mechanism of risk management: A passive component that filters experiential data for possible dangers or risks; an active component that serves to alert others of potential dangers and risks. And a risk management component, that seeks to prevent harm by creating and implementing proactive risk management strategies and enterprises. This discussion continues with examples of how Vigilance can be used to counter all manner of endogenous, exogenous, and heterogenous hazards.

In the case of endogenous hazards, Early Humans could have prevented plant and animal poisoning by maintaining Vigilance when traversing high-risk areas, and bacterial infections by maintaining good hygiene such as washing hands before eating and after defecation. Prevention of parasitic infections requires wearing shoes and cooking meat thoroughly. In each of these cases, the risk of injury or death can be mitigated or eliminated by adopting the necessary preventative measures.

Vigilance is also highly effective in preventing injuries and deaths from exogenous hazards. For example, the adoption of safer hunting techniques such as hunting in large groups or using coordinated attacks against danger-ous game, implementing new techniques such as trapping and avoiding risky hunting scenarios such as nighttime hunting are all effective in the prevention of injuries and deaths. Avoiding hazardous activities such as walking on thin ice, walking near sinkholes, or climbing trees is also effective in preventing injury and death. Preventing exposure-related injuries and deaths requires the avoidance or preparation for thunderstorms, blizzards, and hail. Managing the direct threats posed by animals requires adherence to safety protocols such as traveling in groups of at least four people. And so on.

Vigilance can also be effective in the prevention of heterogenous maladies such as the crimes perpetrated within a social group. Criminologists have confirmed that criminal behavior generally starts at a young age, and as the perpetrator advances in age, the frequency and degree of the crimes often escalate. Thus, the best way to prevent and manage the heterogenous risks is to detect criminal behavior at the early stages to ensure the timely administration of behavioral correction and rehabilitation. Doing so is effective in the prevention of the more serious crimes of assault, rape, and murder.

There is no question that the passive and active components of Vigilance had a positive impact on the safety, security, and viability of human populations. That is because Vigilance includes the steps that are necessary to attenuate, disperse, manage, and negate all species of risk. Understanding these steps, and some of the forms they may take constitutes the first step in understanding the primary role for Sixes. The next section introduces some of the social roles that allow Sixes to perform their evolutionary function of risk management.

Primary Role: Risk Management

From the perspective of risk management, it would have been very sad to witness the plight of Early Humans, because they suffered from a very limited degree of social cooperation. The lack of social cooperation meant that Early Humans operated by the principle of *each to their own*, which meant that there was no safety net in case of injury or disability, thus perpetuating a very selfish culture of survival. The situation was dire, necessitating the evolution of a mechanism that sponsored a specific type of cooperation that supported a mechanism for risk management.

Because social cooperation is a predicate for many types of risk management strategies, Sixes evolved the character traits necessary for securing the necessary cooperation within their communities; coupled with the ability to use that cooperation to create, implement, and supervise various types of risk management initiatives. An example of a basic risk management strategy is the compact formed within a social group, whereby specific social guarantees are contracted, in consideration for specific types of economic cooperation. The most basic of these agreements began to appear soon after Sixes arrived.

Perhaps the earliest example of a basic risk management strategy was the social compact for the provision of security services. This agreement would involve the assignment of a person, basically a security guard, to keep a watchful eye during the time that all other members are sleeping. The security guard could be designated by rotation, or as a permanent post, depending on the scale of the group. But in many cases, the security guard was probably a Six who sponsored, championed, and volunteered for the position. Of course, Sixes are the natural choice to be the security guard, as this role aligns with the primary role of risk management, and the Endeavor to Protect. Indeed, the basic function of a security guard is to Protect others with Vigilance. This type of cooperative agreement is a prime example of an early risk management program initiated by Sixes.

Another example of an early risk management initiative, sponsored and championed by Sixes, was the cooperative agreements for the handling of illness, disability, and death. The agreement would specify that if a member of the group became ill or disabled, all other members would cooperate in providing the necessary food, shelter, clothing, and care to the aggrieved individual. The agreement could also apply to others who are disadvantaged, such as children who have lost their parents, or the elderly who have no caretakers. Such agreements provided aid, care, and protection to those individuals who suffered a loss, injury, or disability.

The above examples correlate with several modern-day risk management concerns. In the case of the security compact, many companies exist to provide uniformed security guards for hire. The essential job duty of modern-day security guards is to identify threats and hazards and alert others as necessary. However, security guards have no responsibility for mitigating or managing risks, as that responsibility is the domain of police forces, such as law enforcement officers commissioned by local, county, state, and federal governmental authorities. In both cases, security guards and police forces have prehistoric analogs, and these analogs closely resemble their modern-day equivalents.

There are also modern-day analogs to the prehistoric cooperative agreements that covered illness, disability, and death such as a plethora of modern-day insurance companies providing indemnity for illness, disease, disability, work injuries, and death. A closer examination of these concerns reveals that Vigilance is the core function in each case. Indeed, no insurance company can operate without personnel who specialize in performing risk assessments such as actuaries, data analysts, loss control managers, auditors, and so on.

There are many other analogs, some of which are not readily apparent such as the prehistoric analogs corresponding to modern-day hedge funds. Fire departments are another example. In all cases, these analogs were the direct result of Sixes, who sponsored, developed, and created them to serve as institutions of risk identification, assessment, and management.

As the ultimate agency of risk management, Sixes understand that risk is a universal phenomenon, as opposed to a local phenomenon having distinct boundaries or dimensions. Risk is omnipresent, operating in the background of reality, a derivative of the immutable laws of the universe. Given the relative obscurity and pervasiveness of risk, all entities must deal with risk, which creates a demand for the talents and skills of Sixes. A discussion of these obscurities, beginning with the Federal Reserve Bank, will help illuminate the need for the risk management skills of Sixes.

Economists had studied risk management since at least the 19th century when the economic cycles of growth and contraction first gained attention, which led to the emergence of a new branch of economics known as macroeconomics. By the early 20th Century, a consensus was building among economists that economic cycles were preventable with an appropriate risk management system. Shortly after the U.S. financial crisis of 1907, Congress created the United States Federal Reserve System (Fed), for the explicit purpose of mitigating the risks posed by economic cycles.

Congress provided the Fed with three objectives: Maximize employment, minimize inflation, and moderate long term interest rates. Employment, inflation, and interest rates constitute the primary risk factors for an economy. Controlling these risk factors is a very difficult balancing act because efforts to control one risk factor will adversely affect other risk factors. For example, expansive monetary policies are generally helpful in maximizing employment, but they have the downside of increasing long term inflation rates. An attempt to control inflation by increasing interest rates (discount rate) has an unpredictable effect on long term economic growth due to its differential effects on employment and investment. And so on.

Interest rates are often used to effect a change in monetary policy, which introduces certain microeconomic shocks to an economy, as a change in discount rate trickles down to the interest rate charged to various concerns. Microeconomic interest rates contain four components: The inflation risk premium, which is the interest rate that is charged to cover for the anticipated future inflation. A liquidity risk premium, which measures the discount necessary for selling a loan before maturity. A default risk premium, which involves the risk of default by the borrower. And finally, there is the real interest rate earned by the lender. Summing the four components yields the nominal interest rate charged.

Another obscure type of risk is the transactional risk between businesses. Here, the risk is that a company will default on its credit obligations to other companies. To mitigate this risk, a company can sell its accounts receivable to a company that specializes in collecting accounts receivable. The essential role of these companies is to assess, quantify, and price the *accounts receivable risk of default* for their clients.

Companies may also face a multitude of risks related to their inventory. There are at least seven types of inventory risk: Input shortage, shrinkage, excess inventory, supply shortfall, value loss, inherent risk, and channel inventory. Input shortages have severe consequences for many businesses, especially when those inputs are integral to the operation of a business. Shrinkage inventory losses occur mostly with food or perishable inventories. Excess inventory is a very common occurrence across many industries. A supply shortfall often occurs during the holiday shopping season, when demand for a product is greater than anticipated, resulting in lost revenues and profits. Value loss is the depreciation that occurs as a product sits on the shelf. Inherent risk is the possibility that inventory will be lost, stolen, or incorrectly accounted. Channel inventory risk occurs when a channel distributor returns items to the manufacturer because they remained unsold. Severally and individually, these risks are sometimes insurmountable for many companies, leading many to file for bankruptcy every year.

Understanding risk management is the predicate for understanding the Endeavor, specializations, and functional adaptations for Sixes. The risk management examples given in this discussion demonstrate that risk is a universal phenomenon that presents seemingly infinite situations for the skills of Sixes. Understanding risk as a universal phenomenon is indispensable to comprehending the specific ways that Sixes assert, compete, and leverage their unique blend of skills and traits. Next, the focus is to understand the functional adaptations that enable Sixes to manage risk effectively.

Functional Adaptations

Fives and Sixes are both adapted with a Thinking Center uniquely tailored for the duties and responsibilities of their respective roles. But that is where their similarities end, as the Thinking Center is hyperactive in the case of Fives; and suppressed in the case of Sixes. The suppression of the Thinking Center is meant to suppress only certain functions, specifically Cognitive Bias, that impedes the ability to manage risk. Understanding why Sixes evolved with a mechanism to suppress Cognitive Bias is very helpful in understanding their inner psychology.

The Thinking Center receives information primarily from the visual and auditory senses. As a rule, the Thinking Center is a closed system, which means that it is generally closed to new information by default, and opens only when extraordinarily narrow conditions occur. The obtuse nature of the Thinking Center is an evolutionary adaptation, serving multiple purposes, most of which are related to the survival of the individual. The fact that Early Humans were obtuse, thick-headed, and close-minded creatures adversely affected the accumulation of new information, knowledge, and wisdom. And it meant that the process by which humans accept or reject new information is subjective, subconscious, and mechanical, which was responsible for a subjective bias within the mind: Cognitive Bias.

Cognitive Bias occurs when there is an identification with past or future information, at the expense of recognizing and accepting the truth of what is happening moment to moment. The tendency to identify with past or future information is ubiquitous among humans because the mind operates according to object relationships. From the perspective of the mind, everything is an object, including the self. Thus, the mind is composed entirely of information from the past, and the identification with that information allows for functioning in the present, albeit a limited degree of functioning.

Of the many problems caused by Cognitive Bias, perhaps the most consequential is that it attenuates the vigilance necessary for risk management. That is because vigilance is a probing, searching, and investigatory type of intelligence that depends on free, unrestricted, and open access to new information. Vigilance operates as an active form of awareness that seeks to acquire, collect, and register what occurs from moment to moment. Thus, when there is vigilance, there is an openness to the flow of new information as it arises moment to moment.

Cognitive Bias obscures what is happening in the present moment, because it restricts, impedes, and rejects the free flow of information, and replaces it with the object relations of past experiences. If Cognitive Bias were a drug, it would be a barbiturate, because it has a tranquilizing effect that reduces sensation, vitality, and awareness. The drug-like effect of cognitive bias provides a familiar sense of self, while at the same time it has an insulating effect, that aims to protect against experiences that have the potential to interfere with an inner sense of security.

The suppression of the Thinking Center eliminates nearly all traces of Cognitive Bias: Creating space for new information, stimuli, and experiences pursued through a newfound sense of curiosity, inquiry, and investigation. This adaptation opens the mind in a rather permanent and perpetual way to new knowledge that would not be possible otherwise. The perpetual curiosity, inquiry, and investigation for new information, stimuli, and experiences precisely define the functional adaptations needed to Protect others. And it also explains why Sixes are deeply insecure, as they have been stripped of Cognitive Bias, leaving them exposed to seeing risk without filters, buffers, or defenses.

The elimination of Cognitive Bias introduces a new form of bias, known as Cognitive Dissonance: The inability to reach logical conclusions due to the attenuation of rational processes. Sixes are afflicted with Cognitive Dissonance by design because it produces the results that were intended by evolution, which in this case was the elimination of Cognitive Bias. The result is that Sixes are functionally adapted to avoid the types of spurious, fallacious, and false conclusions that are so commonly accepted as conventional wisdom. Collateral with this result is a perpetually open-ended thinking style that errors on the side of caution by avoiding, evading, or denying anything that might constitute a false conclusion.

Emerging from this discussion is the revelation that Sixes possess a unique cluster of skills, abilities, and personality traits. To understand these functional adaptations, and how they enable Sixes to perform in their primary role as Risk Managers, recall from the previous discussion that the cooperation of others is a primary hurdle to overcome in the implementation of any risk management strategy. To clear this hurdle, Sixes possess a unique blend of personality traits meant to endear cooperation, including curiosity, openness, loyalty, and commitment. However, at lower levels of functioning, Sixes can be hawkish, condescending, abrasive, demeaning, and cowardly. Whatever level they may be functioning, Sixes are functionally adapted to use their personality traits to great effect.

Although securing cooperation can sometimes be an impossible mission, Sixes employ many methods to bring others within their purview, depending on the level of their psychological development. Overall, Sixes employ a non-threatening, non-confrontational, "matter of fact" demeanor that quickly puts people at ease. Sixes also use an artful blend of humor and banter to align others with their cause. With an easy-going demeanor and lively... unpredictable and humorous conversational style, Sixes have a diplomatic knack for negotiating and securing the cooperation of others.

A diplomatic example rests with the legacy of Benjamin Franklin, a founding father of American independence, who is a testament to the negotiating prowess of Sixes: It was Benjamin Franklin who played a prominent role in securing French cooperation and assistance during the revolutionary war, which culminated in the Treaty of France in 1783. Without Benjamin Franklin's diplomacy, the French may have abstained the war effort, and America's independence from Britain was uncertain.

The late comedian Sam Kinison provides another example of the endearing traits of charm, wit, spontaneity, and unpredictability that Sixes exemplify. Sam was unique among comedians, partly because very few Sixes perform comedy routines, but also because Sam swapped religious sermons with comedy. Sam is best known for his unpredictable rants and screaming, a centerpiece of his unique performance, that brought rave reviews and notoriety. To the end, Sam delivered a wry point of view in a very sarcastic, unapologetic, brash manner that earned him great fame, affection, and distinctions.

Although Sixes have a knack for diplomacy and securing the cooperation of others, they are not well suited for certain categories of occupational endeavors. To understand why this is true, recall the difficulties that Sixes have in reaching a certainty of facts, forming valid arguments, and making logical conclusions. These difficulties are laid bare in many vocational scenarios, especially jobs that require a strong degree of certainty and confidence.

The fundamental problem for Sixes stems from their lack of certainty in their knowledge, character, skills, and abilities. Foremost is their uncertainty about their character, which traces to their affliction with Cognitive Dissonance, and the lack of courage, confidence, and will that it produces. These character traits manifest as an ambivalent, procrastinating, self-doubting, overly cautious, and indecisive personality. Overall, these character deficiencies affect the ability to function in many occupational scenarios.

Sales Representatives are required to be decisive, encouraging, and confident about the products and services that they sell. Sixes are mismatched for sales positions because they tend to be indecisive, discouraging, and uncertain about all things in the world. Their fundamental incompatibility with sales positions becomes clear when considering the three phases of sales. In the phase of sales identification, Sixes struggle because they see the world thru the lens of risk, subconsciously seeing customers as a potential hazard rather than a potential transaction. The situation does not improve as the process continues.

Consider the situation where a customer raises questions or has doubts about whether a product will meet their needs: Sixes may overreact or agree with the customer. For these reasons, Sixes struggle to overcome customer objections; and in many cases, they are likely to say something that repels interest. If they do manage to overcome all objections, Sixes may be inconsistent in the closing phase of the sales process. In some situations, they may do what is required and appropriate, closing the sale with an effective technique. But just as often, they are likely to use the wrong closing technique, if they attempt to close at all.

When Sixes enter the medical professions, they often pursue roles where they can be involved in preventative medicine, which aligns very nicely with their Endeavor to Protect. These roles include that of a primary treating physician, an internal medicine specialist, and medical researcher. However, roles or specialties that require certainty of results, or the expression of certainty, would be very difficult for Sixes; thus, it is rare to find Sixes working as surgeons or in acute care environments.

Sixes sometimes enjoy writing, as confirmed by Benjamin Franklin and his Poor Richard's Almanac. Sixes can be prolific writers for almost any genre, including fiction and non-fiction; indeed, they often find success in subjects that are shrouded in mystery. That is because enigmatic subjects, or subjects where the facts are still in question, invites Sixes to do what they do best: Question, speculate, and surmise. Indeed, many Sixes find success when writing on fictional subjects such as UFO's, horror stories, and futuristic science fiction.

Military service that involves dangerous combat situations, especially combat on the front lines, can be very difficult for many Sixes. Recall that Sixes are risk-averse, and seek to avoid, evade, and escape any situation that poses a threat to their safety or security. Thus, placing Sixes on the front lines of combat against their protest will be met with avoidance, evasion, or paralytic behaviors that will endanger the lives of other soldiers who might depend on them. Militaries around the world should take note of this fact.

When taking the specialization, primary role, and functional adaptations into account, many important revelations begin to emerge, all pointing to the fact that Sixes are the ultimate agency of risk management. Some of the best examples have already been given, such as the discussion of insurance companies, with the key point from those discussions being that insurance companies and Sixes are both agencies of risk management. However, insurance companies are not necessarily the best example of organizations that are created by Sixes to manage risk.

From a risk management perspective, religion is an effective way of managing the risks associated with human behavior. Religious organizations created, founded, and perpetuated by Sixes are without question the least understood phenomenon depicted in this book. Some of these organizations have the characteristics of a cult. However, there is a certain irony of risk involved in the naming of these organizations, as many are fiercely protective of their brand, and some will go to any length necessary to continue what they consider to be a religious prerogative. For these reasons, this book will not cover the religious organizations that have been created by Sixes. However, everyone should understand and appreciate that multiple mechanisms for religion evolved in response to the Nine Factors of Extinction.

The key point of this discussion has been that risk management takes many different forms, and operates at many different levels, depending on the complexity of risk involved. And the greater the complexity, the greater is the level of expertise that is required to manage those risks effectively. Indeed, the highest echelons of risk management require an advanced degree of acumen, for which Sixes are specifically adapted, thus explaining their many accomplishments and achievements. Armed with a bounty of knowledge, experience, and wisdom, Sixes bring a plenary perspective that is fresh, insightful, and penetrating. For these reasons, many of the world's experts and gurus are Enneatype Six.

Basic Delusion

The previous chapter discussed how fallacious thinking prevented Early Humans from acquiring objective knowledge and wisdom. The problem with fallacious thinking is that it leads to spurious, erroneous, or false conclusions. However, fallacious thinking is not always a problem. Many times, the problem is simply a mistaken fact, improper procedure, carelessness, or other type of human error. The most intractable problem was that Early Humans were closed-minded, meaning that they were not open to new information, facts, or experiences. Indeed, Early Humans were hardheaded, thick-skulled, obtuse individuals who were very set in their ways. These traits prevented them from absorbing new knowledge, even when readily handed to them, that might allow them to manage risk more effectively. Thus, a mechanism that sponsored an open-minded approach for accumulating objective knowledge and wisdom was needed.

One of the side effects of controlling Intrinsic Bias is that it creates a vacuum of rational thought, logic, and reasoning. Thus, the ability to assess facts, apply logic, and form valid conclusions is reduced substantially in Sixes. However, this does not mean that Sixes do not engage in rational thought, because they certainly do, but it does imply that they have serious limitations in all activities related to basic cognitive processing. However, these limitations mostly affect the endpoint of the cognitive processing continuum.

At the beginning of the cognitive processing continuum, an assessment of the facts takes place, which necessarily involves an iterative process of research. During the process of gathering information, new questions arise that creates a need for additional research. With their endless questioning, doubting, and skepticism, Sixes ensure that all relevant questions are answered, leaving no stone unturned. However, the endpoint of the cognitive processing continuum where logical conclusions are formed is generally not accounted for by Sixes, which creates a behavioral pattern of endless questioning, inquiry, and reasoning. Thus explaining the difficulty that Sixes have in completing certain cognitive tasks and why they are fearfully uncertain about their own inner experience, spirituality, or character! Without a fundamental sense of certainty, Sixes are prone to perceiving the world as risky, unsafe, and dangerous. The perception of risk, danger, or hazards, in the absence of an objective threat, constitutes the delusion for type Six.

On a physiological level, Sixes have a heightened perception of risk that instigates a never-ending loop of inquiry, questioning, doubt, and skepticism. This never-ending loop means that Sixes are always appraising, calculating, and evaluating risks. Indeed, Sixes possess the needed physiological adaptations for risk management.

Interpersonal Relationships

In previous discussions, an outline of the hazards that confronted Early Humans was presented, which included the interpersonal category of heterogenous hazards. The heterogenous hazards include all manner of interpersonal risks, such as the risk of emotional abuse, various degrees of physical abuse, and capital offenses such as murder. Because of their adversity to risk, Sixes naturally seek to minimize all facets of risk in their life, especially regarding the heterogenous risks.

Risk adversity is associated with a cluster of personality traits, including that of being overly suspicious, cautious, ambivalent, indecisive, evasive, and procrastinating. Collectively, these personality traits tend to create problems when Sixes interact with colleagues, friends, and family. That is because most people have some basic expectations, such as trust, when they interact with others. Most people take offense with those who are suspicious, evasive, or unduly cautious and this is especially true in intimate relationships, which partly explains why Sixes have a higher frequency of relationship difficulties relative to other Enneatypes.

But fortunately for Sixes, they have some positive relationship traits that ameliorate some of their regressive traits, thereby providing some sense of balance. Traits such as loyalty and commitment enable Sixes to enjoy many types of positive, rewarding, and mutually beneficial relationships, especially in their love relationships, where many Sixes enjoy a lifelong marriage that embodies love and trust. And on the question of compatibility, it is estimated that more than 90% of Sixes will pair with Enneatypes One, Five, and Nine; while it is extremely rare for Sixes to pair with Fours.

Because Sixes wish to avoid heterogeneous risks, they try to avoid interactions with people who have character deficiencies, faults, and flaws. Sixes are very good at detecting character aberrations, which explains why they avoid Fours, a type known to struggle with interpersonal relationships. Sixes are most attracted to individuals with a strong character, very few faults, and a high tolerance for skepticism, suspicion, and caution.

Ones are the type with the strongest character, as they tend to be punctilious, dignified, and ethical. Sixes can sense that Ones are the exemplars of law and order, so they can relax and let their guard down, allowing for a relationship to develop. Where they often differ is that Sixes tend to question authority, whereas Ones align themselves with authority, but these dispositions tend to balance one another. Apart from their respective views on authority, Ones and Sixes get along for the most part and can be an effective parenting team.

Nines are perhaps the best match for Sixes because they possess many complementary personality traits such as trust, patience, and supportiveness. Sixes are the least trusting of all Enneatypes, and Nines are the most trusting, so this combination brings a sense of balance and symmetry to the relationship. Nines are also very receptive and patient with all the reactionary venting that Sixes project into their relationships. And in situations where Sixes might go overboard with reactionary venting, Nines are quick to listen, advise, and provide unconditional encouragement and support. These behaviors go a long way toward allaying the fears and insecurities that Sixes bring into their relationships.

Sixes and Fives are also compatible, mostly because Fives do not exhibit the gross character flaws found in other Enneatypes. Fives are low risk for the types of abusive, philandering, tempestuous affairs that Sixes wish to avoid. They often find compatibility thru shared interests, common goals, or social affiliations, such as work, school, or academic life.

Although Sixes enjoy many facets of parenting, there is a bit of hypocrisy involved in their role as a parent. The hypocrisy begins when Sixes question authority, as a matter of general discourse, thus endorsing this behavior in their children. Problems later arise when their children present a challenge to their authority, creating an irreconcilable dilemma that tends to impeach their credibility as a parent. Other parenting issues arise when Sixes are too restrictive, inconsistent, and they inadvertently project their insecurities onto their children. But overall, Sixes are responsibly committed to nurturing and supporting the growth and development of their children.

Psychology of Sixes

Primary Ego Trait: Vigilance

Regressive Traits: Cowardice

In Search Of: Certainty

Focuses On: Contradictory facts

Basic Fear: Catastrophe

Basic Desire: To be protected

Basic Need: Security

Stress Reaction: Complaining; throttled anger

Sense of Self: I'll be ok if I stay out of harm's way.

Motto: Better safe than sorry.

Mental Model: There are no stupid questions.

Motivations:

- Escape the problems, dangers, and risks of the world
- Verify their friends and enemies.
- Find something to believe.
- Be a support for others.

Physical Characteristics

Risk management requires a strong, stout, and durable body due to the very demanding tasks of guarding, protecting, and defending others from harm, injury, and death. That is why evolution has endowed Sixes with a constitution that has, apart from Eights, the most strength, endurance, and toughness. And this explains why Sixes have BMI scores that are second only to Eights.

The next to notice about Sixes is their lack of eye contact. They have an evasive, avoidant, and shifty demeanor when they are in unfamiliar situations, around new people, or under stress. In public speaking engagements, they will often look at the ceiling as a coping mechanism for their anxiety, fears, and insecurities. And Sixes are the type most likely to display the collateral signs of anxiety, such as pacing, tapping feet, swaying, and stepping back and forth.

As a group, Sixes have some eccentricities that can vary tremendously from individual to individual. The overall pattern to these eccentricities stems from the inherent sense of uncertainty that they carry. It's as if Sixes use their bodies as a source of courage to confront their inner fears. In one moment, they may be walking with a very casual posture, and in the next moment, they may be walking with their head tilted to the side.

From most vantage points, Sixes tend to be very neutral in appearance, as they generally wish to avoid anything that might attract attention, harm, or violence. Evasiveness affects their choice of clothing, hairstyle, and accouterments. However, because Sixes are the most unpredictable of all Enneatypes, they often have a flair for clothing, jewelry, hairstyles, automobiles, and housing that is Avant-Garde.

Another distinction is a receding hairline in men. The hairline for male Sixes sometimes begins to recede in their twenties, going from the front to the back, until there is just a small patch of hair left on the back of the head. However, this is not a confirming identifier.

When observing a group of Sixes, they would likely engage in some humorous banter, given their jocular disposition, zany unpredictability, a penchant for improvisation, and unsurpassed wit. They are also the least compliant, as each tends to ignore authority, and do their own thing. But you can always get their attention by sounding the fire alarm.

Facial Tension

Sixes have the only facial tension that does not create an asymmetry in the face, as it is located at the bottom of the chin, making it relatively obscure to the untrained eye. The identification of this facial tension requires some training, and a great deal of practice, making it the most difficult physiological feature to identify among the Enneatypes.

Identifying and Diagnosing Sixes

Sixes are estimated to be only 8% of the U.S. population. They spend most of their time at school or work because they are very hardworking. As a rule, Sixes are rarely found engaging in high-risk activities such as skydiving, parasailing, spelunking, downhill mountain biking, helicoptering, shooting ranges, drag racing, scuba diving, or other very dangerous activities. However, Sixes do enjoy the safest of places, such as churches, malls, restaurants, grocery stores, theaters, work, and home. The following can help to diagnose Sixes:

1. Above-average BMI.
2. Poor eye contact, or shifty demeanor.
3. Signs of anxiety: nervous tapping, fidgety behavior, evasiveness, etc.
4. A pattern of wit, charm, or unpredictable behavior.

CHAPTER 12
TYPE SEVEN: THE OPTIMIZER

Endeavor: Optimization

Despite millions of years of evolution, Early Humans were unable to solve the three basic conundrums of fallacies, risk, and scarcity. The Endeavors of Wisdom, Protection, and Optimization evolved to solve these conundrums. Each of these Endeavors operates within a specific locus of time: Fives are focused on the past, Sixes focus on the present, and Sevens focus on the future to match the locus of time for the factor of extinction from which they evolved. Fallacies are a function of the past, risk is a function of the present, and scarcity is a function of the future. For these reasons, Fives, Sixes, and Sevens are members of the *Time Triad*.

Time plays an important role in the functioning of Fives, Sixes, and Sevens. In the case of Fives, the ego applies logic, reason, and analysis to historical information, as a method for acquiring the objective knowledge and wisdom needed to unravel, analyze, and debunk the various types of fallacies. Sixes apply Vigilance in the assessment, analysis, and implementation of risk management strategies based upon current events, or what Sixes sometimes describe as *Presence* or the *Now*. However, scarcity is a unique type of economic problem:

> **Scarcity**: A condition of limited resources that imposes mental, emotional, and physiological hardships on a group.

Scarcity is a unique type of problem that cannot be solved by the Endeavors of Wisdom and Protection alone. Scarcity is a multivariate phenomenon that is resolved by an economic process of resource optimization. The optimization of resources requires a forward-looking, anticipatory, and strategic type of intelligence, that utilizes experiential knowledge obtained thru reconnaissance, to develop strategies, plans, and solutions to the problem of scarcity. The specialization in this type of intelligence necessarily requires the acquisition of experiential, worldly, and terrestrial knowledge that can be used to overcome the effects of scarcity. Thus, Sevens accumulate knowledge through direct experience and then formulate strategies, plans, and solutions that can be used to resolve scarcity.

Time plays an important role in the functioning of Sevens, as their ego applies logic, reason, and analysis to the experiential, worldly, and terrestrial knowledge that they have acquired, as a method for developing strategies, plans, and solutions to forestall any recurrence of scarcity. A proactive approach is necessary for several reasons, with the main reason being that scarcity has potentially catastrophic effects. As an example, consider the effects of food scarcity: Physical activity immediately declines and ceases within a short time. The implication is that scarcity requires prevention, but specifically a preventative strategy that is spontaneous, forward-looking, and predictive.

Preventing a scarcity of future resources is paramount to human survival. To prevent scarcity, Sevens must arm themselves with the knowledge that is relevant to understanding scarcity, especially its causes and potential solutions. This knowledge is terrestrial, and so it requires physical knowledge of the world that can only be obtained from direct experiences and travel, as those are most relevant, expedient, and reliable. And because this knowledge is experiential, terrestrial, and tangible, it is best described as *Intelligence*.

To understand the importance of Intelligence, recall the example of Neanderthals during the time of major climate change, near the Strait of Gibraltar 24,000 years ago. A major reason that Neanderthals became extinct was due to their lack of Intelligence. In this context, Intelligence would have provided a plan for how to effectively deal with the sudden changes occurring in the local habitat of Neanderthals. Such a plan would be part of the Intelligence put together by Sevens, such as an assessment of game migrations and dwindling forage, followed by a formulation of strategies that would be effective in reversing the effects of scarcity.

No matter the cause of scarcity, whether it was ELE's, changing climates, or the threats posed by a neighboring tribe of hominids, scarcity was responsible for many bottlenecks and extinctions. The evolutionary answer was the introduction of a mechanism for Intelligence, which enables Sevens to meet the heavy burden of protecting all humans from the deprivations of scarcity. This mechanism is forward-looking, experiential in nature, and strategic in accomplishing the goal of reversing scarcity.

Intelligence gathering is a critical behavior among Sevens because it supports the Endeavor of Optimizing resources, which is the evolutionary strategy for preventing, mitigating, and managing scarcity. The Intelligence gathered by Sevens has many uses within the Endeavor to Optimize resources. The following discussion outlines some of the primary uses of Intelligence in the modern world.

Primary Role: Optimization

As a conundrum of grave consequences, scarcity was responsible for the evolution of a new set of human behaviors that forms a process composed of three phases: The first phase is reconnaissance, which is the collection of specific Intelligence on the factors that might influence or be a direct cause of scarcity. Intelligence is then used to identify solutions, develop appropriate strategies, and then analyze the costs and benefits of each strategy. The third phase is the execution of a strategy that aims to prevent, mitigate, or reverse the effects of scarcity. Thus, the first phase of Optimization involves reconnaissance, the second phase is strategic, and the final phase is actionable.

The best way to understand this process is to walk thru a hypothetical situation that occurred many times since the arrival of Modern Humans. The hypothetical setting for this scenario occurred some 20,000 years ago when a Seven named Lightfoot is found living in a tribe composed of 250 members. Lightfoot lives in a valley that extends to the north and south at least 100 miles in each direction. His only known neighbor is about 30 miles to the north, a tribe composed of about 200 members, from which he has had little communication. High mountains are to the west, and a vast, hot, very dry desert runs east. His tribe is facing food scarcity because of a drought that began three years earlier, causing the local river to dry up in the summer, forcing game to migrate beyond the tribes hunting perimeter. The situation for this tribe is dire, as many of its members are experiencing the effects of malnutrition.

As a Seven, Lightfoot has already explored the mountains, desert, and valleys in all directions. During all his travels, Lightfoot found very little variation in resources, except for the area inhabited by the village to the north. The village to the north resides at the confluence of two small streams, which supports a large forest that contains many fruit trees. Thus, the members of the tribe to the north have a better life because of an abundance of fruit trees, vegetation, and small game found in the forests. However, the tribe to the north is not so friendly, and they are very protective of their land and resources. All attempts to trade with the tribe to the north were unsuccessful.

Lightfoot meets with the Chief of his tribe, to explain the reconnaissance he obtained over the years. He goes into detail about the topography, specifically how it would be difficult to relocate their tribe. Any relocation would require more than 200 miles of travel, assuredly reducing the ranks of the very young, weak, and elderly. And there is an imminent risk that relocation would worsen their plight. After weighing all the options, they decide that the best option is to conquer the tribe to the north.

The Chief asks Lightfoot to prepare a strategy, including details on the military mission that will be required. Lightfoot has assessed the situation in detail, knowing that a force of at least 50 men will be needed to overcome the tribe to the north, assuming an advantage of surprise. The only way to gain the advantage of surprise is to travel thru the mountains and then descend to the east during the cover of night, launching an early morning surprise attack just hours before dawn. A stealthy approach will allow them to accost and depose the leader of the tribe, and assuming there is no further resistance, the use of violence will be unnecessary. The Chief admires this strategy and gives his approval. Lightfoot assumes the role of Lead Warrior during a war ceremony, and then prepares and leads the tribal warriors on the fateful mission. As the mission unfolds, the tribe to the north surrenders because of superior tactics, resulting in the unification of the two tribes.

The story of Lightfoot brings many important lessons about scarcity. Foremost is that Intelligence is indispensable to assess the available options. And fewer options are available to those who wait until scarcity has already arrived. And if there is no Intelligence, there may be no options available which might have been the tribe's fate without the Intelligence provided by Lightfoot. Fortunately, the two tribes avoided any loss of life, and economic resources merged, resulting in a certain degree of social and economic parity. However, the post-war merging of tribes was a suboptimal outcome.

An optimized outcome would require that both tribes enter into a mutually beneficial economic compact, basically a trade agreement, that allows both tribes to flourish based on their competitive advantages. A trade agreement would be the optimized outcome because trade always leads to an increase in the standard of living for all participants. The mutual benefits of trade have been studied, detailed, and expounded extensively by many economists.

The important point here is that the optimized outcome always depends on mutually beneficial trade agreements. All other outcomes are less than optimal, including the scenario where the two tribes merged. Even less optimal are those scenarios involving loss of life, as life is the most precious resource. For these reasons, there is a direct correlation between economic Optimization and the conservation of human resources. That is because economic optimization is inversely proportional to the loss of life. Thus, a hierarchy regarding the Optimization of outcomes emerges:

Unrestricted Trade Agreement
Limited Trade Agreement
Relocation, greater resources, no casualties
Voluntary assimilation/merging
Relocation, greater resources, with casualties
War, no casualties
War, minor casualties
War, massive casualties

The hierarchy of outcomes provides a basic example, with the understanding that reality provides an infinitely variable array of options. This ranking includes the implicit understanding that human resources are the most important from an economic perspective. It also depicts options such as the possibility to relocate to places of greater resources that may not exist. Those options would be absent in the ranking, under the assumption that Lightfoot could not relocate his tribe to a new location having much greater resources, thus affecting the total number of options available. Regardless, the ranking shown above contains certain assumptions and scenarios that were not fully delineated here.

Several points emerge from this discussion with the foremost being that Early Humans were not successful partly because they possessed no mechanism to optimize the allocation of resources under the ever-constant threat of scarcity. That is because evolution had not created a mechanism for economic cooperation, commerce, and trade between individuals and groups. Without these mechanisms, the Optimization of resources was not possible, which exacerbated and exposed Early Humans to the ravages of scarcity.

From an economic perspective, Sevens optimize economic resources by acting as a catalyst for trade; and if that fails, other options are considered and executed as necessary. Thus, the core function of Sevens is to optimize resources thru competitive trading activities; and if that fails, then resources are subject to competition using involuntary methods such as war. Because Sevens act as a catalyst for trade, and as a last resort, they become a catalyst for war; they are aptly named the Trader or the Optimizer. However, the term Optimizer is preferable because the Optimization of resources is the overarching prerogative of this Enneatype.

The primary role of resource Optimization has many dimensions, facets, and levels, and so it presents a variety of challenges that require a unique set of skills related to the phenomenon of scarcity. Sevens are infinitely capable of addressing the problems associated with scarcity, including different strategies for resource allocation, trading initiatives, cooperative agreements, strategic planning, and so on. For these reasons, Sevens possess traits, abilities, and skills that support and encompass all matters related to trade, commerce, and war.

Part of their primary role is to use their specialization in Intelligence to support military operations. In this context, the terminology of military intelligence and the Endeavor of Intelligence are very similar. And when viewed from this perspective, it becomes clear that war serves the purpose of eradicating scarcity, by optimizing resources to those possessing superior power, technology, and civilization. Indeed, history teaches that a primary method for eradicating scarcity has always been to raid the food, weapons, tools, and land of neighboring tribes. Raiding a neighbor has proven itself to be an overwhelmingly successful method for eradicating scarcity, leading to the specialization in skills that are necessary for that Endeavor.

As the Optimizer, Sevens evolved to be an integral part of the natural selection process, as they are the mechanism by which resources are tracked, cataloged, and optimized. The Optimization of resources is part of the natural selection process that endorses the strongest genes, specifically the genes needed to survive ELE's, bottlenecks, and wars. Thus, the Optimization of resources includes a mechanism of competition, whether it is accomplished thru trade or accomplished thru war. Either way, evolution has endorsed competition as the mechanism by which resources are allocated to the fittest, strongest, and most advanced, as a means for perpetuating the human species.

There are nearly infinite ways that Sevens work to optimize resources. A book could be devoted to this subject, shedding light on resource Optimization across industries, countries, and the planet. Indeed, many economists have already expounded on this subject. However, the focus here was to shed light on the primary role of Sevens, along with their basic methods of operation, to illuminate how they fulfill their evolutionary purpose of trade and resource Optimization.

Functional Adaptations

The story of Lightfoot highlighted a range of possibilities for optimizing resources to illustrate the fundamental traits and behaviors that are necessary for the very important role of resource Optimization. That discussion continues with a focus on the behaviors and functional adaptations that are necessary for optimizing resources at the extremes. Recall that the highest degree of Optimization occurs when there is peaceful trading, and the least optimized outcome is the forceful reallocation of resources between social groups. The Optimization possibilities from the highest to lowest, and everything in-between forms a continuum of economic outcomes. This continuum is a function of both economics and psychology.

Trade is the peaceful exchange of resources having equal value, whereas war is the forceful reallocation of resources from the weakest to the strongest. The behaviors necessary for trade and war overlap: Strategic Thinking, an adventurous spirit, an uninhibited approach to life, a materialistic disposition, and the pursuit of experiential Intelligence. Sevens exhibit each of these behaviors as part of the functional adaptations that support the Endeavor to Optimize.

Experiential Intelligence is typically acquired thru the Instinctive Center by way of direct experiences with the physical world, such as thru sports, traveling, occupations, performing experiments, and so on. Although everyone has some capacity for acquiring knowledge in this manner, Sevens are a special case in that they are continuously driven to seek experiential knowledge from all possible sources including books, television, the internet, gurus, friendships, relationships, seminars, exhibitions, sports, hobbies, and so on.

Sevens have certain adaptations that allow them to acquire vast amounts of experiential knowledge, including an evolved physiology of great endurance, and an ability to acquire and process information with great speed. The most important adaptation is the ability to absorb, process, and utilize information faster than all other Enneatypes. Certainly, no other Enneatype can match their speed in the acquisition of new ideas, concepts, and theories for how the world works. The adaptation for quick thinking is a uniquely human trait, especially when compared to the thinking ability of Early Humans.

The Thinking Center is the slowest of the three centers, mostly because it operates at a low frequency, which hinders the ability to absorb, analyze, and utilize information quickly. The sluggish capabilities of the Thinking Center would have been the chief obstacle that prevented Early Humans from solving all manner of problems related to scarcity. Evolution responded with the development of a new mechanism that is unique to Sevens, just as

Vigilance is unique to Sixes and Wisdom is unique to Fives, that couples the Instinctive Center with the Thinking Center to boost the speed at which information is absorbed, analyzed, and utilized.

A good example of the speed of the Instinctive Center occurs in the squinting reflex of the eye, which is reflexively (instinctively) triggered when a moving object approaches the eye. The efficiency of the squint reflex, measured in milliseconds, is a testament to the speed of the Instinctive Center. The speed is partly due to the higher frequency of the Instinctive Center, yielding reaction times that are a fraction of those coming from the Thinking Center. By coupling these centers, the Thinking Center receives a major speed boost for all mental processes.

Faster mental processing provides the necessary foundation for Strategic Thinking, a thinking style that is unique for its speed, tactical, and problem-solving abilities. Strategic Thinking evolved as an adaptation that combines the speed of the Instinctive Center, with logical reasoning, to create an experientially based mechanism for solving problems. The game of chess provides a situation where this mechanism provides a subjective advantage.

Chess is a game of strategy where success is proportional to an ability to formulate, implement, and adopt a strategy for capturing an opponent's King. Success requires the formulation of a superior strategy in response to the strategy put forward by an opponent. The ability to anticipate, adapt, and strategize depends primarily on three factors: Memory, thinking speed, and objective reasoning.

Although memory is a very important factor, it is highly correlated with general intellectual ability, as revealed by many studies of intelligence. Thus, memory capacity or general intellectual ability is a constant that is unique to the individual. To control for this constant, assume that each player has roughly the same intellectual ability, which leaves the variables of thinking speed and objective reasoning unaccounted.

Because Fives have a competitive advantage with objective reasoning, they are more likely to win a chess match against opponents of identical intellectual ability assuming the opponent is not a Seven. In matches between

Enneatypes Five and Seven, assuming equal intellectual and logical reasoning ability, the outcome will depend on the time constraint for the game. That is because a time constraint will necessarily confer an advantage to the player with the fastest thinking speed. Thus, Strategic Thinking provides Sevens with the advantage in shorter games, as against all other Enneatypes having the same intelligence.

Despite having a competitive advantage in playing speed chess, Sevens are not likely to be chess players at all since it is played almost entirely thru the mind, thus involving very little interaction with the physical world. Fives are the type most adapted for chess because they focus most of their energy on abstractions of the physical world, which more closely aligns with the skills needed for chess. However, Sevens are focused on acquiring knowledge of the physical world, at a very rapid pace, as the primary input for Strategic Thinking. The result is that Sevens focus on the acquisition of experiential, rather than theoretical, knowledge of the world.

Strategic Thinking is an ego function, unique to type Seven, that is an integral part of Intelligence. Although everyone has some ability to think strategically, Strategic Thinking is not very effective in most Enneatypes, due to the numbingly slow speed of the Thinking Center. However, in the case of Sevens, the Thinking Center is enhanced by a unique connection with the Instinctive Center, which substantially boosts the quality, quantity, and speed of their Strategic Thinking ability.

The Endeavor for Intelligence, especially the ability to think quickly, is closely aligned with the traits that are needed to solve the problem of scarcity. For example, consider the amount of time that it would take to distill the infinite range of possible solutions for scarcity down to a short, feasible, and manageable list. Analyzing scarcity and its possible solutions is a daunting task that is susceptible to fallacies, differing opinions, and subjective viewpoints. For Early Humans, it was a near impossibility, especially in consideration of the time constraints imposed by the effects of scarcity.

The Endeavor for Intelligence also includes the skills necessary to act upon, execute, and implement the continuum of solutions to scarcity, from trading initiatives to war. At first glance, the skills needed for trading and war would not appear to be the same. Trading requires a vast knowledge of resources, especially the economic knowledge of the supply and demand for factor inputs, labor, goods, and services. And a professional Trader must have exemplary skills in negotiating. A Trader who possesses exemplary economic and negotiating prowess can create wealth with only their Intelligence. A true story will illustrate this phenomenon.

The late Michael Hirsch was an aficionado of photography who attended various technology exhibitions in the Midwest during the 1980s to 1990s. He would typically appear at a photography exhibition early on a Saturday morning with only a small sum of money and leave at the end of the weekend with a treasure of several thousand dollars and multiple pieces of equipment. In some cases, he would begin with nothing and still achieve impressive results. In every case, Michael utilized his Intelligence to create wealth based simply on the skills that are secondary to the Endeavor of Optimization. And in every case, Michael satisfied the wants and needs of many technology consumers.

The story of Michael Hirsch highlights the functional adaptation for arbitrage, which is an economic activity whereby an economic asset is acquired and then resold for a higher value. Success in arbitrage requires near-perfect knowledge of the supply and demand for economic assets, accompanied by the skills necessary to complete multiple transactions. The innate ability to arbitrage is one of the many functional adaptations within the specialization of Intelligence.

The adaptation for arbitrage closely aligns with the skills needed for sales and marketing positions, which explains why Sevens have distinct competitive advantages in marketing, as they possess the requisite demographic, sociographic, and economic knowledge. Even without formal education, Sevens are often successful in marketing endeavors, as proven by arranging a small group of Sevens to brainstorm an advertising campaign for a client. In a matter of minutes, the fast minds of Sevens will produce a bevy of viable advertising slogans, masterfully integrated into a web of possible supporting media; such as commercials, online advertising, social media advertising, and much more. Sevens can see the synergistic effects of various media, within a multidimensional framework that is not immediately apparent to others, due to a prescience this is unique among the Enneatypes.

In addition to having the powers of prediction and foresight, Sevens possess all the fundamental skills required to be effective in the three phases of the sales process. In the phase of identifying sales opportunities, Sevens are exceptionally skilled, as they have a natural talent for making conversation with everyone. They relate with a very casual conversational style, so they do not come across like they are trying to sell something, which puts people at ease. During a conversation with a prospective customer, Sevens can surreptitiously weave some questions into the conversation related to the customer's needs, which is an excellent approach for identifying a potential sales opportunity. Many customers come away with the feeling of hanging out with a friend, rather than the experience of a commercial transaction. For these reasons, Sevens are a textbook example for relating to potential sales customers.

After the first phase, Sevens are generally very adept at positioning products in such a way to match the features with a customer's needs. Although this phase takes some practice, Sevens will typically rise faster than all other Enneatypes. And Sevens are quite astute in overcoming customer objections and closing deals. The only issue for Sevens is that they may sometimes be a little pushy in closing a deal, and that may backfire by turning some customers away. However, if Sevens can slow down the process, and match the closing technique with the personality type of the customer, they can be extremely effective closers.

At the other end of the resource Optimization continuum, Sevens use their Intelligence to develop effective war strategies by adopting, modifying, and implementing the necessary tactics for success. The skills required for wartime operations are closely aligned with the skills necessary for trading, in that both require a vast amount of experiential knowledge, including the geographic, logistical, terrestrial, and economic facts on the ground. And both require thinking that is fast, precise, informed, and decisive.

Sevens are the natural tacticians of war, as they embody the Intelligence that is indispensable to formulating the tactics and strategies that are necessary for addressing the effects of scarcity. What is not often understood is that the Endeavor for Intelligence aims to conserve human resources, as highlighted in the story of Lightfoot, who developed the tactics and strategy necessary to avoid a loss of lives. Indeed, Sevens wish to avoid scarcity of all resources, including the very human resources they evolved to Optimize.

Basic Delusion

Sevens are perpetual, hyperactive, and materialistic extroverts who never seem satisfied with what they have. They are perpetually driven to acquire what they don't have and upgrade what they do have, in a never-ending cycle of consumerism. It doesn't matter what they have attained, or what they have accomplished; it is never enough. Sevens are easily mesmerized by new technologies, devices, and accouterments. When they see a shiny new object, they must have it, and they will go to great lengths to get whatever captures their fancy.

Many Sevens become blinded by their drive to consume, to the point of addiction, which is a direct reflection of the primary role of Optimization. The greater the scarcity of resources, the greater that Sevens will be driven to optimize resources. Thus, the attitudes and behaviors of Sevens are a direct reflection of the relative degree of scarcity that persists in their locale. Beneath the façade of these attitudes and behaviors lies a basic fear of scarcity.

Eons of experience with scarcity eventually formed an archetype in the collective subconscious of humanity. Emanating from this archetype are feelings of deprivation, and the agony of pain that goes with it, that are the precursors of death and destruction. The archetype of scarcity is a very powerful and moving experience; as is the evolutionary response manifesting as Enneatype Seven.

Sevens have a basic fear of scarcity, which creates a bias within the ego because it effectively filters, reduces, and limits the ability to appreciate the resources that are available in the world. The inability to appreciate resources is tantamount to an inability to perceive resources, meaning that Sevens will subconsciously perceive a scarcity of resources regardless of the diversity, density, or abundance of resources available. And it is the subconscious perception of universal scarcity, as opposed to scarcity as a local phenomenon, that constitutes the delusion for type Seven.

Interpersonal Relationships

On a subconscious level, the basic fear of scarcity creates a perpetual desire for economic improvement. The most expeditious, efficient, and expedient method for economic improvement is thru trade, thus explaining the basic behaviors of engaging, negotiating, and transacting observed with Sevens. Thus, the compulsory drive to trade, whether it is ideas, experiences, goods, or services, naturally colors their interpersonal encounters as opportunities for some degree of economic improvement.

The interminable need for economic improvement becomes a limiting factor in all their interpersonal interactions, as Sevens seek economic gains whenever possible, which sometimes leads their trading partners to feel exploited. These behaviors are sometimes considered narcissistic, even by many psychologists, instead of a manifestation of the basic fear of scarcity. This understanding can be helpful to those having close relationships with Sevens.

From the perspective of Sevens, people are simply another economic resource to be optimized thru trade. Optimization opportunities take many forms. Exchanging commercial knowledge is the most common, followed by the bartering of personal goods and services. Bartering is where many of the complaints against Sevens arise because they sometimes fail to meet their obligation, or they change the terms after reaching an agreement. But the greatest economic advantage is obtained when Sevens can purchase items at prices that are significantly below market value. These items are then resold at full market value (arbitraged), yielding substantial profits because of their superior knowledge in market pricing.

Thus, the basic behavioral framework exhibited by Sevens is to negotiate, remarket, and upsell for a profit. This framework necessarily requires a substantial degree of personal detachment from subjective feelings, emotions, and compassion. Silly notions like fairness, ethics, and honor do not apply.

That is because Sevens believe everyone is equal under the laws of commerce; thus, all transactions between willing and consenting adults results in substantial benefits to each party. Everyone who trades is a winner; there are no losers.

Economic theory coincides with the Seven point of view that trade does benefit all willing and consenting parties. However, what matters is that evolution has endorsed trade as the primary method to optimize resources. Sevens are the primary mechanism for trade, and once this is understood, a newfound appreciation for Sevens will emerge. Appreciation for Sevens is overdue, as they embody the fundamental economic behaviors that are critical to the success of the human species.

As a group, Sevens are very witty, playful, and fun to be around. They are consummate socializers and are known to be the life of the party. These traits are attractive to the opposite sex, so Sevens often attract attention, but they are perhaps the type least likely to engage in long term relationships. The problem for Sevens stems from their commercial orientation, and how that colors their attitude, priorities, and behaviors in relationships. For these reasons, Sevens are known for passing through many relationships until they reach a stage in their life where they feel satisfied enough to settle down. However, for many Sevens, that day never comes.

Relationships with Sevens are generally short, inconsequential, and unemotional affairs that center around activities such as traveling, sports, and recreational pursuits because these are the easiest ways to keep Sevens engaged. After the fun is over, things tend to fizzle very quickly, as Sevens move on when they get bored. And it is very easy for Sevens to become bored.

Although relationships with Sevens are often negative, it's important to avoid generalizing the characteristics of a group to every individual in that group. There are certainly many Sevens who have enough self-awareness to know their tendencies and deficiencies in relationships. Those that do will work on developing greater intimacy, emotion, caring, compassion, and commitment to complement all their positive traits. But those Sevens are rare to find.

In the area of parenting, Sevens are known to provide stimulating and exciting experiences for their children. But where Sevens tend to fall short is in providing a structured, disciplined, and consistent environment where children can flourish. That is because Sevens are the type most likely to divorce, leaving their children to deal with a broken family. But if there is a strong marriage, then Sevens can be part of a very effective team that stimulates, inspires, and motivates children to actualize their potential.

Sevens have the most compatibility with Enneatypes One, Six, and Nine. Ones help Sevens to settle down and adopt a strict, disciplined approach to life. Sixes bring an unpredictable sense of humor that Sevens enjoy, while at the same time inspiring them to settle down. And Nines are patient and accepting of all the little eccentricities that Sevens bring into their relationships. Other relationship possibilities with Sevens do occur, but they are less likely to endure.

Emerging from this discussion is an understanding that fear of scarcity is the foundation for the attitudes, behaviors, and character traits associated with Sevens. And this foundation leads to the perception of deficiency, shortage, and deficits of the necessities of life. And out of adversity rises the perspective that conditions can be improved if resources are optimized appropriately. Sevens embody this perspective, and in the process, they become the coercive agents of trade, commerce, and war. All other pursuits, including relationships, parenting, and family, are subsumed by the Endeavor to Optimize the limited resources of the world.

Psychology of Sevens

Primary Ego Trait: Intelligence

Regressive Traits: Greed

In Search Of: Experiential Knowledge

Focuses On: Probabilities

Basic Fear: Scarcity

Basic Desire: To experience everything

Basic Need: Pleasure

Stress Reaction: Various mood disorders

Sense of Self: Plan well, feel well

Motto: The future has unlimited possibilities

Mental Model: The outcome depends on the probabilities involved

Motivations:

- To learn something new every day
- Trading ideas, concepts, theories, and experiences with others
- Overcoming boundaries, limitations, restrictions, and impediments
- Keeping a step ahead of problems, conflicts, and disagreements

Physical Characteristics

Although Sevens have a range of BMI possibilities, many have a very slim constitution that reflects the needs of a very active body adapted for reconnaissance. Having a slimmer constitution is a testament to the unique physiology that supports the drive for experiential knowledge. This phenomenon becomes clear when engaging Sevens, as they are very difficult to keep up with, as they seem to have boundless energy. Threes are the only other Enneatype that comes close to the boundless energy exhibited by Sevens.

Sevens have exceptional proprioceptive abilities, which enables them to perform at above-average levels concerning sports, recreational, and other physical endeavors. Their proprioceptive abilities provide excellent agility and physical coordination, that when combined with their fast minds, allows them to become proficient in almost any sport or recreational activity. These skills are highly transferable to many vocations that require an exacting degree of timing, agility, and proprioception.

In consideration of the superficial characteristics, such as their outward appearance, Sevens have a pattern of presenting themselves in a very commercial, affluent, and material kind of way. The presentation of affluence means that Sevens can typically be found wearing the latest trends in clothing, including the best name brands, no matter the cost. Accouterments of affluence, such as the latest smartwatch, cellphone, and jewelry, are noticeably visible in many cases. Their proclivity towards displays of affluence reflects a penchant for indulgences that allay their fears of scarcity.

Female Sevens tend to be well dressed, but with a low maintenance appearance, and minimal use of makeup. Male Sevens tend to have thinning hair, especially by age 50, with some balding possible after middle age. The combination of these superficial characteristics enables Sevens to blend into their environment unnoticed.

Facial Tension

The facial tension for type Seven is like type Five, except that it occurs on the left side of the mouth. The tension has the effect of moving the left corner of the mouth closer to the midline of the body. Thus, the left half of the mouth will appear to be smaller than the right half of the mouth. Also, the left half of the mouth may appear to be raised or elevated, relative to the right side of the mouth, especially while talking.

Identifying and Diagnosing Sevens

Although Sevens are very extroverted and outgoing, as would be expected for a type that specializes in trade and war, they are estimated to be only 2% of the population in the USA. Thus, there are few opportunities for diagnosing Sevens. Nonetheless, the following traits can be used to identify Sevens:

1. Material displays of affluence (expensive jewelry, watches, cars, etc.)
2. Humorous disposition.
3. Skittish, unsettled, fidgety, flighty demeanor.
4. Positive, optimistic, futuristic thinking.
5. Very rapid speech, rapid eye movements, nervous jerks, etc.

CHAPTER 13

THE GENIUS OF EVOLUTION

The journey to understand the Nine Factors of Extinction, and how evolution responded with the Nine Human Endeavors, is not complete without a basic understanding of how the Enneatypes are organized, arranged, and combined. Recall the arrangement of the Endeavors around a circle, with every human being corresponding to a unique point on the circle, and each point corresponding with two Enneatypes. The Endeavors are combined according to a certain logic, to achieve a certain balance, parity, or synergy between the Enneatypes, which becomes the subject of further analysis.

The primary condition for placement of the Endeavors is the maximization of synergies. For example, it would make no sense to combine the Endeavors of Conservation and Protection, because this combination has very little synergistic value. Likewise, there is little to be gained by combining Entrepreneurism with Optimization, Civilization with Economization, or Economization with Conservation.

The second condition for placement of the Endeavors is to create a system of checks and balances that aims to prevent any potential abuses of power. Also, the overall system must balance the Enneatype negatives and positives to achieve a certain harmonic balance. From this perspective, each Enneatype has the potential to be a check against another Enneatype, depending on their placement within the system. Thus, the precise arrangement of the

Enneatypes is crucial to maximizing the synergies, parity, and objectives of the overall system.

The key point in this discussion is that the relationships formed between the Endeavors are just as important as the Endeavors themselves. This assertion is not fully explained here, because the objective is to identify some of the most important congruities in the Enneagram system. The following discussion gives some basic clues to the genius, and supreme intelligence, that was behind the evolutionary process of Enneciation.

Eight/Nine

As a mechanism of resource conservation, Eights have the responsibility of ensuring the allocation of resources to the strongest, fittest, and most capable members of the human species. To meet this responsibility, Eights possess the capability of adapting and transforming to the needs of their environment, resulting in a type that has an astonishing ability to wield power. However, evolution recognized that concentrating power in this manner can be problematic, necessitating a mechanism to hold it in check, and that mechanism is Enneatype Nine.

Nines have a power that is equal to or greater than that of Eights. The key to understanding this truth is to realize that Eights assert power in physical ways, whereas Nines assert power by way of a stabilizing attitude. The relationship between supernovas and black holes provides an analogy, where supernovas represent the physical power of Eights, and black holes represent the stabilizing power of Nines. In this analogy, Nines have a power that is analogous to a massive black hole, with all the gravity that entails.

Eights project power in extroverted ways, whereas Nines project power in introverted ways, so combining Eights with Nines is an effective way to govern the concentration of power. As a practical matter, the Eight/Nine combination ensures the exploration of peaceful means before there is an escalation in violence. Thus, the Eight/Nine combination ensures that non-violent options for resource allocation are given a priority, as opposed to the approach of Early Humans, where violence was the primary method of resource allocation.

Nine/One

On the surface, Nines seem to draw their power from having a nearly flawless character. However, a close examination of Nines reveals several weaknesses, with perhaps the chief weakness being an absence of purpose, which manifests as an attitude of apathy. A closer examination of Nines reveals a fundamental lack of psychic structure, that if left unchecked, would leave them grossly incapable of performing their primary role. Evolution recognized this dilemma and paired Nines with the most structured of all Enneatypes.

Ones are responsible for creating the structures of civilization, especially the basic pillars of education, government, and religion. Combining Nines with Ones provides the structure necessary for Nines to matriculate throughout society, enabling them to perform their basic role of counseling others. Indeed, many of the roles that Nines fill are complementary with the structures created by Ones. For example, the primary role of counseling is complementary to the role of religion, as counseling is one of the fundamental services provided by many priests. Evolution recognized that the primary roles for Nines and Ones are complementary, and combined them into a very powerful force that aims to eliminate barbarism.

One/Two

Ones are the embodiment of discipline, order, and structure, which are the foundations of civilization, and the prerequisites to eliminating barbarism. One of the primary functions of civilization, not previously mentioned, is to provide the structure necessary for Commerce. Indeed, it is the role of government to provide the social structure, institutions, laws, and regulations that are necessary for Commerce to flourish. For these reasons, government and commerce are inextricably linked.

Twos help to fulfill the important prerequisites to civilization, which are the behavioral standards relating to language, communication, etiquette, and conduct. As an example, consider that without a common language, it would be nearly impossible to implement the three pillars of civilization. More important is that Twos hold Ones in check, by preventing government and religion from infringing on the freedom of the individual, thereby balancing the needs of civilization with the interests of Commerce.

The marriage of Ones and Twos reflects the importance of balancing order, structure, and the rule of law with the needs of Commerce. This arrangement prevents the errors that might occur when either function is out of balance, such as governments that squelch the fundamental economic behaviors responsible for Commerce. Or the economic damage that might occur when one culture attempts to subvert another culture. Finding the right balance between these prerogatives is accomplished when Ones and Twos are combined.

Two/Three

Twos create the basic social structures necessary for Commerce by way of the time-consuming and tedious process of social networking. Twos develop social networks that are both broad and deep, which explains why they tend to have far more interpersonal contacts during their lifetimes, as compared to the other Enneatypes. The key point is that Twos hold the keys to social power, as they Endeavor to Govern others, and this power has the potential for abuse thru nepotism, partisanship, and other social biases.

Threes hold Twos in check by ensuring that commercial decisions are merit-based, instead of by nepotism, favoritism, or graft. Threes embody the principles of merit, and champion meritocratic causes, by emphasizing the importance of an incorruptible system that values the contributions of the individual. As Economists, Threes evolved to root out the inefficiencies, waste, and incompetence connected with the abuses of social power.

The Two/Three combination reflects a fundamental truth, which is that economic growth and excellence requires a balanced approach. There is a fine line between a culture that inspires excellence and a culture that is fraught with nepotism, hubris, sloth, and free riders. The answer was to combine Governance with a mechanism that emphasizes the Merit of the individual. This combination recognizes the need to balance cooperation, conduct, ethics, and merit in all matters of economic decision making.

Three/Four

The primary directive of Threes is to economize resources, especially human resources, to increase the per capita output of the human species. Significant increases in output are possible by focusing on the economization of factor inputs, which over time will lead to additional increases from economies of scale, specialization, and Pareto Efficiency. Perhaps most important to understand is that the economization of resources evolves alongside changes that occur in factor inputs, innovations, and technology.

When the economization of resources reaches an equilibrium point, where no further increases in output are possible, a catalyst that resets the process is required. The catalyst must be external to the system, such as an innovation that increases economic output through automation, efficiency, specialization, or economies of scale. Fours are the mechanism of innovation, and history provides many examples where Fours have introduced new technologies that have been instrumental to the advancement of the human species.

Because Fours are the mechanism of innovation, they are complementary with the prime directive of Threes; and together, they provide a powerful hedge against economic stagnation. That is because this combination is highly effective in the innovation of new technologies that enhance economic output through automation, efficiency gains, and the deployment of labor enhancing technologies. Here, the focus is to innovate and deploy technologies that will have a measurable impact on economic behavior, economic output, or the economic standard of living for all humans.

Four/Five

At the core of all entrepreneurial endeavors resides a creative spirit that wishes to introduce something new to the world. However, the physical world places very restrictive limits on creative talent, and these limits often take the form of problems or conundrums that must be solved. The solution to these problems often depends on objective knowledge and wisdom.

Fives provide the objective knowledge and wisdom that is necessary to solve all manner of problems and conundrums. This knowledge provides the basic information that is needed by all Enneatypes; however, in the case of Fours, this knowledge is indispensable to the creation of innovations, inventions, and technologies. Without this knowledge, Fours are stymied and unable to achieve their evolutionary purpose.

Because the wisdom provided by Fives is indispensable to the entrepreneurial endeavors of Fours, it was necessary to combine these Enneatypes, thereby ensuring that the introduction of innovations, inventions, and technologies would continue unabated. This combination is responsible for the *inventive mind*, which aims to change human behaviors with inventions that enhance the standard of living, well-being, or general interests of humanity. Indeed, this combination has been responsible for many of the greatest human inventions ever created.

Five/Six

Fives are adapted for the rigorous investigation, reasoning, and logic, formally known as the scientific method, that is necessary to quash the effects of fallacious thinking. This adaptation ensures that Fives are effective at replacing fallacies with objective knowledge and wisdom. However, as the custodians of knowledge and wisdom, Fives are subjected to its corrosive effects, including a manifestly destructive form of nihilism.

Sixes use an entirely different approach to acquire objective knowledge and wisdom. This approach relies on Vigilance, which is a never-ending, relentless, and open-ended inquiry into the present moment. This approach to knowledge is resolute, practical, and timeless, making it effective in the prevention of fallacies, while simultaneously avoiding the problems associated with nihilism.

Because the close-ended thinking style of Fives balances with the open-ended thinking style of Sixes, this combination effectively merges the benefits of the scientific method with the open-ended inquiry of Sixes. This combination ensures that research is conducted thoroughly, while it also places a check on the concentration of knowledge and wisdom. This check is necessary to prevent the corrosive effects of nihilism from replacing all forms of fallacy.

Six/Seven

Sixes use their Vigilance and inquiring minds to develop knowledge that is grounded in the moment. Although this type of knowledge has many uses and applications, especially in the areas of risk management and prevention, it also has many limitations. These limitations become obvious when dealing with certain intractable problems, such as certain types of catastrophic problems that might occur in the future, as these are typically beyond the scope of inquiry and Vigilance.

Among the various problems encountered by humanity, scarcity is unique in that it is an ever-present existential threat that is preventable if detected early enough. Sixes provide the early warning signs for scarcity, which provides more time for reconnaissance and an assessment of options, thereby increasing the odds of survival. However, Sixes are lacking in the experiential knowledge necessary to formulate viable solutions to scarcity.

Combining Sixes with Sevens merges the experiential knowledge required to prevent or reverse scarcity with a mechanism for early detection. Apart from its efficacy in resolving scarcity, the combination of early detection and experiential knowledge is remarkable for its problem-solving power in a multitude of different situations apart from scarcity. These situations include the detection and prevention of many types of disasters, catastrophes, and ELE's.

Seven/Eight

A scarcity of resources has the potential to decimate populations in a very short time. For this reason, Sevens take a proactive, experiential, and logical approach to elucidate the options available. Trading is the option of choice, as it confers the most economic benefits, and provides the best long-term outcomes. War is the least preferable outcome, as it generally reduces the total resources that are available to a species. Between these extremes lies a multitude of possible options, which is a daunting task, even for extroverted Sevens.

Fortunately, Sevens have some help, which is the conservation of resources provided by Eights. The specialization to conserve resources overlaps, and is in direct alignment with, the mandate to resolve scarcity. That is because the activities associated with conserving resources are effective remedies for scarcity. Thus, the Endeavors for Sevens and Eights naturally overlap.

The combination of Sevens/Eights brings a surge of human energy, and synergy, to bear on the problem of scarcity. Compounding these synergies is the fact that both Sevens and Eights are extroverted Enneatypes. Thus, the effect of combining these Enneatypes is multiplied, rather than added, which underscores the importance that evolution has placed on the intractable problem of scarcity.

The Dawn of Enduction

By endowing every human being with two Endeavors, evolution created nine hybrid Enneatypes, within a scientific framework that is as intuitive as it is logical. However, because humanity started with a very limited fund of knowledge, eons of time passed before the Nine Human Endeavors gained the traction needed for substantial progress. Of course, there were many other impediments to progress. Severally and individually, these impediments explain why human progress was excruciatingly slow even after the arrival of the Nine Human Endeavors, such that approximately 190,000 years would pass before humans began keeping historical records.

Viewing history thru the lens of the Enneagram, a deeper appreciation for the struggles of humanity emerges from the rubble of wars, the ravages of disease, and the decimations of famine. Through it all, the Enneagram was the only constant: Guiding, shaping, and empowering humans to persevere the vicissitudes of life. The Enneagram is a constant, in the sense that it provides a consistent process for eliminating barbarism, achieving economic prosperity, and solving conundrums. Because the Enneagram is the foundation of this process, and the process results in a reduction in the NFE, a logical term for this process would be Enduction.

Although the past, present, and future success of the human species is almost wholly dependent upon Enduction, it is perhaps the least understood scientific phenomenon, especially concerning the unity of its operation. The key to understanding this unity is to recognize that it is very fragile, and because of this fragility, it is susceptible to suppression by various factors. Since recorded history, the most important factor of suppression has been the mechanisms of civilization. For example, the Catholic Church was responsible for the suppression of knowledge for much of the past two millennia, while during the same period, many governments instituted policies that interfered with Enduction.

Enduction requires a certain degree of protection for each of the Nine Human Endeavors, so that each Endeavor may function unmolested. Any restrictions that impede the NHE will necessarily restrict Enduction. Thus, Enduction depends on the unfettered operation of the NHE, which in turn depends on the freedom of the individual. For these reasons, Enduction depends on the freedom of the individual.

When the freedoms of the individual are protected, the Endeavors that are unique to the individual may be activated, unleashing the most powerful phenomenon on Earth. But to the extent that individual freedoms are limited, the qualitative contributions made will be limited, and those limits have measurable economic consequences. The first step in measuring the economic consequences of restricting individual freedoms is to identify the specific protections that are necessary for each Endeavor. The following list demonstrates the Nine Protections, which are the basic protections that are needed by each Enneatype:

Eight: Due process

Nine: Association

One: Religion

Two: Speech

Three: Merit

Four: Entrepreneurism

Five: Intellectual

Six: Organizing

Seven: Mobility

Eights require a very structured, transparent, and equitable environment to be effective in their role as Conservationists. Most important is an environment that provides for due process to prevent the abuses of authority that Eights detest. Due process ensures that the rules, regulations, and laws are applied fairly, equally, and judiciously, to ensure that justice prevails. From the perspective of Eights, justice requires absolute objectivity, to ensure that the law is applied uniformly. If there is no justice, there will be no conservation of resources, as Eights view their role of conserving resources to be the ultimate form of justice.

Nines require the freedom to associate so that they can perform their basic role of stabilizing the collective human psyche. Any restrictions placed on the formation of groups, associations, or social enterprises will impede Nines in their primary role. That is because Nines depend on the fundamental freedom of association that allows them to matriculate into the various spheres of human endeavor. Thus, their efficacy in the Endeavor of Stabilization is directly dependent on their ability to associate, and matriculate, into all aspects of human endeavor.

Religion is perhaps the most important pillar of civilization, as it is very effective in maintaining law and order, especially in the remote areas of the world that are beyond the reach of government. And because the institutions of religion tend to be fragile, the freedom of religion must be protected, so that Ones can manage this important pillar of civilization unmolested.

Unfortunately, where religion and government coexist, jurisdictional conflicts sometimes arise, resulting in religious censorship. To the extent that there is religious censorship, there will be censorship in the mechanism responsible for creating a perfect civilization. Thus, religious freedom is paramount and must be protected, so that Ones can pursue their religious prerogatives unmolested.

Because speech is the basic currency of Commerce, evolution provided a mechanism for regulating speech within the specialization for Enneatype Two. This arrangement balances the exercise of free speech against the needs of Commerce. A check and balance is required since a failure to protect speech at the absolute encroaches, eclipses, or eliminates the primary role of Governance.

Threes inherently recognize that competition is the most effective and expedient method for economizing resources, and the best way to encourage competition is through the adoption of merit-based social systems. These realizations explain why Threes are the champions of merit-based social systems, and why they stress that individual accomplishments, achievements, and merit be the only criteria for economic remuneration. Accomplishing their evolutionary purpose requires that Threes have the flexibility, and the authority, to implement merit-based systems in their primary role as Economists.

Fours bear the economic risks associated with entrepreneurial endeavors, in the hopes that their creations, innovations, and inventions will change human behaviors, and bring economic rewards that are commensurate with the value-added. The entrepreneurial risk cycle is conditional, and one of those conditions is the development of a system that guarantees the entrepreneur will receive all economic credits associated with their work. Such a system is the predicate for all manner of entrepreneurial risk-taking because, without specific guarantees for economic rewards, Entrepreneurs will not engage in the risks that are necessary for successful innovations.

The knowledge that Economists classify as intellectual property has many similarities to the innovations of entrepreneurs, and so it requires the same types of protections afforded to entrepreneurs, as any system that fails to protect intellectual property will fail in providing the economic protections that are necessary for Fives to engage their Endeavor. In practice, a failure to protect the Endeavor of Wisdom effectively nullifies the evolutionary role that Fives perform, thereby impeding humanities accretion of knowledge. Thus, the evolution of human knowledge is dependent on the economic guarantees that go hand in hand with intellectual property rights.

The right to free assembly, and to organize, is germane to the risk management function of Sixes. Because without the protections related to the right of free assembly, Sixes would be unable to form basic risk management organizations; and thus, they would be unable to fulfill the objective of Protecting humanity from risk. For these reasons, the Endeavor to Protect others is directly dependent upon the protections for peacefully organizing and assembling.

Sevens acquire knowledge from activities, experiences, and reconnaissance, which requires that they have the mobility to travel and explore their unlimited curiosity. Unfortunately, international travel restrictions impede the ability of Sevens to engage their Endeavor for Intelligence, which in turn impedes their ability to fulfill their primary role. The unfortunate consequence is that many Sevens, especially those in third world countries, do not have the freedom or means to engage their evolutionary Endeavor.

The Economics of Enduction

Enduction is an evolutionary phenomenon that produces measurable increases in economic output. A straightforward way to measure Enduction is to rank the countries of the world according to their provision of the Nine Protections. Such a ranking will test the Theory of Enduction, which states that the relative per capita economic output of a country is proportional to the provision of the Nine Protections. Thus, the Theory of Enduction holds that the per capita output for each country will, holding other factors constant, be proportional to the efficacy of the Nine Protections.

The USA is a prime example of what is possible after the implementation of the Nine Protections. Founded in 1776, the USA was among the poorest countries of the world. However, the American Founders had the wisdom and foresight to add a Bill of Rights to the constitution of the USA. The Bill of Rights correlates roughly with most of the Nine Protections necessary for Enduction, as indicated in the following list:

Eight: Due process – 5th, 6th & 8th Amendment

Nine: Association – 1st Amendment

One: Religion – 1st Amendment

Two: Speech – 1st Amendment

Three: Merit – 5th & 7th Amendment

Four: Entrepreneurial – 5th & 7thAmendment

Five: Intellectual – 5th & 7th Amendment

Six: Organizational – 1st Amendment

Seven: Mobility – 1st Amendment

Within 100 years of its founding, the USA moved from the bottom of the list to the top of the list of wealthy and powerful countries. Soon after that, the USA became the wealthiest and most powerful country in the world. Economic historians have long debated the reasons that explain the rise of American hegemony. Some historians have cited that the freedoms of the individual, as guaranteed in the American constitution, were responsible for America's rise to power: And they were correct.

Enduction is a fragile phenomenon, consisting of Nine Human Endeavors, each dependent on specific protection for its operation. When the Endeavors receive the protections that they require, as was the case in the USA, the power of Enduction is activated. Enduction has the power to transform a developing country into the richest country within the space of a few generations. Such transformations are easy to verify because that is what happened in the case of the USA. And it has happened in other countries, too.

As compared to all other countries, the fact remains that the USA has been more effective in reaping the benefits of Enduction. And while that may be true, it does not mean the USA has unleashed the full power of Enduction. On the contrary, the USA has achieved a small fraction of what is possible.

For the USA to reach their full potential requires the realization of the Nine Human Endeavors on an individual level, and their seamless integration at the organizational level, in alignment with the intent of evolution. The next chapter continues with a discussion of Integration.

CHAPTER 14

THE FOURTH WAY

When Gurdjieff described the Enneagram as perpetual motion, he was referring to the fact that the Enneagram is a catalyst for infinite change, in the sense that it is a mechanism that produces continuous improvement. This analogy was very prescient, as Enduction has been highly effective against the NFE. Perhaps most interesting is that the Enneagram operates subconsciously; and thus, it does not depend on the conscious will of the individual. Rather, every individual is preordained to pursue one of the Nine Human Endeavors. This arrangement is meant to ensure that humanity conforms to the dictates of evolution.

Clues to the power of the Enneagram appears within a circle containing nine interconnected points. The circle represents the unity of humanity, with each of the infinite points on the circle representing a unique individual human being, each endowed with preprogrammed skills, abilities, and talents. When taking an individualistic perspective of the Enneagram, an understanding emerges that each person is a device of perpetual motion, designed with skills, abilities, and talents that are predestined to serve an evolutionary purpose.

Every human is biologically programmed, through the DNA, with an Endeavor, specialization, primary role, and functional adaptations for eradicating a factor of extinction. As a consequence of biology, this programming cannot be altered, diluted, or changed, which has several repercussions.

The most important being that Enneciation effectively places a stamp on every human being, under the guise of a delusion that effectively limits consciousness, thereby restricting the ability of that individual to otherwise engage with reality in an open and unrestricted way. This knowledge reveals a startling fact, which is that Enneciation was the shackle placed on Early Humans as a remedy for barbarism, economic stagnation, and conundrums.

The knowledge that Enneciation constitutes a restriction, subordination, or tribulation has been described in several ways. In the Christian Bible, an allegory for Enneciation appears in the story of Adam and Eve, which depicts the fall of humanity that occurs when Eve partakes of a forbidden apple. The apple symbolizes a forbidden level of consciousness that Eve actualizes immediately after eating the apple. Eve experienced this change in consciousness as a new perspective, knowledge, and self-consciousness.

The story of Adam and Eve illustrates the paradoxical transformation that occurred, in the leap from Early Humans to Modern Humans, manifesting as new perspectives, knowledge, and self-consciousness that had not existed before. It was the fall of humanity, in the sense that the primal innocence that had existed before Eve ate the apple was lost forever, and replaced by the nine subconscious delusions — resulting in a restriction (fall) to an Endeavor (consciousness) that was preordained by evolution (God). From the Christian perspective, the fall of humanity was a regression in a certain sense, in that it restricted human consciousness in painful ways. And there is plenty of evidence to support the Christian perspective.

For many thousands of years, humans have attempted to circumvent their evolutionary programming, to achieve an unbridled, unrestricted, expansive consciousness. Understanding these attempts requires an examination of the three traditional religious paths, the way of the Monk, Yogi, and Ascetic, from the perspective of the Enneagram. Each of these paths focuses on liberating one of the three centers of the human psyche. Monks focus on the heart, Yogis focus on the mind, and Ascetics focus on their instincts.

Despite the ubiquity of the three traditional paths, their efficacy is very low, given an overall success rate of less than one percent. A 99% failure rate is astonishingly high, given the decades of devotion to chants, meditations, singing, movements, dances, prayers, and contemplations that each path requires. As a consequence, the three traditional paths provide no guarantees; and in the end, they provide no sense of purpose or meaning. And for those reaching a point of ego liberation, it rarely confers new skills, abilities, or talents. On the contrary, liberation generally constitutes a reduction in the ability of the ego to perform its evolutionary functions.

The persistent failures in the three traditional paths of liberation led to the development of what is known as a Fourth Way Path. Fourth Way Schools emerged thousands of years ago, on the wisdom that the Enneagram provides a path to liberation, but only to those who align themselves with their evolutionary purpose. The wisdom provided by Fourth Way Schools brings several distinct advantages over the paths of the monk, yogi, and ascetic.

The primary advantage of Fourth Way Schools was in how they were structured. Some were structured so that students could remain in society during their participation in the school, allowing students to continue working in the world to support their families. If a school required full-time participation, it was generally for a short period of a few years, at which point the individual would matriculate back to society; and resume their life with new vigor. Graduates of Fourth Way Schools would return to society all the wiser, which was very appealing to many students.

The teachings of several world religions trace to the Fourth Way Schools that preceded them. Indeed, the imprint of the earliest Fourth Way Schools persists in the teachings, practices, and rituals of the major religions in existence today. Having a common origin explains why many modern religions use similar concepts, such as the concepts of Heaven and Hell, to explain the predicament of humanity. But these concepts also serve to conjure certain archetypes.

Many religions use the concept of Hell to describe the conditions of Early Human life. For example, many world religions describe Hell as a place of exile for the irredeemable souls who failed to conform to the will of God. The misbehaviors that qualify for Hell, which vary somewhat from religion to religion, have a direct correlation with the regressive behaviors that underlie the Nine Factors of Extinction. Thus, the concept of Hell is a substitute for, or an analogy of, the primitive conditions of Early Human life. From this perspective, many religions have relied on the depictions of Hell as an allegory for the Nine Factors of Extinction.

The concept of Hell provides a major deterrent for behaviors that are repugnant to the intent of evolution. On the other hand, the major religions depict Heaven as the greatest possible reward, to incentivize the behaviors that are in alignment with evolution. Thus, the concepts of Heaven and Hell are an implicit acknowledgment by the religious establishment that evolution is not only important, but that evolution has provided humans with a path to liberation.

As an open matter of discussion, religious organizations depict liberation in different ways. Some describe liberation as Heaven, while others describe various types of transcendental states of enlightenment. There are various rites and rituals associated with liberation, such as baptisms, confessions, whirling dances, meditations, and many more. What they all have in common is the notion that alignment with the Laws of the Universe, manifesting as Gods Will or the Will of the Supreme Creator, will be rewarded with unfathomable riches, treasure, happiness, and contentment.

The concept of liberation might be recognizable to some people, due to its ubiquity, and the fact that it traces to the earliest of the world religions. However, what is generally not understood is that the major world religions are the progeny of the ancient Fourth Way teachings of liberation. So, it should come as no surprise that Fourth Way Schools possessed even greater knowledge of the process for liberation, including the understanding that liberation requires individuals to align their consciousness with the intentions of evolution.

The Enneagram provides the road map to liberation, self-actualization, and enlightenment. A background in psychology is not necessary to understand it, as the Enneagram is remarkable in its simplicity and very easy to follow. The starting point for every individual begins with the realization of one's primary Enneatype, which provides the knowledge of one's Endeavor, specialization, primary role, and functional adaptations. This knowledge empowers the individual to fully engage their Endeavor, in the manner intended by evolution, to prevent, minimize, and eradicate a factor of extinction.

Upon mastery of the primary Endeavor, the focus turns to the Endeavor that is in the path of integration. The path of integration follows the lines connecting each of the Enneatypes according to the directional pattern detailed in Chapter Three. For example, Sixes would integrate to Nine, and Eights would integrate to Two. Enneatypes Three, Six, and Nine have only three steps in their path of integration, which is equivalent in overall difficulty to the six steps that types 1, 2, 4, 5, 7, 8 must complete.

The process of Integration provides an important lesson, which is that human consciousness was shattered by evolution into pieces that can be reassembled by following a graduated process of reintegration. The first stage of human development is complete upon reintegration of the fragments of consciousness. However, the process of reintegration depends on several factors that are independent of the individual. And that is where things get sticky because the factors that affect reintegration are not always within the control of the individual.

Reintegration depends foremost on the freedom of the individual, especially the freedom to master and apply each of the Endeavors. Chapter 14 discussed the specific protections necessary, which allows each of the Endeavors to operate without restrictions so that all individuals can apply and master all aspects of their Enneatype. To the extent that the necessary protections are in place, every individual has the freedom to engage their evolutionary Endeavor; and follow their path of integration. Unfortunately, the Endeavors have historically not received the protections that are necessary for the optimal development of every individual. And the Endeavors are under constant attack by various mechanisms.

A key point from Chapter 14 was that the USA provides a model for the protections that are necessary for each of the Endeavors. However, this does not imply that the USA provides optimal conditions for Integration, just that the USA does a better job of protecting the Endeavors than other countries. Thus, it's important to point out that the USA could improve. For example, the USA wastes a tremendous amount of its human resources, by way of the highest incarceration rate in the world, which runs contrary to the Endeavors related to Conservation and Economization. This wasting of resources comes with a certain irony, which is that most incarcerations in the USA are of Eights, whose criminal acts are often a derivative of their Endeavor to Conserve!

Another irony is that the incarceration of Eights is mostly related to the difficulties of applying their Endeavor in socially acceptable ways. The failure to master resources is tantamount to poverty, and this outcome is often not the fault of the individual, as it is at least partly a reflection of the socio-economic environment. So, incarceration is not always the best solution, as many times the better approach is to ensure that Eights have the freedom to engage their Endeavor; and as a last resort, military roles should go to those who qualify. The military provides the structured environment that many Eights need, while simultaneously providing opportunities for conserving resources by way of force, in alignment with their evolutionary purpose.

When individuals become incarcerated, regardless of which Enneatype they are, it is sometimes because the socio-economic environment did not allow an individual to engage their Endeavor in constructive ways. Thus, the goal of a society should be to provide certain structures, such as the protections that are necessary for each of the Endeavors, accompanied by incentives and coercive policies that ensure individuals will fulfill their evolutionary purpose. And conversely, socio-economic policies that undermine, circumvent, or restrict the Nine Human Endeavors should be avoided.

When the Nine Human Endeavors are adequately protected, they will naturally create an economic system of free markets. The application of free-market principles to all sectors of an economy results in an economic system known as capitalism, which denotes a system where resources can move freely. In a capitalist economy, each Enneatype has the freedom to engage their Endeavor: Eights have the freedom to conserve resources, Twos stimulate markets and enterprise, Threes are free to economize resources based on merit, Fours take entrepreneurial risks, and so on. Emerging from this perspective is the realization that free markets and capitalism are the product of evolution.

Unfortunately, humans are known to create economic systems that interfere with the Nine Human Endeavors; and in each case, these systems trace to the regressive traits and mechanisms of the psyche. Some of these traits were discussed previously, including greed, envy, and gluttony, in the context of the Nine Factors of Extinction. And they are relevant in this context, as they are responsible for policies that undermine capitalism and free markets. This discussion continues with an overview of the factors and systems that undermine free-market capitalism.

To the extent that an economic system does not allow the Enneatypes to exercise and engage their Endeavors, it will resurrect the full force and effect of the Nine Factors of Extinction. For that reason, it is very important to give careful consideration to the economic policies chosen, especially when governments regulate Commerce, to prevent unintentional interference with Enduction. Along these lines, several economic systems must be avoided entirely, precisely because they interfere with Enduction.

Collectivism refers to a broad category of socio-economic systems administered under various names such as socialism, fascism, and communism. The differences between these systems lie in how and to what degree they interfere with Enduction. Thus, it is necessary to discuss the characteristics that they share and how those characteristics are known to interfere with Enduction.

Collectivism is a socio-economic phenomenon that aggregates, controls, and redistributes the economic factors of production according to the dictates of a social group. Collectivism may take different forms, depending on the form of government and the extent of economic freedoms allowed. The most stringent forms of Collectivism prohibit individuals from owning land, geological resources, houses, buildings, machinery, commercial equipment, public facilities, public transportation systems, banks, banking systems, markets, cooperatives, businesses, corporations, proprietorships, utilities, and most other non-personal assets of value. The main difference between the various brands of Collectivism is the extent to which the factors of production are owned and administered by the Collective.

Collectivism can be administered by different forms of government, ranging from democracies to totalitarian regimes, depending on the degree of individual freedoms that are allowed. In cases where individuals have relatively few freedoms, a totalitarian government is generally required, as that is the only form of government that can maintain a vice-like control over the factors of production. The same is true for countries having a greater endowment of resources.

The defining feature of Collectivism is that it transfers the ownership of assets, and the decision-making authority that goes with that ownership, from individuals to the Collective. The crucial point here is that the authority to make economic decisions goes from the individual to the Collective. Consequently, individuals are stripped of their economic authority by the Collective, thereby allowing the Collective to control all aspects of the economy, including markets, prices, and assets.

The transfer of assets from individuals to the Collective constitutes a transfer of economic power from individuals to the Collective, which effectively sabotages Enduction in ways that are immediate, personal, and catastrophic. Although economists have studied this phenomenon for many decades, those analyses were independent of the scientific framework provided by the Enneagram, which presents an opportunity for recapitulation. Along those lines, a summary of how Enduction is affected by Collectivism follows.

The Economic Five

The fact that five of the Nine Human Endeavors are devoted to resolving economic problems underscores the importance that evolution placed on developing the economic capabilities of humans. Indeed, three Enneatypes (2,3,4) are devoted to resolving economic stagnation, and two Enneatypes (7,8) focus on resolving economic scarcity, which illustrates that Enduction is mostly an economic phenomenon. Altogether, these are the *Economic Five* of the Enneagram.

The ignominious transfer of economic power from individuals to the Collective has profound consequences for each Enneatype, and severe consequences in the case of the Economic Five, whose evolutionary purpose is directly dependent on the freedom to engage in economic behaviors.

The main consequence of stripping the economic power of the Economic Five is that they are rendered impotent; therefore, incapable of performing their evolutionary purpose. Rendering the Economic Five impotent brings Enduction to a grinding halt. Some elaboration may help to explain.

Twos use their networking skills to create markets, form enterprises, and engage in all types of commerce. However, when a Collective takes over, the economic stimulus provided by Twos is replaced with a bureaucratic machine that is antisocial, antimarket, and antienterprise. Even worse, the Collective also usurps the Governance of language, etiquette, and the code of conduct as it pertains to Commerce. The economic fallout caused by the Collective is catastrophic, as Twos have no incentive to improve social learning channels, apply their networking skills, or promote commerce, as these are all eclipsed by government rules and regulations. In the end, Twos have virtually no opportunities or incentives to engage their Endeavor in a collectivistic economy.

Threes inject a strong work ethic into their local economy, and champion merit-based economic systems, both of which serve the purpose of eliminating the economic problem of free riders. When the Collective takes over, all traces of a strong work ethic and merit-based economic system are annihilated and replaced with production quotas, wage parities, and economic planning. Moreover, all functions related to resource economization are also handled by the Collective, which means that the Collective effectively eclipses the specializations, primary role, and functions of Threes.

Fours accept the Entrepreneurial risks that are necessary for innovation, in the hopes of introducing an invention or technology that changes human behavior in meaningful ways. Unfortunately, the innovative process grinds to a halt when the Collective takes over, as the entire entrepreneurial process is replaced by a bureaucratic machine that blows the candle on the creative spirit that drives innovation. The problem is that after the Collective takes over, Fours have no means or incentives to innovate, due to the elimination of the entrepreneurial predicates. Underscoring these problems is the fact that the Collective is anti-entrepreneurial, while at the same time, it has no veritable interest in innovation.

The reconnaissance and trading initiatives sponsored by Sevens become obsolete when the Collective takes over, which effectively disables the evolutionary mechanism of optimizing resources, resulting in a rapid deoptimization of Commerce. The collateral effects of Collectivism explain the rapid economic decline, Exogenous Barbarism, and warlike atmosphere that sometimes follows a substitution of capitalism with Collectivism. When this substitution occurs, Sevens are left with no opportunities to trade, arbitrage, or optimize markets. All is not lost, as collectivistic systems do utilize the Strategic Thinking ability of Sevens in various types of military operations. However, the fact that Collectivism does not allow Sevens the unrestricted opportunity to peacefully apply the benign aspects of their specializations should be alarming to anyone reading this book.

When Collectivism replaces capitalism, economic productivity crashes to a small fraction of what is possible, thereby reducing the overall amount of resources that are available in an economy. The reduction of economic resources constitutes a reversion to a subsistence level of existence, where everyone is in fear of not having enough resources to survive. Eights respond to this survival scenario through various activities that aim to conserve resources for the survival of their group. These activities may include gangs, criminal organizations, syndicates, or posse's, whose mission is to ensure the just allocation of resources. From the perspective of many Eights, the only other option they have is to join the military or to form a militia.

Collectivism also interferes with the Endeavors of the noneconomic Enneatypes: Nine, One, Five, and Six. For example, Collectivism often restricts religious choice, which interferes with the Endeavor of Ones, who use religion as a means for maintaining law and order. Collectivism may also restrict the vocations related to psychology, which has the effect of displacing Nines, who are generally seeking to improve the psychological stability of their social group. Fives will complain that they are unable to pursue research in their chosen field of knowledge. And collectivistic societies have little need for risk management or Protection so that Sixes will be relegated mostly to teaching and policing functions.

The fact that Collectivism interferes with the evolutionary purpose of each Enneatype means that it constitutes a regression, specifically a regression back to the conditions that existed before Enneciation, which was a subsistence level of economic stagnation. The regression from affluence to poverty is rapid, as demonstrated by the country of Venezuela, which implemented Collectivism in 1999. In just 20 years, the capitalist economy of Venezuela spiraled into poverty conditions with greater speed than many economists thought possible. However, for countries that have few natural resources, and are therefore heavily dependent on Enduction, the decline to poverty may happen in a matter of months.

Denoting Collectivism as a regressive phenomenon is ironically accurate, as it refers to a regression back to the Nine Factors of Extinction that occurs when free-market capitalism is displaced. The irony is that Collectivism is often touted as a progressive advancement as if it will bring greater progress to humanity, or in the very least that it will bring greater economic equality. Despite any claims that are made by its proponents, Collectivism fails to increase the long-term per capita standard of living of its members. What it does do, with varying degrees of cruelty, is strip the humanity from every human being: The Endeavor, specialization, and primary role, along with the opportunities for growth, maturity, and Integration.

CHAPTER 15

THE EVOLUTIONARY PURPOSE OF EVERY HUMAN BEING

In documenting the story of the human species, the focus has been on the later phases of human evolution, from Homo Erectus to the present. During this period, Modern Humans have fundamentally transformed the narrative of the Nine Factors of Extinction; given that military organizations have replaced Exogenous Barbarism, civilization has replaced Endogenous Barbarism, international trade has replaced scarcity, knowledge has replaced fallacies, economic power has replaced economic stagnation, and so on. Amid these changes, a new narrative for humanity has emerged, which provides new insights, revelations, and guidance to individuals.

A key insight is that Enduction is a scalable phenomenon, which means that Enduction operates at different levels, such as the level of a species, country, organization, family, or individual. As Enduction moves down the levels, the conditions predicate for the next level are satisfied, and so on. This process continues until the Enneagram reaches the level of the individual, which happened near the end of the second millennium, as evidenced by the emergence of a new phenomenon.

The protection of the Nine Human Endeavors during the 18th and 19th centuries was responsible for the emergence of Nine Human Virtues that effectively replaced the Nine Factors of Extinction. These virtues are a direct result of humanities struggle to evolve toward higher states of being, and so they hold the key for continued evolution, especially the evolution of the individual. The Nine Human Virtues appear on the back cover of this book.

The Nine Human Virtues reflect the universal struggles of Early Humans that crystallized into the timeless wisdom of universal truth. The arrival of this knowledge portends great possibilities for humanity, as it indicates the attainment of a certain degree of perspective, maturity, and wisdom, which can now be applied and utilized by individuals. To the extent that this knowledge is applied to individuals, and utilized in a manner intended by evolution, human progress has infinite potential. For these reasons, it is incumbent upon every human being to understand, Integrate, and practice the Nine Human Virtues.

The Evolution of the Individual

Evolution operates by authority of the Laws of the Universe, to ensure that life succeeds whenever and wherever possible. The primary mechanism of evolution is to create the basic parameters of behavior that each species must follow for survival. The success of every species and the individual members within a species depends on conformity with the behaviors that are expected by evolution. Humans must also conform as no creature is immune to the expectations or authority of evolution. There are no exceptions to this rule.

In the case of humans, evolution has very high expectations of behavior, and those expectations are very clear. Every human is expected to contribute to the advancement of the human species, by aligning themselves with their evolutionary purpose, according to their Endeavor, specializations, and functional adaptations. Alignment necessarily requires every human to be conscious of the strengths and weaknesses of their Enneatype, so that their strengths can be applied in a meaningful way, while at the same time they work to mitigate their weaknesses.

Also, every human being is expected to align themselves with the Nine Human Virtues, by exemplifying the attitudes, behaviors, and actions that are consistent with each virtue. The objective religions of the world teach some variation of the Nine Human Virtues, with some that are in near-perfect alignment, and others that teach a simplified version. However, the origin of the Nine Human Virtues traces to the most proficient Fourth Way Schools.

In its purest form, the realization of the Nine Human Virtues depends on the process of Integration, which is the process of mastering the Endeavors, primary role, and functional adaptations in the path of Integration demarked by the Enneagram. Thus, Integration is the process of human development, growth, and maturity that occurs as individuals struggle to align themselves with their evolutionary purpose. As a universal process of growth, Integration requires each person to struggle in ways that are uniquely personal to acquire the facets of consciousness that were eclipsed by Enneciation.

Every individual begins their journey of Integration with the realization of their primary Enneatype. Many people will recognize their Enneatype by simply reading this book. (For those having difficulty, or those who are not certain, please see the end of this book for additional resources.) The next step is to do a self-assessment, which includes taking a historical perspective, to reconstruct how one's Enneatype has interacted with past events. This assessment must be exhaustive and can be very time consuming, even when conducted on a full-time basis.

The next step is to apply the wisdom gained from self-assessment, and combine that with the knowledge of one's Enneatype, to formulate a strategy for mastering all aspects of one's Enneatype. Here, the strategy takes the form of an aim, and the aim is to master the Endeavor, specializations, and functional adaptations of an Enneatype. The aim must include a timeline, including a start and finish date, and a clearly defined goal or objective. Most important is that the aim is in alignment with the evolutionary purpose of the individual, which requires that the tasks, goals, and objectives align with the intent of evolution. Although this step can be very complicated, some individuals may accomplish this step on their own volition.

Upon mastery of the primary Enneatype, the focus moves to the Enneatype in the path of Integration, which now becomes the new aim. The first two steps of the process are repeated to integrate the Endeavor, specialization, and functional adaptations of the next Enneatype. This process continues, until all Endeavors in the path of Integration have been integrated, at which point the process of Integration is complete,

The process of Integration is multi-dimensional, in the sense that each step requires the integration of the Universal Quality of Consciousness that corresponds to each point on the Enneagram. The integration of these qualities is difficult, as each Enneatype evolved without certain qualities of consciousness as a predicate for tethering each ego to a specific Endeavor. Lifting this restriction requires curiosity, dedication, and love for the truth of reality. Curiosity is a rare phenomenon, and alignment with Truth is even more rare, which partly explains why the process of Integration does not proceed on its own.

The process of Integration is very difficult to accomplish without the help of a teacher, whose role is to provide the necessary structure and support that is needed for Integration to proceed unabated. The necessary structure may take various forms, such as group exercises that stimulate the process of Integration. To be effective, a teacher must have the requisite knowledge, experience, and wisdom to guide others along their uniquely individuated path of Integration. Thus, the choice of a teacher, or the enrollment in a path that supports Integration, must be evaluated carefully.

The best way to evaluate any path of human development is to apply the Enneagram as a litmus test of objectivity. The Enneagram provides the objective knowledge necessary to assess, evaluate, and validate all paths and teachings. Utilizing the Enneagram in this manner, a ranking of the various paths of human development emerges, each according to their alignment with Truth. The result is a ranking of religions, spiritual paths, and schools of human development, based on an objective assessment of their teachings, methods, and results.

When the paths of human development are ranked, an important revelation emerges, which is that the purpose and meaning of life will reveal itself only when there is an alignment with the Truth. Thus, the purpose and meaning of life, which everyone is born to realize, can only be found in the Truth that emerges from the struggle to Integrate the fragments of perspective that are secondary to evolution. For these reasons, it is necessary to include this criterion when ranking paths because doing so reveals that very few paths lead to the realization, actualization, and Integration of the purpose and meaning of life.

This book has documented that every human being was preordained to Endeavor against a factor of extinction, using the specializations, adaptations, and roles that support their Endeavor, for the advancement of the human species. However, most humans are completely unaware of their Endeavor, which means they are asleep to their evolutionary purpose. Awakening from this sleep may occur in several ways, but the most common way is to undergo a process of awakening, vis-à-vis a path of human development. Awakening allows individuals to consciously align with their purpose and begin the work of Integration on the pathway provided by evolution. The purpose and meaning of life are found only on this pathway.

Perspectives

From the perspective of evolution, the process of Integration is an important step forward for humanity, as it empowers every individual to reach their full potential. The evolution of the individual is paramount because only when every individual reaches their full potential will the full potential of humanity be reached. Thus, every human being shares a common purpose in actualizing their full potential and helping others to actualize theirs.

From the perspective of government, the Nine Human Endeavors must be protected, supported, and nurtured, so that every human being has the freedom to align themselves with their evolutionary purpose. These prerogatives require all levels of government to work in unison, to provide the structures that are necessary for Enduction to thrive while avoiding policies and schemes that interfere with individual freedoms. These guidelines do not manifest on their own. They only happen when an advanced degree of consciousness translates the Truth of the human condition, including the predicates for self-realization, into governmental policies that further the advancement of the human species.

From the perspective of various types of organizations, each type of organization must have a mission statement that aligns with at least one of the Nine Human Endeavors, with a precise delineation of the roles that are necessary to carry out that mission. Upon meeting these requirements, the next step is to match roles with Enneatypes that evolved for the requirement of each position. To the extent that an organization operates within these guidelines, such organizations will take a leadership role for their industry, as they become a model that others strive to follow. And conversely, those organizations that fail to align themselves with the edicts of evolution will achieve suboptimal results. There are no exceptions to this rule.

From the perspective of the individual, the journey of Integration is a process of reunification, where the fragments of the soul are unified to form a complete human being. As the journey of Integration unfolds, there is a greater alignment with the Truth of reality, until a realization of the unity of reality occurs. Along the way, an understanding of the inherent purpose of life deepens, followed by revelations that are insightful, personal, intimate, and transformative. These revelations provide answers to the most elusive questions, including those related to the uniquely individualized purpose and meaning of life.

APPENDIX A
ANALYSIS OF THE ID

This discussion is limited to the genesis of the Id, its basic framework, along with a summary of how it functions. The emigrating tendency of Homo Erectus provides evidence to suggest that the genesis of the Id coincided just before their appearance throughout Asia approximately 2 MYA. Thus, the operation of the Id, and the behavioral effects that it produces provide the strongest evidence for the hypothesis that the Id was responsible for the emigrating tendencies of Homo Erectus.

Fossil record data supports that Early Humans have always faced three categories of threat: Food scarcity, environmental threats, and accidents. These ever-present threats led to the development of three survival mechanisms operating by way of three distinct mechanisms of fear conditioning: A fear of starvation from food scarcity; fear of isolation from environmental threats; and a fear of pain from the ever-present risk of accidents and personal injury. Evolution responded to these general threats with the development of the Id, which is an Environmental Archetype based survival mechanism within the psyche, that is responsible for creating three distinct instinctive drives: Self-Preservation, Socialization, and Hedonism.

Self-Preservation Instinct

Although Early Humans often experienced nutrient scarcity, they had no way of monitoring their nutritional status, so that appropriate steps could be taken to prevent nutritional deficiency. They certainly possessed the hunger instinct, and they had some constitutional awareness, such as weakness and fatigue. But the operation of the hunger instinct, weakness, and fatigue is very primitive and does not advise on the nutritional status of the body. Indeed, the hunger instinct arises only during the first two or three days of a complete fast; and does not return until the body is near death. Thus, a healthy body can function for several weeks without food, as facilitated by a hunger instinct that fades after the first three or four days. However, a body that is already nutritionally deficient may survive only up to a few weeks without food. The implication here is that the hunger instinct, weakness, and fatigue do not provide reliable feedback on the nutritional status of the body.

After eons of experience with food scarcity, an Environmental Archetype developed linking the experience of food scarcity with death, which crystallized as a fear of food scarcity. The subconscious fear of food scarcity eventually evolved the Self-Preservation Instinct. The essence of the Self-Preservation Instinct is that it heightens awareness of the body, operates by the Law of Conservation, and creates response mechanisms aimed at securing the survival of the individual. The gross interoceptive senses, such as the awareness of body functions, becomes deeper, more refined, and multidimensional: Including temperature, space, hunger, comfort, grooming, exhaustion, sleep cycle, proximity, balance, etc. Everyone possesses some degree of constitutional awareness; but with the Self-Preservation Instinct, the awareness is richer, fuller, and more immediate. Moreover, the Self-Preservation Instinct has an amplifying effect on an individual's awareness of their physiology, as a compensatory mechanism for the threats posed by nutrient scarcity.

By amplifying awareness of physiological processes, the Self-Preservation Instinct ensures that the constitutional needs of the body take priority. Egoic needs, interests, and desires lag behind the unmistakably ardent feedback of the body. The needs of others may be delayed, or become secondary to, the immediate physiological needs of the individual. These experiences are understandable, as the Self-Preservation Instinct creates a drive to do something about any physiological deficiencies that rise to the surface.

The Self-Preservation Instinct also operates by the law of conservation, in that it conserves the body's energy and resources. The goal is to provide a slow but steady metabolism, hard-wired to store extra energy when possible while keeping energy expenditures to a minimum. The result often coincides with heavier, thicker body types, after accounting for other factors such as the body type classification (endomorph, ectomorph, mesomorph).

As an example of how the Self-Preservation Instinct creates response mechanisms within the body, consider an individual who accepts an invitation to a party at a new friend's house. When she walks into her new surroundings, she may notice the room is very warm, so she looks for a safe and reliable place to put her jacket. She will locate the rest facility, and then may notice others eating and drinking, so she grabs a plate of food. With her plate of food, she might look for a comfortable place to sit. She may limit her drinking, as she feels dizziness after a few drinks. The Self-Preservation Instinct controls her comportment so that she addresses the immediate needs and comforting of her body, whatever her situation. Her focus is not on the people, the events of the party, or the details of her environment. If you ask her about the party, she will describe in ample detail the food, how much she ate, what she drank, and so on. But she may have difficulty describing all the people in attendance, or the activities that occurred because those were of secondary importance.

Self-Preservationists focus on their physical security by planning, forecasting, and anticipating their future, rather than acting spontaneously. Achieving security means having a stable career, purchasing a home, and saving for future needs. The goal is to ensure that the needs of the body will always be taken care of, by creating a safe, secure, comfortable living environment.

Those with the Self-Preservation instinct take care of the body in many ways: Regular exercise such as running or swimming, bodybuilding, taking vitamins, and dieting. They conserve energy as homebodies, preferring to stay close to home whenever possible. If they do go out, they avoid wandering too far from home. The aversion to travel is not absolute; it just means there is a distinct pattern of preference for remaining home whenever possible. For these reasons, Self-Preservationists are homebodies, with a certain degree of rigidity, inflexibility, and conservation of energy. For these reasons, the Self-Preservation Instinct is synonymous with the homebody instinct.

Social Instinct

Early Humans were poorly equipped to handle the dangers that arise when living in isolation. These dangers included predator attacks, sickness, temporary disability, resource scarcity, barbarism, accidents, and many others. There are also economic consequences for living alone. An individual living by himself will have a much lower standard of living, compared to those living in small communities, because he will be required to provide everything for his survival: water, vegetables, nuts, meat, all types of clothing, shelter, tools, weapons, etc. However, if he lived in a community setting, he might specialize in hunting meat for all community members. By specializing in providing meat, economic theory informs that he would have a higher quantity and quality of clothing, water, shelter, and other food sources because of gains achieved through economic specialization, economies of scale, and economic trade. However, a man living alone would have a lower standard of living, and consequently, a shorter life span. In all of the above cases, the probability of survival was proportional to the group size.

The economic consequences and direct threats to survival under discussion were consolidated by evolution into an Environmental Archetype that instilled a fear of living in isolation. The archetypal experience of living in isolation and the fear that it induced was the predicate for the Social Instinct. The Social Instinct counteracts the fear and vulnerability of aloneness through a process of social bonding. The need for social bonding, or the need to connect with others, spurs traveling and exploring, seeking new experiences, learning new languages, or organizing groups and associations. The Social Instinct supports any activity which might bring a person into contact with new groups of people, new cultures, new communities, or new experiences.

The Social Instinct sponsors an empathic awareness, operating at a macro level, which allows an individual to focus on the needs, objectives, and psyche of the group. There is a special attunement to the group, and a willingness to go along with the group's agenda. There is a need to belong, to fit in, to find one's place within the group as if one's survival depends on it. All of this requires openness and flexibility; there is little room for racial prejudice, intolerance to others, or pretentious attitudes and behaviors. "When in Rome, do as the Romans" for the alternative might be death by exile.

Whereas the Self-Preservation Instinct operates by conserving energy, the Social Instinct wires a person for perpetual motion, allowing for the tremendous energy expenditures that are required to conquer the Id's underlying fear of aloneness. For these reasons, Socials are blessed with excellent endurance and enjoy social endurance events such as marathons. Socials are generous with their energy and enjoy putting energy toward group projects. For these reasons, Socials tend to have faster metabolisms and body types that are generally slimmer when compared to Self-Preservation.

If a Social accepts an invitation to a party at a new friend's house, upon arriving they will immediately take notice of who is there, and what groups or "cliques" of people have formed. Also, the demeanor of the groups, and which groups they might fit in. They generally will prefer to join a group instead of seeking one-on-one conversations. They may bounce between groups, until they have combed the entire party, and have a feel for where they fit in. They may do recruiting for a special social cause that they are affiliated with, or discuss their political positions, being careful to assess how others respond. Socials enjoy group dancing, a wide range of music, learning about other cultures, and trying different cuisines. The Social Instinct is about gatherings of people

The need for bonding, the need for connection, makes social status very important to Socials. Socials will often accept a lower-paying career, so they can advance a social cause they believe. Or, lower pay for more prestige and social status. For example, many politicians are known to leave a private-sector job to accept a political position because it offered greater social status and recognition.

Modern Humans that have the Social Instinct have a greater awareness of social issues; and thus, they tend to be more politically active, and more likely to participate in social causes. Socials are also responsible for a litany of lesser-known activities, from secret societies to groups that are preoccupied with extraterrestrial matters. These types of activities provide evidence for the supreme openness to new experiences that Socials exhibit.

Hedonism (Pleasure) Instinct

The occurrence rate of accidental deaths among Early Humans was high, mostly because of the deficiencies in attendant care that were imposed by very primitive living conditions. Without hospitals, advanced medicines, or surgery to repair accidental injuries, imagine the consequences of an Early Human who suffered an accidental compound fracture of his leg: There would be intense pain, followed by a slow and torturous death from being left unattended in the wilds of nature. In response to this dilemma, Early Humans developed an association between accidents and pain, which eventually crystallized into an Environmental Archetype.

Although pain serves as an effective deterrent for risky behaviors, the demands of survival often require situations and circumstances that are inherently risky. Indeed, Early Humans were required on many occasions to take risks, such as when hunting, crossing rivers or walking over icy terrain. Hunting large game might have posed the greatest risk for Early Humans because large game could cause irreparable damage by severing important arteries with their teeth, breaking bones, or maiming vital organs. If an injury did not result in death, it would certainly reduce the chances of reproductive success, because the maimed and crippled were considered less desirable by the opposite sex. Fighting is another example of a risky situation which might lead to death. Certainly, Early Humans associated risk-taking behaviors such as large game hunting, with pain, reproductive compromise, and death. In this way, an Environmental Archetype between risk-taking and death was born.

Among Modern Humans, accidents and risk-taking behaviors continue to be a leading cause of death for individuals aged 15 - 39. Examples include death from an unintentional fall, mishandling a weapon, exposure to inanimate forces, drowning, or fire. From the perspective of evolution, the question was how to deal with the risk and threat of accidents, and their association with pain, reproductive compromise, and death? A pain (risk) avoidance mechanism was needed, which would maximize the chances of survival and reproductive success while minimizing risk and the probability of being in an accident. The answer was the Pleasure Instinct.

The Pleasure Instinct filters the conscious experience of reality, sorting, and categorizing information about the immediate environment, thereby enabling an individual to respond to threats or pleasurable opportunities. Information that is not a threat or pleasure opportunity is filtered, creating a refined focus of attention, vigilance, and awareness for what is happening in the instant moment. Individuals endowed with the Pleasure Instinct have eyes which appear to be larger, as the eyelids are positioned in a wide-open position, thus increasing the reception of visual cues.

The anatomical basis for the Pleasure Instinct is in the ratio of pain receptors relative to pleasure receptors. Individuals who possess the Pleasure Instinct have a much higher ratio of pain receptors, which causes pleasurable experiences to register with less intensity relative to painful experiences. The central nervous system is fundamentally biased toward pain because it is metered to amplify painful experiences while discounting pleasurable experiences. In this way, the nervous system is in a state of disequilibrium due partly to the high ratio of negative stimulation versus positive stimulation. To restore equilibrium, the individual must seek out positive stimulation, excitement, or any pleasurable experience; while avoiding any negative stimulation. This discussion continues with the anatomical differences that are a product of the Pleasure Instinct, alongside the three fundamental sources of pleasure: exogenous, endogenous, and abstract.

The Pleasure Instinct is also known as the sexual instinct, because sexual intercourse fulfills the instinctive drive for pleasure, thus correcting the pleasure-pain imbalance endemic to the central nervous system. But the Pleasure Instinct is much more than a boosted sex drive, as it is responsible for acts, attitudes, and behaviors before the consummation of the sex act. A good place to look for evidence of the Pleasure Instinct is with grooming because there is an emphasis on grooming oneself to be more attractive to the opposite sex. Men pursue means and methods to enhance their masculinity, while women may seek to embellish their femininity with make-up, clothes, jewelry, and so on.

Those endowed with the Pleasure Instinct have certain anatomical adaptations. Thus, the hormonal differences between the sexes are exaggerated, which creates a greater range of femininity versus masculinity. For example, the feminine voice is noticeably more feminine, while the male voice is deeper, fuller, and more masculine. Another anatomical difference endemic to the Pleasure Instinct lies with the olfactory pleasure receptors, which are more developed, thus creating a need to block or cover up negative smells using strong-smelling colognes and perfumes. Learning to identify the superficial characteristics that are associated with the Pleasure Instinct, such as colognes, body enhancements, makeup, and so on, can be very helpful in its identification.

Verbal communication is an important precursor to human sexual relations. For this reason, the Pleasure Instinct is also known as the Relational Instinct, because it enhances verbal fluency. Those endowed with the Pleasure Instinct have a veritable skill for engaging conversations that are generally fast-paced, witty, and humorous. It can be difficult for those of the other instinctive types to keep up. Here, the preference is for one-on-one conversations involving direct eye contact, because group conversations are much less stimulating, and do not generally lead to more pleasure. One-on-one conversations provide the positive stimulation that is needed to satisfy the Pleasure Instinct, and this stimulation is often a prelude to more intimate and pleasurable experiences. For these reasons, the term *Relational* can be used to describe those who possess the Pleasure Instinct.

The key point here is that the Pleasure Instinct creates an awareness, interest, and investment in matters of relationships. The focus on pleasure explains the moniker *Sexual Instinct* or the *Relational Instinct*. Understanding Relationals helps to explain many of the differences observed among Modern Humans, including exaggerated masculinity/femininity, and an emphasis on fashion. The Pleasure Instinct is partly responsible for a culture that values beauty over character, and favors appearance over function, thereby promoting a superficial orientation toward reality.

The Pleasure Instinct also played a role in the Early Human use of mind-altering recreational substances. The historical record for Early Human recreational drug use dates to the Paleolithic, supported by finds at the Shanidar Cave and art from Tassilli. Early Human recreational drug use increased substantially during the Neolithic period, where there is evidence of marijuana, opium, mushrooms, and tobacco use in various parts of the world. And the last two hundred years has witnessed a global explosion of recreational drug use, as hundreds of controlled substances have become available, including dozens that are used solely on a recreational basis. Over time, the availability of mind-altering substances has increased from a mere handful fifty thousand years ago, to over one hundred recreational drugs and narcotics in use today. The drive for stimulation stemming from the Pleasure Instinct explains part of the increase in recreational drugs.

The Pleasure Instinct is certainly not responsible for all recreational substance use, but it does play a major role in substance abuse. That's because the Pleasure Instinct creates a biological drive for pleasure-seeking that can only be temporarily satisfied, setting the stage for a vicious cycle of indulgence, fading, withdrawal, and indulgence. Thus, the Pleasure Instinct can also be called the Addiction Instinct.

In modern societies, the most common addictions are for drugs, gambling, sex, alcohol, and smoking. In many cases, the Pleasure Instinct is the common denominator behind the addiction, as the individual seeks pleasure to correct the underlying neurocognitive imbalance.

Using the earlier example, going to a party for Relationals means an opportunity for pleasure. Upon entering a party scene, the focus is to find something fun and exciting to do such as a conversation aimed toward a sexual encounter, participating in a game, or partaking in libations or other recreational substances. Relationals naturally gravitate toward the center of high energy, such as loud voices, dancing, or a physical altercation.

Whereas the Social Instinct is associated with endurance, the Pleasure

Instinct aligns with short, high-intensity movements. And while Socials enjoy team sports, Relationals are better equipped to handle situations that require quick reflexes, anaerobic sprinting, and excellent proprioception: The Pleasure Instinct provides all of these. For these reasons, Relationals are generally more successful at dealing with high-risk situations and avoiding accidents; thus, allowing for the procreation and survival of the Human Species.

FORM AND FUNCTION

The three instinctual adaptations work in concert, according to a paradigm that is encoded genetically, which gives rise to six possible instinctive types. As illustrated in Table 2.1:

Alias	Dominant	Secondary	Tertiary
The Foodie	Self-Preservation	Social	Relational
The Homebody	Self-Preservation	Relational	Social
The Explorer	Social	Self-Preservation	Relational
The Model	Social	Relational	Self-Preservation
The Comedian	Relational	Social	Self-Preservation
The Monogamist	Relational	Self-Preservation	Social

Table 2.1 - Level Four

The expression of the instinctual variants depends on the level of functional integrity discussed in Chapter Three. The functional integrity level describes the level of maturity, or functional abilities, on a scale of one thru seven. The Instinctual Variants operate in different ways, depending on the level. At functional levels of one thru three, the instinctual variants are in balance, and they function in the manner described earlier in this chapter. At functional integrity level four, the instincts may have some mild distortion, and there is a substantial difference in the relative degree of instinctual expression. Moving down the levels toward level seven, the expression of the instincts becomes more and more distorted, reaching a point at level seven where the expression becomes mostly unintelligible.

Level four is perhaps the most important level for understanding the expression of the instincts, as approximately 50% of the population functions at this level; and because level four is the level where mild distortions in the operation of the instincts emerge. Table 2.1 demonstrates how the rank order of the instinctual variants determines which instinct will be dominant, and which instincts will serve in a subordinate role, for individuals at the fourth level of functional integrity. Because the functional integrity level determines the relative degree of expression for the instincts, the focus turns to how the instincts are expressed within the context of functional integrity level four, followed by a discussion of how the instincts become more distorted at the lower levels.

At level four, the dominant instinct accounts for a disproportionate amount of the instinctive expression, and the secondary and tertiary instincts play a limited role. Notably, level four marks the emergence of dysfunction. The best way to understand the dysfunction is by examples, requiring a brief look at each of the instinctive types at level four.

The Foodie's love of food derives from the Self-Preservation instinct, which is the dominant instinct for this type, and it creates a drive for satisfying all manner of physiological needs. But because the tertiary instinct is essentially not expressed, which in this case is the Relational Instinct, Foodie's tend to neglect important relationships. Because the Social instinct is secondary, Foodie's have an appreciation for all types of cuisine, and often enjoy eating at new restaurants. Whereas most people eat to live, Foodie's live to eat, and think about food more than most people. Most Foodie's rarely miss a meal; and this instinctive combination will tend to eat more calories than are required, especially at integrity level four (or lower). And individuals at level four often have difficulty maintaining regular exercise, which when combined with excess calories and slow metabolism, may eventually produce an obese individual. Individuals above level four have a reduced propensity for obesity, whereas those below level four have a stronger inclination toward overt obesity. Of course, this discussion excludes other factors affecting obesity, such as body type (endomorph, ectomorph, mesomorph), age, Enneatype, and other genetic factors.

The Homebody is like the Foodie, except that the Social instinct is a blind spot, so the desire to travel and socialize is almost nonexistent at integrity level four. For this reason, Homebodies spend as much time at home as possible; and because the relational instinct is secondary, they often wish to share the safety and security of home-life with a companion. Homebodies enjoy monogamous relationships, creating a family legacy, and preparing their favorite foods at home. Homebodies need to maintain a strong sense of security, which they accomplish by planning, controlling, and managing the details of their life. The need for micro-managing their life makes the Homebody the least spontaneous of the instinctive types. They exhibit a strong need for security thru relationship, but their need for control spills over to their relationships, which creates a fundamental incompatibility with other instinctive combinations. Thus, compatibility with other instinctive combinations becomes an important factor in this case.

Explorer's enjoy travel or other social activities, taking rest at home between their social engagements. Explorer's share a common interest with the Foodie, in that they enjoy trying many different types of food, especially while traveling. And because Self-Preservation is the secondary instinct, Explorer's like to combine travel with exercise: Bagging mountain peaks, trekking across continents, or sailing oceans. Although the Social and Self-Preservation instincts combine to form an individual who is at once flexible and rugged, the fact remains that the Relational instinct is a blind spot, which explains their limited compatibility with Relational's.

The Social-Relational-Self-Preservation instinctive combination is referred to as the *Model* because as a group, this instinctive combination stands out as the most charismatic. This truth becomes clear when dividing a large group of people by their respective instinctive combinations, under the direction of a skillful practitioner, and then polling to determine the most attractive group. Winning popularity contests is second nature for this group, as they easily navigate social channels, and take relationships in stride. While they do well in their careers and relationships, the Self-Preservation instinct is the blind spot; and in this case, the blind spot leads to neglect for taking care of fiduciary and health matters. Many pop-culture stars, including Elvis Presley, fall into this genre.

Improvisational comedy, which requires a fast and witty mind, is the domain of those who possess the Relational-Social-Self-Preservation instinctive combination. For functional integrity levels above four, the relational style is direct and straightforward. But at level four, the relational style shifts towards a more sarcastic style of presentation, which can be a source of confusion and misunderstanding for the other instinctive types. The Comedian seeks to express excitement and intensity, but in the same way as the Model, their Achilles heel is in taking care of fiduciary and health matters. The sarcastic presentation style of the Comedian appears in the comedy performed by Chris Rock.

Some general observations are that the secondary instinct is expressed in moderation, while the tertiary instinct is much less important. As an example, Self-Preservation is the dominant instinct for the Foodie, followed by the Social instinct, which has some degree of expression; while the Relational instinct is dormant. Indeed, the tertiary instinct constitutes a blind spot, such that it is rendered inactive, especially for individuals at or below level four.

This discussion is meant to be an introduction to the Id, provided as an aid for diagnosing the mechanisms of personality. The astute observer will notice that the functions of the Id overlap with some of the Enneatype functions. The implication here is that evolution attempted to resolve the impediments to survival with a basic mechanism, which was later eclipsed by a more sophisticated mechanism, resulting in the duplication of certain functions. Despite some overlap in function, the Id and Ego are distinct survival mechanisms distinguishable with practice.

APPENDIX B
ENNEAGRAM VS. JUNGIAN MODEL

Chapter Three's discussion of the Enneagram model continues with a direct comparison to the Jungian personality model. The main difference between these models is in how each depicts the basic structure of the ego: The Enneagram depicts the ego as having three basic mechanisms; whereas, the Jungian model depicts an ego with four basic mechanisms. Anyone that understands the three basic laws of the universe will immediately recognize that the Jungian model is flawed, as evolution does not produce mechanisms having four components. That argument aside, a probative analysis is required to elucidate the critical errors in the Jungian model. Figures 1.1 and 1.2 illustrates the basic difference between the Enneagram and Jungian models:

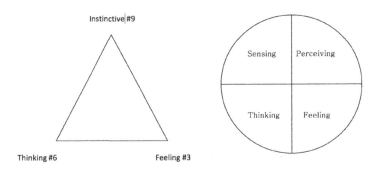

Figure 1.1 - Enneagram   *Figure 1.2 – Jungian Model*

Figure 1.1 displays the equilateral triangle from the Enneagram symbol. The points on the equilateral triangle pair with the three fundamental centers of the ego, Thinking, Feeling, and Instinctive, which is consistent with Freud's depiction of the basic structure of the ego. However, knowing the structure of the ego is not the same as describing its functions. If figure 1.1 delineated functions, a function of each center would be listed. For example, functional monikers might include the "interoceptive sense" of the Instinctive Center, paired with "concept rationalization" (Thinking), and "mentoring" (Feeling). Instead, the Enneagram maps the structure of the ego, not the functions of those structures, which is a critical first step in recognizing the structure of the ego.

Figure 1.2 displays the four basic functions of the ego, as described by Jung in the behavioral model he published in 1922. Jung established that his model delineated the functions of personality. At first glance, the Enneagram and Jungian models appear vaguely similar, yet they are different in that the Enneagram delineates the structure inherent to the ego, whereas the Jungian model delineates egoic functions. Indeed, the Enneagram maps the structure of the survival mechanism known as the ego, while the Jungian model demonstrates some of the basic functional (behavioral) patterns manifesting within the ego.

The first step in discerning the ego types is to map the overall structure, which in this case consists of three basic appendages, followed by the differentiation of the functions that manifest within each appendage. The Enneagram is effective in both cases; whereas, the Jungian model fails in both regards. Further analysis of Figures 1.1 and 1.2 reveals that the Jungian model has three problems: It emphasizes function over form, is overreaching in scope, and it fails to precisely differentiate the underlying survival mechanisms. Some examples will help to explain.

Independent of his personality model, Jung conceived that "intuition" is a type of "perception"; and when individuals are "sensing" and "feeling" they are "perceiving" because sensing and feeling are perceptual ways of absorbing information about the immediate environment. However, "Intuition" is redundant with the Sensing and Feeling functions. Removing "Intuition" from Jung's model reduces it to the same form and structure as the Enneagram: Thinking, Feeling, and Instinctive (sensing) Centers. Jung's inclusion of "Intuition" meant that he failed to correctly discern the underlying structures from the functional offspring of those structures; thus, he made the classic error of confusing form and function.

The major problem with the Jungian model is its overreaching scope. Consider that when Jung added "intuition" to his model, he put greater emphasis on the Feeling and Instinctive centers, thus irrevocably skewing his model. And Jung further increased the scope of his model by including the function of "judging," which is derivative to the "Thinking" and "Feeling" functions, thereby including some of the functions of the superego in his model. The inclusion of "judging" was a substantial mistake as it is an aspect of the Superego and must be differentiated accordingly.

Even more problematic, Jung's personality model does not differentiate the survival instincts of the Id, from the instinctive functions of the ego mechanism of personality. Unfortunately, Jung attempted to model all the mechanisms of personality, so Jung's model is not an ego model per se. For these reasons, the Jungian personality model has very little utility, as it does not differentiate, define, or map the ego. Whereas, the Enneagram model precisely defines, differentiates, and maps the human ego.

Contrasting the Enneagram with the Jungian model underscores the importance of treating the Id, ego, and superego as distinct structural elements of personality. Holding these distinctions can be difficult at times, especially since the ego, superego, and Id have characteristics that are both distinct and overlapping. However, the difficulty arises because of an inadequate understanding of the Law of Three. Without the Law of Three, it becomes difficult to separate the Id as a distinct and autonomous locus of function from the ego, while appreciating the Superego as a distinct element. The autonomy of the superego is rarely discussed in this book since the focus is on the evolutionary functions of the ego.

If the aim is to identify the Enneatypes, and the Id is distinct and autonomous from the ego, then it can be said that personality typing involves a method of subtraction. The first step is to observe the elements of personality, and then the qualitative elements of the Id are subtracted, leaving only the Ego and Superego elements of personality. Thus, an objective map of the elements of personality is required at the starting point so that the Id and ego can be differentiated.

BIBLIOGRAPHY

The conceptualizations, accounts, descriptions, terminology, and depictions appearing in this book required an expert understanding of economics, psychology, and most importantly, the Enneagram. Indeed, the Enneagram framework provided a discrete starting point for the conceptualization of the Nine Factors of Extinction and the Nine Human Endeavors. However, a great deal of contextual knowledge was also necessary, requiring a working knowledge of anthropology, history, philosophy, and sociology, which was obtained mostly through academic coursework and extensive research. For these reasons, it is not possible to cite every source of knowledge that was instrumental in the writing of this book. With these points in mind, an effort was made to cite the most indispensable post-collegiate sources of knowledge, especially those aligned with the thesis of this book.

Almaas, A.H., *Facets of Unity: The Enneagram of Holy Ideas*, 2000. Shambhala

Almaas, A.H., *The Void: Inner Spaciousness and Ego Structure,* (2nd Ed.) 2000, Shambhala

American Psychiatric Association. (2013). *Diagnostic and Statistical Manual of Mental Disorders*, (5th edition). Arlington, VA, 2013.

Freud, Sigmund. *The Ego and the Id.* New York: W. W. Norton & Co., 1960. Original publication in 1923.

Freud, Sigmund. *A General Introduction to Psychoanalysis.* New York: Washington Square Press, 1952. Original publication in 1915 to 1917.

Jung, Carl. *Psychological Types.* New Haven: Princeton University Press, 1971. Original publication in 1921.

Kernberg, Otto. *Borderline Conditions and Pathological Narcissism.* New York: Jason Aronson, 1975.

Kohut, Heinz, *The Restoration of the Self,* (1977). International Universities Press. New York.

Ouspensky, P.D. *In Search of the Miraculous.* New York: Harcourt, Brace, and World, 1949.

Oxford University Press. (2017). *The Oxford Handbook of THE FIVE FACTOR MODEL,* New York, NY, 2017.

Porter, M. E. (1990) *The Competitive Advantage of Nations.* Free Press, New York, 1990.

Riso, Don Richard & Hudson, Russ, *Personality Types: Using the Enneagram for Self-Discovery.* 1996. Houghton Mifflin

Wilber, Ken. *The Atman Project: A Transpersonal View of Human Development,* 1980, 2nd Ed.

ADDITIONAL RESOURCES

Universal Paradigms was founded by Richard Colter as a non-profit organization in 2019 to advance the capabilities of all peoples, organizations, and countries. The Enneagram paradigm is central to the teaching of various human development subjects related to leadership, Integration, organizational development, and macroeconomic development. Information related to the programs and services offered by Universal Paradigms is available by request:

Universal Paradigms
Richard Colter
P.O. Box 11312
Pleasanton, CA 94588
richard@universalparadigms.org
Youtube Channel: UniversalParadigms
(925) 388-6220

For information related to seminars, future publications, organizational development, and speaking engagements, please subscribe to the Universal Paradigms periodic newsletter at: *subscribe@universalparadigms.org*

Please send organizational development and speaking engagement inquiries to: *consulting@universalparadigms.org*

General information can be found at *www.universalparadigms.org*

BIOGRAPHY

RICHARD COLTER (above) is the founder of Universal Paradigms, an organization that edifies individuals and organizations, through the promotion and implementation of various initiatives. These initiatives include teaching the Nine Human Endeavors, as part of a certification program in the Enneagram Paradigm, and authoring books related to the human condition. He is currently working on the next book in the Understanding Human Evolution series. Before working with the Enneagram Paradigm, Richard completed the coursework for a master's in economics at Ball State University, as part of the academic requirements for a doctoral degree. However, after reading Personality Types in 1997, Richard ceased work toward a Ph.D. in economics, and he began mastering the Nine Human Endeavors. His interests include mountaineering, snow skiing, and traveling. He currently resides in California's Bay Area.